The Typewriting Dictionary

The Typewriting Dictionary

Edith Mackay

BA (Hons), FRSA, FSCT

Examiner to the Royal Society of
Arts in the Diploma for Personal
Assistants

Former Chief Examiner to the
Royal Society of Arts in
Shorthand-typewriting and
Audio-typewriting

Moderator in Shorthand,
Typewriting, and Shorthand-
typewriting to the
Middlesex C.S.E. Board

PITMAN

First published 1977

Pitman Publishing Ltd
Pitman House, Parker Street, Kingsway, London WC2B 5PB
PO Box 46038, Banda Street, Nairobi, Kenya

Pitman Publishing Pty Ltd
Pitman House, 158 Bouverie Street, Carlton, Victoria 3053, Australia

Pitman Publishing Corporation
6 East 43 Street, New York, NY 10017, USA

Sir Isaac Pitman (Canada) Ltd
495 Wellington Street West, Toronto M5V 1G1, Canada

The Copp Clark Publishing Company
517 Wellington Street West, Toronto M5V 1G1, Canada

ISBN: 0 273 31721 0

Text set in 10/11 pt. Monotype Plantin, printed by photolithography,
and bound in Great Britain at The Pitman Press, Bath

(Q7: 41)

Introduction

The original *Dictionary of Typewriting* by Maxwell Crooks was first published in 1919 and for nearly fifty years provided valuable guidance to teachers and students alike. However, typewriting 'theory' and techniques are not static but are constantly changing with use. As with the English language itself, Typewriting is a living thing in which constant changes are taking place: sometimes they are obvious and dramatic, but frequently they are subtle and almost indiscernible. Looking at typewriting textbooks that were in use twenty-five years ago and comparing them with forward-looking and currently-used ones, we can only be amazed and wonder how the radical changes came about.

Changes in typewriting outlook and practice have been prompted by several factors. Great advances have been made in typewriter design and performance and this has gone hand in hand with greater mechanization and sophistication of office procedures in general. Wider educational and career opportunities for women led to a recognized general decline in the standard of students studying Typewriting— although there are, of course, very many excellent students. Employers tended to become dissatisfied with the typewriting skill and English ability of their typists and this, coupled with soaring labour rates, led to a quest for rationalization of practice. It became widely accepted in commerce and industry that speedily-produced and mailable copy should be the top priorities.

One result of this search for speed and accurate copy was the introduction of the blocked style of layout and open punctuation. Although 'traditionalists' sometimes express horror at some of the new practices in Typewriting, this is often only a natural reaction to change. Most students, teachers and office workers who at first detested the blocked method of letter layout, for instance, now accept it without question and even admire the simple symmetry of a well-typed letter in one of the blocked styles (there is no single 'correct' method!).

Because of the fundamental changes that have taken place in type-writing thought and practice there is a wide divergence of styles used in different offices. This often presents a great problem to teachers and students of Typewriting as well as to the examining bodies. Many teachers and examiners tend to think that their particular way of typing is 'correct': they swear by the methods they learned and teach, and by what is said in their pet textbook. Often they overstress the importance of minor points of practice and layout and overlook the prime need for speedy and accurate output. Naturally, this can lead to inconsistent and illogical marking of examination scripts.

Fortunately, an invigorating wind of change is blowing throughout the typewriting educational world and the main emphasis is being placed where it rightly should be—on speed of production combined with accurate copy. Minor, unimportant points of style and practice (for which there is no sound and logical reason), and which could fail a candidate in an examination, are now viewed with a very liberal outlook. For instance, why should roman numerals always be lined up to the right? Yet typewriting textbooks stated this 'rule' for many years, although there is no sound reason for it. This was but one of a host of irksome points that typewriting students had to master. Roman numerals are now accepted aligned either to the right *or* left. In addition, examination candidates were penalized if they underscored punctuation marks at the beginning and/or the end of the underscoring. One's natural reaction when underlining with ruler and pen is *not* to stop short at the puncutation marks. Typewriting students actually had to learn and be taught the 'typewriting method'—again a waste of time and mental effort that could have been better applied elsewhere. Fortunately this senseless 'rule', together with numerous others, no longer applies.

The Royal Society of Arts working party, which looked into all such matters when its Typewriting syllabuses and marking scheme underwent a major review (1973–1976), did much good work in ruthlessly examining petty and illogical 'rules' which often failed candidates in examinations. Careful analysis of examination papers and results revealed that some candidates had failed largely through minor, arbitrary 'display' errors. The revised marking scheme will enable more candidates who produce reasonably accurate and reasonably displayed work to pass.

Students are confused because when they enter an office after their training they frequently find they are required to set out documents in a completely different way from what was the custom in school or college. So many different offices have their own particular 'house style' with regard to typewriting, that no teacher could possibly expect to acquaint the pupil with all of them. A good typewriting teacher should, however, teach students to be *flexible in approach*. Although the teacher may favour and expect students to work largely in a particular style of layout, this should not be taught to the exclusion of all else: it should be stressed that there is seldom only one 'correct' way of performing a task, and, in addition to giving the students some practice in various different methods, the teacher should make it clear that the preferences of employers should always be observed in the work situation.

This new typewriting dictionary has attempted to present typewriting theory and practice in an enlightened way. There are very few strict do's and don'ts.

In addition, the layout is different from the former *Dictionary of Typewriting*, in that all information about a particular topic is, as far as possible, presented together. For instance, all the different parts of a typewriter and their uses are described together under **Parts of a typewriter and their uses** but, for ease of location, each one is cross referenced. The author considers this arrangement better than having all the different parts scattered alphabetically throughout the book and hopes that this format will be more acceptable and will enable the reader to study the topics as entities. Also, subject matter that comes within the sphere of Office Practice—the method of operating a duplicating machine, for instance—has been omitted. Attention is directed almost exclusively to aspects of typewriting.

It is desirable that this book should set out principles which readers in different countries can apply to their own situation. If the variants in different countries were included, some sections of the book would become over-complicated. For example, in the section on money, it is clearer, in the interests of simplicity, to use the sterling system, which is widely known, leaving the reader to apply the principles to his or her own system; similarly, the section on references sets out the type of books in which information of a particular kind might be found.

A great deal of hard work has gone into the writing of this title but if it helps the student, teacher, and worker in typewriting to obtain a firm but liberal grasp of the subject, the author will consider all the effort well worthwhile.

Edith Mackay

Abbreviations. There are many hundreds of abbreviations in common use—and the number is constantly growing. It does not come within the scope of this typewriting work to attempt to list abbreviations and their meaning: there are separate titles devoted entirely to them— *The Complete Dictionary of Abbreviations*, compiled by R. Schwartz (Harrap) and *Everyman's Dictionary of Abbreviations* (Dent), to mention but two. In addition, there is a useful list of general abbreviations at the end of most English dictionaries; also a handy list for the typist in *The Typist's Desk Book* (Pitman).

At one time it was general usage to type a full stop at the end of each letter or group of letters that formed an abbreviation, with the following exceptions:

1. Ordinal numbers—1st, 2nd, 3rd, 4th, etc.

2. Abbreviations separated by the solidus—a/c (account), c/o (care of), B/L (Bill of Lading), c/f (carried forward), etc.

3. A few isolated abbreviations, such as per cent, re.

In addition, abbreviating symbols formed on the typewriter have, traditionally, never been followed by a stop. These are:

(a) &—(ampersand) meaning 'and'.

(b) @—meaning *at* or at the price of.

(c) £ or $ etc.—meaning the pound, dollar or other currency symbol.

(d) %—meaning per cent.

In the interests of simplification and speed it is increasingly becoming the practice to omit stops completely after abbreviations—particularly in conjunction with the blocked style of layout. Some typists who still type stops after abbreviations in the traditional manner, omit to insert them in acronyms—which are becoming a popular form of abbreviation because they are easy to pronounce and remember. In fact, many people who use acronyms as part of their everyday speech often do not know what the letters stand for even though they understand the meaning of the acronym. An acronym is an abbreviation in the form of a word, made up from initial letters. Examples are NASA (National Aeronautical and Space Administration), NALGO (National Association of Local Government Officers), RADA (Royal Academy of Dramatic Art), and UNESCO (United Nations Educational, Scientific, and Cultural Organization).

Some examples follow, illustrating both the traditional and modern method of typing abbreviations. Note the spacing, where applicable.

Typed Without Stops	Traditional Method
Mr J T Longman OBE MA	Mr. J.T. Longman, O.B.E., M.A.
	or
	Mr. J. T. Longman, O.B.E., M.A.
PS The concert tickets are enclosed.	P.S. The concert tickets are enclosed.
I flew to Spain on a BEA plane.	I flew to Spain on a B.E.A. plane.
It was flight No BE 21634.	It was flight No. B.E. 21634.
She ordered 6 kg of apples.	She ordered 6 kg. of apples.
Please arrive at 10 am.	Please arrive at 10 a.m.
She applied for a job with the BBC.	She applied for a job with the B.B.C.

Manuscript abbreviations. Most people, when writing matter which is to be typed, use various abbreviations to speed up production of the manuscript draft. Examples are: shd (should), wd (would), ffy (faithfully), yr (your). There are many others and people often use their own individual ones—although the meaning should be clear, particularly if the matter is to be typed by someone other than the writer. All such manuscript abbreviations should always be typed in full: only the generally used abbreviations such as i.e., e.g., viz., N.B., B.B.C., etc., should be left in their abbreviated form.

Accents. Increasingly, typists are being called upon to type matter in foreign languages. For most other European languages the use of various accents is necessary, the most important being the following:

´	(acute)	`	(grave)
^	(circumflex)	″	(umlaut)

In addition, the following two complete characters are frequently required:

ç	(cedilla)	ñ	(tilde)

If a typewriter is frequently required for typing in a foreign language, it should have the necessary accents fitted to it, or it will be necessary to ink these in later. Not only is inking in tedious and unreliable (unless the work is very carefully checked) but it tends to give the typewritten work an untidy appearance.

Typewriters are built to a standard size and it is not possible to extend the type basket to accommodate these extra characters. Therefore it would be necessary to dispense with some seldom-used characters (e.g. certain fractions) and replace the typefaces with the required accents and characters.

Modern practice is to fit the accents to 'dead' keys so that the carriage does not move forward one space when the key is struck: the required accompanying letter is then struck without the need for backspacing. If the accents are not fitted to 'dead keys', use of the backspace key is obviously necessary.

Acronyms. See **Abbreviations.**

Addendum. See **Literary work.**

Addressing machines. These obviously save time and money in that a typist does not have to type each individual envelope and invoice, delivery note, statement heading, etc., and absolute accuracy is ensured from a correct master. Once masters have been prepared, envelopes, etc., can be rapidly addressed by passing the masters through the machine.

A wide variety of addressing machines is available ranging from small, hand-operated types to large, rapidly-operated, sophisticated machines. Masters for the machines are made by embossing plastic or metal plates or by typing spirit or stencil masters.

Stencil masters for addressing machines are prepared on the type-writer, using a fibrous material similar to that used for ordinary stencils (see **Ink duplicating**). A special attachment is available to enable a typewriter to easily take the stencil cards, which are mounted in card-board frames. Two types of frame are obtainable: one is narrow, intended only to hold the stencil firm; and the other has a wider top on which can be recorded the information contained on the stencil (in addition to other required matter)—a feature that has several valuable uses in the office. An ordinary ink duplicator will not handle stencil addressing cards: a special stencil-operated addressing machine is necessary.

Spirit masters for addressing machines use the same principles outlined in **Spirit duplicating.** Hectograph carbon paper is used for typing the masters on special continuous master sheets, which are perforated so the sections can be easily separated and fitted into plastic frames (available in different colours for selection purposes).

A different type of addressing machine that uses a typed master is the Elliott Addressall 6000. This is electrically operated and incorporates the sophisticated features of automatic print, skip and repeat controls. The masters are typed on plastic cards and slide easily into special grooved frames—which can be used to take a new card when a previous one is no longer required.

Adjustment of paper. When paper is fed into a typewriter crookedly, adjustment is necessary to straighten it. The paper release lever should be pulled forward to release pressure on the feed rollers: this will allow free movement of the paper so it can be aligned with the paper bail.

When the paper has been satisfactorily straightened, the paper release lever should be returned to its position for typing. (See also **Correcting errors** (*Erasing*) and **Inserting paper into the typewriter.**)

Agenda. See **Meetings.**

Alignment. This term refers to the straightness of the line of typing. If any character appears above or below the normal typing line, it is said to be out of alignment.

With manual typewriters, characters usually appear out of alignment because of faulty key operation on the part of the typist. In some cases, however, the typewriter may be to blame and will therefore require the attention of a skilled mechanic. Faulty alignment with electric machines is nearly always caused by faulty typewriter mechanism.

The most common touch fault of type being out of alignment is incorrect manipulation of the shift key. If the typist does not ensure that a shift key is held down firmly while an upper case character is struck, it will appear either above or below its correct position. In addition, if she strikes a lower case character before completely releasing the shift key, the lower case key will appear out of alignment. Lower case characters also sometimes appear out of alignment if the keys are not struck firmly and sharply.

Alignment scale. See **Parts of a typewriter.**

Alphabetic drills. See **Drills.**

Alphabetic sentences. These, as the name implies, are sentences that contain all the letters of the alphabet. Such sentences provide useful practice for typing all the letter reaches.

In the early stages of training, when the students have been introduced to all the letter keys, the teacher should regularly watch each student type an alphabetic sentence so she can check on correct fingering and techniques (use of shift key, carriage return, etc.).

Some examples of alphabetic sentences
1. The crazy pavement was quickly fixed by a jolly old gardener.
2. The quick brown fox jumps right over the lazy dog.
3. The firm quickly realized that expenditure on the building was very injudicious.
4. In consequence of his love of luxury, the wealthy journalist did not take part in the mountain climb that the young people organized.
5. Do not be discouraged just because you find a particular exercise to be extra difficult; you may have tried to type too quickly without realizing that accuracy comes first.

Many teachers establish the habit of writing an alphabetic sentence on the chalkboard (or overhead projector) for their students to repeatedly copy for a few minutes at the beginning of a lesson, e.g. while they are assembling, etc. In this situation it provides a useful 'warming-up drill' (see **Drills**).

Alternate hand drills. See **Drills**.

Ampersand. See **Extra typewriter characters**.

Apostrophe. See **Punctuation marks**.

Arrangement of the keyboard. The typewriter keyboard that we all know and use is generally called the 'universal keyboard'; its arrangement varies little from one make of machine to another. Everyone who has studied the working arrangement of this keyboard agrees that it is illogical and unscientific.

Many of the early inventors of typewriters were printers and it is thought that most of them based their keyboard arrangement on the letter order of a printer's case or frame for holding type. The first practical typewriter was manufactured by Remington in 1873, its basic keyboard arrangement being as follows:

```
2 3 4 5 6 7 8 9 - , -
Q W E R T Y U I O P :
; A S D F G H J K L M
& Z C X V B N ? ; . '
```

It will be seen that today's keyboard arrangement differs very little from this, so Christopher Sholes (who, in 1868, patented the first Remington-produced typewriter) can be called the originator of the universal keyboard. However, Sholes and his fellow workers decided upon this arrangement only after considerable experiments. It is thought that Sholes at one point arranged his keyboard in alphabetical sequence, but the early clumsy typebars would not bounce back quickly enough to prevent a skilled operator from frequently jamming them. Therefore Sholes juggled the letters around and, quite deliberately, positioned the most frequently used keys *to slow down the operator* and thus prevent the typebars colliding and sticking at the printing point.

Any scientific study of the typewriter keyboard must take into consideration the comparative frequency of use of the twenty-six letters of the alphabet. In 1926, a Dr Hoke made an extensive study of the alphabet from this point of view and placed the letters in the following frequency order:

e t a o s i n r h l d c u m y b p w f g v k j x q z

Dr Hoke claimed that the first six letters (e t a o s i) are used *more frequently than the remaining twenty*. Of these six letters it will be seen

9

that only two are struck with the right hand. Hoke claimed that the letter **e** is used more frequently than twelve other letters combined (y b p w t g v k j x q z).

A more recent study than Dr Hoke's places the letters of the alphabet in the following order from the point of view of frequency of use:

e t a o n i r s h d l c w u m f y g p b v k x q j z

Common digrams in English are: th er on an re he in ed nd ha at en es of or ut ea ti to it st io le is on ar as de rt ve.

Common double letters are: ss ee tt ff ll mm (the latter two only being struck with the right hand). Common trigrams are: the and ent ion for has nce man.

Disadvantages of the universal keyboard

1. The weaker left hand (for most people) performs 57% of all key striking; the right hand thus being responsible for only 43%.

2. A number of words of high frequency are typed using only the left hand (e.g., are, as, were, at, address). Many people quite rightly assert that we are using a left-handed typewriter in a right-handed world.

3. Only 32% of all key striking is on the home row, 52% being on the third bank of keys and 16% on the first bank.

4. The weak little finger of the left hand is responsible for 8.2% of key striking whilst, for instance, the strong second finger of the right hand accomplishes only 7.2%.

5. It is generally agreed that more speedy typewritten work is produced when the hands are used alternately. On average, less than 50% of typewritten matter is thus produced.

In the face of these facts it is hardly surprising that attempts have been made to change the arrangement of the universal keyboard. However, all such attempts have failed largely because of the economic and retraining factors involved.

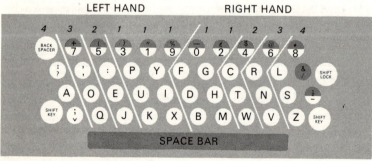

The Dvorak keyboard

Two suggestions for a re-arranged keyboard are most worthy of mention. The first was patented in 1932 (after years of work) by an American, August Dvorak, and is shown on p. 10.

Dvorak's proposed new keyboard arrangement is based on the following principles:

1. The most frequently used letters are placed on the home row so the fingers do not have to reach up or down to strike them.

2. Dvorak claims that 70% of key striking is done on the home row, 22% on the third bank and 8% on the first bank.

3. There is an improved balance between the action of the right and left hands (56% and 44% respectively).

4. There is a better balance of alternate key striking with opposite hands—66% compared with 48% on the universal keyboard.

5. Since every syllable contains at least one vowel, the vowels are all positioned on the left of the home row—so that no word has to be typed with the right hand alone, and very few with just the left hand.

In controlled experiments it was found that students trained on the Dvorak keyboard were superior to those trained on the universal keyboard. Nevertheless, all Dvorak's attempts at reform met with no success. Dvorak once dolefully remarked: 'Proposing a new keyboard was like proposing to reverse the Ten Commandments and the Golden Rule, discarding every moral principle and ridiculing motherhood.'

Mrs Lillian Malt, an English woman, has done considerable work in producing what is known as the Maltron keyboard, which follows.

```
1 2 3 4 5        6 7 8 9 0
B W F L M        Y G U P C
A N E H R        D O T I S
Z X . Q .        . . V J K
```

Some important points about the Maltron keyboard

1. The home row does not concentrate all the vowels on the left side (considered by some a weakness of the Dvorak keyboard). The home row A N E H R (left), D O T I S (right) divides them up.

2. The figures are sequenced in the normal way (cf. the Dvorak keyboard) since Mrs. Malt claims this is easier for the typist.

3. Less key striking is required of the third and little fingers than on the Dvorak keyboard; it is generally considered that these are the weakest fingers.

4. All the twenty most common digrams and fifteen of the twenty most common trigrams are on the home row.

Asterisk. See **Combination characters and special signs** and **Literary work** (*Footnotes*).

At the price of sign—@. See **Extra typewriter characters.**

Audio-typing. Audio-typing is typing direct from the spoken word. This is normally done by the audio typist listening (through a headset or earpiece) to pre-recorded dictation which is played back on a special audio machine. She can stop and start the machine whenever required and backtrack to listen again to part of the recording if it was not clear and she did not fully understand the meaning.

Types of machine. There are two basic types of recording machine for audio work—magnetic and non-magnetic. Non-magnetic machines are now hardly used since the medium can be used only once and mistakes cannot be easily and immediately rectified as on magnetic machines.

With magnetic machines, recordings can be erased and the same medium used over and over again. Also, if the dictator makes a mistake or changes his mind about what he is going to say or how to say it, he can backtrack and re-record. After backtracking a suitable distance, he should listen to his recording until he comes to the end of the last correct sentence or phrase, then switch the machine to 'record' and continue dictating. This process automatically erases the unwanted part and the revised dictation replaces it on the recording medium.

A variety of media is available for dictating purposes, i.e., tapes, discs, sheets, foils, belts and wires—although the two in most common use are tapes and discs.

The following illustrations show the Philips 96 (tape), the Agavox 2B (disc), the IBM 170 (belt) and the Dictaphone 400 (sheet).

The Philips 97

Discs resemble gramophone records in appearance and some types are rigid and others flexible. Most discs can be used for recording on both sides. Discs are unbreakable, easy to handle, and any part of the recording may be quickly located by turning a knob and moving the pointer to the required spot on the index strip.

Tapes for transcription machines are made of thin, magnetically-coated plastic. For most tape machines in current use, the tapes are

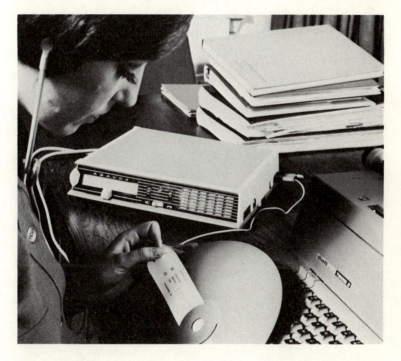

The Agavox 2B

provided in cassettes—plastic containers that hold two spools—so that no threading of tape is involved. In general, tapes provide a longer recording time than discs. Tapes for some machines have a playing time of thirty-five minutes on each track. However, tapes have the slight disadvantage that it is slower to locate a particular point since the tape has to be wound until the required position is reached. Moreover, many offices prefer a medium with a relatively short recording time since this helps to speed up the turn-round of a piece of dictation.

Index strips. The design of index strips varies to some extent according to the make of machine but the basic principle is the same. An index strip shows the audio-typist where a particular piece of dictation begins and ends. With most makes of machine, the length of playing time agrees with the divisions on the index strip. For instance, if the strip is numbered from 0 to 10 or from 0 to 20, this usually means that the recording time is 10 or 20 minutes respectively.

The IBM 170

Since the dictator indicates on the strip where he begins and ends each piece of dictation, the transcriber is able to gauge the approximate length of the passage and therefore the size of paper to use, margins, etc. Some dictators, of course, tend to speak more quickly than others, but if the audio-typist is used to transcribing for a particular person or group of persons, she soon becomes familiar with the general speed and characteristics of each dictator. For instance, if the index strip shows that a letter has taken four minutes to dictate and the transcriber knows that the dictator records at an average speed of 100 words a minute, including instructions and dictating conventions, she will know that the letter will consist of approximately 300–350 words and will select A4 paper and adjust her margins accordingly.

The Dictaphone 400

Index strips are, of course, essential to the audio-typist in a business situation. However, in audio-typing examinations it is common practice to give the number of dictated words for transcription as an alternative method of indicating the size of paper and margins to use, etc. Some examining bodies, however, insist on the realistic office situation and use index strips.

Some advantages and disadvantages of audio-typing. The end result of audio-typing and shorthand-typing is the same—transcription of material that has been dictated.

Dictating onto a machine is more flexible in some ways than dictating to a shorthand-typist. For instance, a person can dictate onto a recording machine at any time during the day or night. He can compose and dictate each letter, memo, report, etc., when the matter is fresh in his mind, instead of having to get together a batch of dictation before calling in a shorthand-typist and dictating it all together—when his original thoughts have probably gone from his mind. In addition, some of the shorthand-typist's time may be wasted during 'dictating sessions' by interruptions of various kinds (telephone, visitors, etc.).

Nevertheless, dictation onto a machine has its disadvantages as well. Accurate and speedy transcription requires good quality and consistent recording. No matter how skilled she may be, the audio-typist cannot produce satisfactory transcription from poor and muffled dictation. The question of dictation is a significant one and many organizations that installed audio equipment reported many difficulties at first. Success was only achieved where the dictators followed a strict code of instructions regarding method and punctuation. After all, if a dictator starts a piece of dictation by giving every punctuation mark, including commas, he cannot really blame the audio-typist if he suddenly forgets to dictate them—and the audio-typist follows suit!

Firms with audio equipment are increasingly realizing the fact that dictators need instruction in how to dictate efficiently. Many concerns either run their own courses on dictation methods and conventions, or send their executives on such a course at a local technical college or college of further education, if the suppliers of the equipment are unable to provide such a course.

It is generally accepted that a strict and full code of dictating instructions is necessary. Many dictators find following such a code so irksome and distracting to the flow of their thoughts that they prefer to write out their correspondence and reports in longhand to be copy-typed.

Ideally, perhaps, the only punctuation marks that should be dictated are those that cannot be anticipated by the typist, such as the start of a new paragraph or punctuation that is stylistic, such as semi-colons and colons.

Dictating machines are versatile in that they can be used not only in the office but also in many situations outside where the services of a shorthand-typist might be difficult, costly, or impossible. For instance, a surveyor inspecting premises can record his findings direct onto a recording machine, rather than laboriously write them out by hand. Many other such examples could be cited, such as a tailor or curtain maker recording vital measurements for a particular order, or a stock-taker calling out his list of items instead of having to write them out, thus leaving his hands free to maintain the uninterrupted flow of his checking.

Working as an audio-typist. Without doubt, audio-typing is here to stay. The demand for audio-typists increases yearly and even top secretaries who work mainly in shorthand often find that they need to be able to audio-type as well. More and more employers are expecting their employees to be able to transcribe from audio machines as well as from shorthand.

Pay for an audio-typist is in some cases lower than for a good short-hand-typist—but the gap is steadily narrowing and many firms pay a good audio-typist as much as (and in some cases more than) a good shorthand-typist. However, financial gain is not all-important to many people: job satisfaction is an important factor and before embarking on an audio-typing job one should enquire about the conditions of work, promotion prospects, etc.

When starting work as an audio-typist one will, in general, work in one of two ways: either in a small firm where audio-typing will be only one of a variety of duties, or alternatively in a firm where it is the main occupation—in which case one will be working with a number of other audio-typists in a centralized or departmental system.

(*a*) *The one or two machine situation.* Many small firms and organizations own only one or two audio machines. Often one machine is sufficient to handle the dictation requirements of the few persons who will dictate correspondence and other matter, and also be used by the audio-typist for transcription. In other cases, a second machine is provided solely for use by the transcriber. In such a situation the audio-typist will be required to carry out, in addition, various office duties, such as filing, copy-typing, and answering the telephone. Many audio-typists prefer this situation because of the variety of work it provides, and they also like the frequent personal contact with the people for whom they work.

(*b*) *Centralized and departmental audio-typing.* An audio-typist in a centralized system will spend most of her working time doing audio transcription. She will be one of a number of people working in a large, pleasant room and will work under the control of a supervisor who will oversee and distribute the transcription requirements of a whole organization.

With this system all the recording machines are situated in a single room and there are a number of dictating points scattered throughout the building. Dictation is recorded direct onto a free machine by dialling a certain number on an ordinary telephone handset. It is the duty of the supervisor to ensure that an even flow of work is maintained in the transcription room and that pleasant relations are established both with her transcribers and with the dictators.

If it is necessary for the audio-typist to refer to correspondence, reports, etc., these are often taken to the transcription room by messenger—or by the dictator himself, as many dictators like to establish personal contact with the people transcribing for them.

Many firms have organized their audio-typing in small departmental units since it is generally recognized that a girl likes to work for a particular man or group of men. In this situation the audio-typist works close to the related department and gets to know the different people in it. If she has a problem in transcribing she can often consult the dictator direct, and personal relationships are established and maintained. This is good for the morale of all concerned.

Departmental audio-typing also helps solve the problems of specialized vocabularies. For instance, audio-typists in the Engineers' Department soon master the specific vocabulary that is necessary, and the audio-typists in the Town Clerk's Department likewise become familiar with the necessary legal terminology.

In most concerns where centralized or departmental audio-typing is successful, the working conditions are especially good. Fitted carpets are provided in light, airy, and well-planned offices with modern décor. It is now widely recognized that audio-typing involves a high degree of concentration and a feeling of isolation. To help counteract this, many offices provide easy chairs, coffee tables, magazines, vending machines— so the girls can really relax and get to know each other when work is slack. In addition, coffee, tea, and lunch breaks are often taken all together for the same reason.

Several enlightened firms, recognizing that audio-typing taxes a worker's concentration and resources to the full, intersperse spells in the audio pool with other forms of clerical and secretarial work. Under good and enlightened management, audio systems are working very happily and efficiently.

Learning to audio-type. A skilled audio-typist types continuously. This means that she types almost non-stop and purely listens only occasionally: she listens to a long phrase or a whole sentence and then stops her machine and types; before she has completed typing what she has heard she starts her machine again and listens to the next long phrase or sentence. Most typists find this a difficult skill to master and are not expected to be able to do it in their first lesson. At first the pattern of work will be:

1. Start the transcribing machine, listen to a complete short sentence and retain it in the memory *word for word*.

2. When the dictator says 'full stop', stop the machine and type the sentence.

3. When typing of the sentence is complete, start the machine again and listen to the next whole sentence before stopping and typing it.

If necessary, the beginner in audio-typing should listen to a sentence more than once since it is important that she transcribes accurately word for word. Every effort should be made to type these early short sentences as single units—otherwise the learner may develop the habit of listening to only two or three words at a time before typing. This would hinder development of sound audio-typing skill since it would make it difficult for the audio-typist to *understand* the meaning of what she was typing— which is vital. As audio skill develops the learner will acquire the ability to break down long sentences into meaningful phrases.

Since it is vitally important that an audio-typist understands what she hears and types, she should always listen for meaning or she will make unnecessary mistakes. If what she hears does not make sense, she should backtrack and listen again and, if necessary, listen a little way ahead until the meaning becomes quite clear.

To become a really skilled audio-typist takes much time and practice and it is important that the learner uses a well-graded course: one that begins with short sentences, proceeds to longer ones, then to short and longer paragraphs, simple letters, and so on.

All typists need a good command of the English language, but this is obviously even more important in audio-typing since the operator does not have the assistance of copy. On this point see also **Punctuation marks** and **English, knowledge of**.

In most schools and colleges audio-typing is taught in one of three ways. If the secretarial course is a **full-time** one, audio-typing can be successfully integrated with the typing lessons. For instance, once the students have mastered the keyboard they can learn the controls of an audio-machine and type simple sentences: when they can type para- graphs they can then proceed to do this in the audio lessons; then letters, memos, etc. With **part-time** classes (e.g., day release and evening) where little additional instruction is given in typewriting layout and theory the students should be at least at RSA Stage I Typewriting standard before beginning an audio course. In addition, a well-designed audio course is suitable as short, **intensive** training for competent typists whose English is good.

Automatic typewriters. See **Special purpose typewriters.**

Backing sheets. A backing sheet should always be used when typing on a single sheet of paper or on thin paper, taking only one or two carbon copies. Not only does this help prevent wear on the platen but it also improves the appearance of the typewritten work and reduces the noise made by the typewriter. If one types on a single sheet of paper, especially if the typist's touch is heavy, the platen soon becomes pitted: this produces typewritten matter with a poor, uneven appearance and necessitates replacement of the platen.

Backing sheets are made of stout paper or thin plastic. (Thin plastic backing sheets are used when typing spirit masters.) Some have a turnover flap at one end, which assists the typist when feeding several sheets of thin paper and carbons into the typewriter.

See **End of paper** for suggestions about using backing sheets to ensure a uniform space at foot of paper.

Backspace key. See **Parts of a typewriter.**

Backspace key drills. See **Drills.**

Balance sheets. A balance sheet is a statement of the assets and liabilities of a firm or company and shows its financial position at any given time. Liabilities are usually shown on the left-hand side and assets on the right-hand side. Note, however, that the Continental style of typing balance sheets differs from the British one in that assets are typed on the left and liabilities on the right.

In offices where lengthy balance sheets are frequently typed, A3, draft or brief paper and long-carriage typewriters are used so that the whole balance sheet will appear across the width of one sheet of paper. However, in offices where long-carriage typewriters are not available, a balance sheet, if required, has to be typed on A4 paper, either on a single sheet of paper (with the wider side at the top) or on two sheets (with the shorter sides at the top), which are later joined together.

When balance sheets can be typed across a single sheet of paper, their typing presents few difficulties, apart from the usual ones of display and correct setting out of money items. Alternate sides should be typed until the shorter side is complete (apart from the total). Then one should continue until the longer side is finished, when both totals should be typed *on the same line*. Each side should occupy exactly half the width of the paper. The main heading should be centred over the width of the paper; there should be a space between the two halves of the balance sheet, and the left and right margins should be equal.

If a balance sheet is typed on two sheets of paper that must later be joined together, the task is a more complicated one as great care has to be taken to see that the two sides align when joined together. The main heading of the balance sheet should run right across the two sheets without a break, half the heading being typed on the left, ending flush with the right-hand edge of the paper, and the other half typed on the right-hand sheet of paper starting at the left-hand edge of the paper. There should be narrow and equal margins on the right (or left, if the Continental method is used) side of the liabilities sheet and on the left side of the assets sheet; also, the left margin on the liabilities side and the right margin on the assets side should be equal. The side with the larger number of items should be typed first and, before starting to type the second sheet, it is helpful if a light pencil mark is made at the points where the heading is to be continued, where the first line begins, and where the totals should be typed. When the typing is complete, the two sheets of paper should be carefully stuck together (using transparent tape) on the back, making sure that the alignment is correct and that the two edges of the paper just meet. The light pencil guide marks should then be cleanly erased.

As in all column work, tab stops should be set for each column.

Banker envelopes. See **Envelopes.**

Bell, warning (see also **Division of words at line ends**). The bell, warning a typist that the end of her line is approaching, rings approximately six spaces before the point at which she has set her right-hand margin stop—where the carriage locks and the margin release key has to be used for typing beyond that point. It will be found that the number of characters one can type between the sounding of the bell and the locking of the carriage varies with different makes of typewriter. Every typist should familiarize herself with her machine on this point and when reading the following points should take this factor into account.

If equal margins are required, the right-hand margin stop should be set a few spaces to the right of where the typist aims to end her line, or there will be a tendency for the right-hand margin to become wider than the left-hand one (which is generally considered bad typing practice), or alternatively there will be excessive use of the margin release key, with a resulting loss of time.

A meticulous typist will maintain as even a right-hand margin as possible and should observe the following procedure upon the sounding of the bell.

1. If the typist is in the middle of a medium-length word, she should complete typing it before turning up to the next line.

2. If the typist has just started typing a long word, she should decide upon a suitable point for division.

3. If the typist has just completed typing a word and the next word is a short one, she should proceed to type it before turning up.

4. If the typist has just completed typing a word and the next one is lengthy but suitable for dividing, she should do so, and after hyphenating at a suitable point, turn up to the next line and complete typing the word.

5. If the typist has just completed typing a word and the next word or group of characters should not be divided, she should immediately turn up. However, if the typing of the next word would extend not more than two characters into the margin, the margin release key should be used, rather than allowing a long gap at the end of the line.

Bibliography. See **Literary work.**

Bills of quantities (see also **Specifications** and **Tender**). Most building or engineering projects are put out to tender and each interested contractor submits his tender on the basis of a supplied bill of quantities. Some variations in layout are often found from firm to firm and the typist should always follow the particular style and preferences of her employers.

When a building or engineering project has been designed and planned by an architect or engineer, he has usually drawn up a document which analyses the work, item by item, the standards to be adhered to and the materials to be used. Such a document is known as a bill of quantities. A copy of the bill of quantities is sent out to interested contractors who carefully price it, item by item (usually employing the services of a quantity surveyor), and the total figure becomes the tender figure. Usually the contractor submitting the lowest tender figure is given the job, although this is not always the case as other factors are sometimes taken into account.

As with specifications, the trades and items are listed in the order in which the work will normally be carried out. For instance, on a large building project, after any preliminaries, details of excavation work will be given, followed by concrete work, brickwork and blockwork—and so on. If only a few copies of a bill of quantities are required, carbon copies are usually taken. However, if a large number is needed (as would be the case with a major project) they are normally duplicated or photocopied.

Bills of quantities are usually typed on specially ruled A4 paper with vertical lines running the full length of the paper. If plain A4 paper has to be used for practice purposes in schools and colleges, it should be ruled prior to the typing. Each item is numbered or lettered and the pages are numbered, in the middle at the bottom of each page. As with specifications, use is made of spaced capitals for main headings and closed capitals for sub-headings.

There are usually six or seven vertical columns on the specially ruled paper. The first one is narrow and in it is typed the appropriate reference number or letter for the item. The second column is a wide one, occupying nearly half the width of the paper: this is for a description of the relevant details, and also includes any headings. The third column is narrow and gives the required measurements, with the fourth column naming the nature of the measurements (cubic metres, litres, etc.). The fifth column contains the unit price of the particular item and the sixth and seventh columns give the total price for the item (pounds in the first column and pence in the second one). Sometimes only one column is given for the total price—in which case the typist should head the column with the £ symbol and use the decimal point (see **Money, typing of**). The total at the foot of each page is preceded by the words 'To Collection' and these totals are carried forward to a summary of the collections at the end of the bill of quantities. If the bill of quantities is a very long one, it may be divided into quite separate units for the different trades, and each will have its own summary of collections: in this case there will be a Final Summary of the whole at the end of the document.

Endorsement. Short bills of quantities are folded (and creased) from left to right and the endorsement typed on the side then uppermost. Long bills of quantities are bound and the pages kept flat, the endorsement appearing on the top sheet. The endorsement is worded in a similar manner to that of a specification: an example is given under **Specifications.**

Blank keyboard. This is a typewriter keyboard on which the letters and other characters are covered. The keys are usually blanked out by using plain circular stickers.

Some teachers favour blank keyboards when teaching the keyboard, in an attempt to prevent learners from developing the habit of looking at the keys. Many people consider the method of dubious value. Most teachers agree that looking at the keys is essential when new keys are first introduced, and prefer to rely on the students' good sense and self discipline in getting them to understand that *frequent* key-looking prevents the development of efficient typing skill. (See also **Touch typewriting.**)

Blind carbon copy. See **Carbon copying** (*Circulation of copies*).

Blind typists. People who are blind often make excellent typists. Their lack of sight often helps them develop other senses and related skills. The one great disadvantage they experience in typing is their inability to read any copy or instructions. Blind people who type are therefore mainly employed as audio-typists—all instructions being given in the form of the spoken word.

Nevertheless, although dictating machines and touch typing make employment possible, it is not possible for blind people to correct their work—thus rendering them uneconomic from an employer's point of view.

A new machine, called the Phylab Brailler, enables a blind typist independently to read, proof-read and correct typewritten texts with ease. This self-contained typing-transcribing system automatically and simultaneously produces a Braille copy of the black and white type-written text. As the typist works, the Phylab Brailler embosses, simultaneously with the typewritten text, a Braille copy on paper teleprinter tape.

A useful aspect is that the tape automatically advances *one* space after embossing one Braille character, *two* spaces when the tabulator is pressed and *three* when the carriage is returned, thus providing the Braille copy with a clear indication of the typed text form. Students can use the tape as a 'carbon copy' which they themselves can read, thus providing material in a form that will help blind typists in their own studies.

Blocked headings. See **Headings.**

Blocked layout (see also **Display work**). Increasingly, firms are using blocked methods of layout for the typing of letters and other documents, and abandoning the once widely-used complicated styles.

Blocked layout has several advantages. It saves valuable typing time since blocked documents are the quickest to type. The style presents information in a clear, easily-assimilated form. In addition, after one has become used to the radical differences in style layout, it presents a very pleasing appearance to the eye.

When it was first recommended that letters—the most common form of commercial document—would be best typed in the fully-blocked style, many 'traditionalists' threw up their hands in horror and revolted against what at first appeared a repugnant style. Many continued to prefer and use the indented method with all its time-consuming rami-fications (centring of headings and signature block, backspacing from the right-hand margin point for typing the date, and so on). Nevertheless, the new style rapidly gained ground, largely for the economic reason that the typist using it produced a greater output of work. Blocked and semi-blocked letter styles (see *Business letters* under **Letters**) are now very widely used and most people have come to admit that their un-cluttered appearance is eminently readable and attractive.

From the point of view of learning and teaching typewriting, blocked forms of layout are by far the easiest and quickest to master. Most teachers and students dislike complicated documents—specifications, for example—but, adapted to the blocked method, they present few problems and many people now approach 'traditional' styles with considerable apprehension and caution. Open punctuation (see separate entry) is usually used in conjunction with blocked layout.

From the initial somewhat shaky start of blocked letters, the method has gone from strength to strength and is now widely used for a varied range of documents. Many organizations have adopted their own slight individual modifications to the blocked form and typists should, of course, always follow the preferences of their employers. If they have been well taught, the minor changes from that which they are accustomed to are soon overcome.

Under the sections **Meetings** and **Specifications** the reader will be able to find examples of documents laid out according to both the traditional and blocked methods: the clarity and simplicity of the latter will at once be obvious. Of course, any type of document can be adapted to a blocked layout and a page of a typical report, together with its title page (again in the blocked style), follow.

STOCK CONTROL AND STOCK PURCHASE

AST.MK.43

August 1976

Report prepared by AZTEC CONSULTANTS
on behalf of

PLASTICS PRODUCTION LIMITED, FAVERSHAM, KENT

CONTENTS

1.1-1.8.4   Stock Control

2.1-2.4.3   Purchasing Administration

3.1-3.4.2   Purchasing Rules

4.1-4.4.5   Accounting Procedure

STOCK   CONTROL

GENERAL

1.1   The main purpose of the introduction of
         a new system of stock control is to
         ensure that at no time do we run out of
         stock of any item. It is realized that
         such a goal is difficult to attain but
         at least most of the serious errors of
         the past will be obviated if the system
         now described is implemented.

INDEXING SYSTEMS

1.2.1   <u>Letter Series</u>   The cards to be used
         (specimens are enclosed with the report)
         are designed so that the new alphabetic
         letter series to indicate subsidiary
         companies and departments may be used
         for all stocks.

1.2.2   <u>Numeral Series</u>   Since every separate
         item of stock must be identified indivi-
         dually by a four-figure number, it will
         be necessary to allow the departments at
         least 2 months in order to establish a
         numerical series. The series for each
         letter is to begin at 0001 and go pro-
         gressively forward. At the moment the
         highest number likely to be reached is
         6500.

1.2.3   <u>Method of Entry-Making</u>   Job cards will
         be created at the same time as stock
         cards using the Anderson Numeration and
         Data Processing Machine for the oper-
         ation. Typed lists, treble-checked by
         departments, will be needed in duplicate
         before this process can be undertaken.

INPUT INFORMATION

1.3.1   Computer Services   The system once set up will be geared to the computer bank in Canterbury and arrangements are already in hand to provide departments with monthly tabulations giving the following information: Stock Letter Number, Opening Stock, Closing Stock, Sales, OSR (on sale or return), AC (approved or complimentary items), Cumulative Annual Sales, 2 years' past comparison, Minimum Stock, Warehousing Unit Cost, Current Retail Price, Current Discounts graded as at present under Codes 0, 1, 2, 3, 4, 5.

Blocked paragraphs. See **Paragraphs.**

Brace. See **Combination characters and special signs.**

Brackets (square). See **Combination characters and special signs.**

Business letters. See **Letters.**

Carbon copying (see also **NCR (no carbon required) paper** and **Reprography processes**). This is the most widely used means of producing copies since, in virtually every office, at least one carbon copy is normally taken of every letter, memo, etc. In some offices carbon copies are no longer taken—the required copies being made on a copying machine. However, this is a comparatively costly process, and unless the copying machine is readily to hand, it is impracticable. The normal method of taking one or two copies is by use of carbon paper. Thus the immediacy and cheapness of the copies makes carbon copying ideal for routine typing when only a few copies are required. Its importance is reflected in the fact that most public examinations in Typewriting require the candidates to show that they can use carbon paper satisfactorily.

There are two main types of carbon paper. Single carbon paper has the carbon coating on one side only whereas double carbon paper is coated on both sides.

Single carbon paper. This is the type in most general use and special flimsy paper (available in a variety of tints) is used for the copy or copies. Single carbon paper is available in various weights: heavyweight produces only one or two good copies at a time but has a long working life; mediumweight gives up to five copies at a time; and lightweight will produce more than five copies, but can be used effectively only a few times.

In addition, it is possible to obtain 'once-only' carbon paper which, as its name implies, can be used only once. This paper is very thin and cheap. It is used extensively in the manufacture of assembled sets of paper and carbon where a number of copies is required of a document—as in billing. This obviously saves the typist much time in the handling of papers. It is also sometimes used in continuous stationery, and provided for use with stencil cutting.

One can also obtain what is commonly known as 'long-life' carbon paper. Whereas the conventional carbon papers are made with a wax-pigment coating, long-life carbons do not contain any wax and use instead a microporous plastic coating impregnated with a quick-drying ink. This coating is applied to an extra strong base tissue or alternatively to a resilient film material. These waxless solvent carbons have a number of advantages:

1. They produce clearer copies because the coating wears down evenly and prevents broken outlines to the characters.

2. They are clean and easy to handle as there are no particle deposits. The copies produced are smudge-free because the ink *penetrates* the copy paper: this makes for cleaner correcting.

3. They are crease-resistant and will not 'curl'.

4. Wastage of materials and time is reduced and the extra strength and wearing qualities give a good all-round performance.

5. They are obtainable in various weights: standard weight for up to four copies; manifold weight suitable for taking up to eight copies. In general, each sheet can be used about two hundred times.

Double carbon paper. This is used only if a large number of copies is needed by the carbon-copying method. Using very thin, almost transparent paper and double carbons it is possible to take up to about twenty copies (more with an electric typewriter using the special pressure control) at one typing. If the maximum number possible is being taken, the ribbon should be disengaged so that the type bars strike directly and sharply on to the top sheet of paper. Two sheets of copy paper are required for each sheet of double carbon paper. Each sheet of carbon produces a reverse copy on the paper above it (this reverse copy being read *through* the paper) and a normal copy on the paper underneath.

Corrections are obviously very difficult to make with double carbon paper. Because of this and the now widespread use of photocopiers, double carbon paper is becoming less and less used.

Colours. Carbon paper is available in a variety of colours—blue, black, purple, green, red, and brown. The different colours can be used in a variety of ways. For example, the habit can be established that a copy in a particular colour is always used for a certain department or person; a different colour can be used to highlight a particular document or part of it; and, in some cases, the carbon colour can be selected to match the ribbon colour of the original.

Hectograph carbon paper. See **Spirit duplicating.** This is used when typing masters for spirit duplicating.

Insertion into the typewriter. If only a single carbon copy is required, the typist should place a sheet of flimsy paper on the desk and on top of it place a sheet of carbon paper of the same size—with the carbonized side facing the flimsy. She should then place the paper on which she will type (the top copy as it is always known) above the carbon paper with the typewriting side uppermost. The papers should then be picked up with the flimsy paper facing the typist; the papers should be aligned at the top by gently tapping them on the desk and manipulating them with the fingers. The typist should then insert the papers into the typewriter with the *top* of the typewriting paper first entering the machine and the flimsy paper facing her. If the papers need further aligning, the paper release lever should be used.

Many typist experience difficulty when using several sheets of carbon paper. The method of arranging the papers before insertion into the typewriter is basically the same as the one described above. The typist places above the first flimsy and carbon as many further flimsies and carbons as are required before placing the top copy above the last sheet of carbon paper.

To facilitate the insertion of numerous sheets into a typewriter, one can use a special backing sheet with a folded end, to help keep the edges straight and in line. Alternatively, it helps if the typist pulls forward the paper release lever before inserting the papers into the machine and, after careful insertion, replaces it so that the feed rollers grip together all the papers.

Another method frequently adopted with numerous carbons is first to insert the papers into the typewriter without the carbons. When the feed rollers have gripped them about half an inch, the sheets of paper should be brought forward and turned back separately after insertion of a carbon for each flimsy. This method also assists removal of the carbons when the typing is complete and the papers have been taken from the machine. It is a simple matter to hold the top edges of the paper in one hand and neatly pull all the protruding bottom edges of the carbons with the other hand.

Some typists use carbon paper with the top right or left corner cut away. After the papers have been removed from the typewriter, she holds the papers at the corner where there is no carbon and gives a little shake so the carbons all fall out on to the desk. This method is quicker and cleaner than handling the individual sheets.

Points to observe when carbon copying

1. The type faces should be clean and in good condition for the production of clear, incisive copies.

2. The platen should be hard if a large number of carbons is required. Some typewriters can be fitted with interchangeable platens so that it is an easy matter to substitute a hard platen when numerous copies are required. The platen should be kept free from pitting and a backing sheet always used when only one copy is being taken.

3. With manual typewriters the typist should use a sharp, even touch. Any unevenness in striking the keys will show clearly on the carbons.

Handling and storage. Carbons should be handled lightly and carefully or the carbon deposit will get on to the typist's hands, resulting in messy work. Carbon paper should be frequently turned upside down and a strip cut off the top or bottom edge when it gets very worn: this will ensure that the maximum use is obtained from each carbon sheet.

The habit should be established of fully using each carbon or group of carbons before starting new sheets.

Carbon paper should always be kept away from heat. It should be stored flat, preferably in a box or drawer in a cool place. The 'treed' effect produced by carbons is caused when they are creased. Creasing sometimes happens if carbons are badly inserted into the typewriter. Such creasing, however, may not be the typist's fault and if it happens despite all care being taken, she should check whether the feed-roller mechanism of the typewriter requires adjustment.

Correcting carbon copies. To correct an error when carbon paper is being used, the following procedure should be adopted.

1. Lift the paper bail and turn the sheets forward until the error rests on the erasure table.

2. Move the carriage to the extreme right or left (which is nearer the error) by using the margin release key. This will help prevent any eraser particles from falling into the type basket.

3. Insert a slip of paper behind each sheet of carbon at the point of the error.

4. Erase on the top copy (see **Correcting errors** (*Erasing*)). Then erase on the first carbon copy, using only a soft eraser, and remove the first slip of paper. Proceed to the second carbon—and so on until all copies have been corrected and all the slips of paper removed.

5. Replace the paper bail and turn the platen back to the correct position for typing the correction.

6. If corrections have to be made to carbon copies after they have been

removed from the typewriter, a small piece of carbon paper should be placed between the ribbon and the paper before each correction is separately typed, to secure uniformity in the appearance of the carbon copies.

If a note needs to be typed on the carbon(s) but should not appear on the top copy, a small piece of paper should be inserted between the ribbon and the paper at the printing point before the note is typed. Conversely, if something must be typed on the top copy but not on the carbons, a slip of paper should be inserted behind each carbon where the note will appear on the top copy.

When letters, etc., are presented for signature, the carbon copy or copies should always be attached. If the person signing makes any alterations, he normally immediately marks up the carbon(s): otherwise the typist must make sure she carefully marks them up herself. If a number of errors have been made, the typist will obviously need to retype. However, alterations may not always be the typist's fault and may result from new information or second thoughts on the part of the dictator. Carbon copies should, of course, always be an exact record of the original.

Circulation of carbon copies. When carbon copies are sent to persons other than the addressee, it is common practice to type at the foot of the letter or other documents, 'cc' (copy circulated to) followed by the names, in alphabetical order, of all the other recipients, each starting on a new line at the same point of the scale. This information usually appears on all the copies so that everyone concerned is aware of the distribution. The name of the person for whom each copy is intended is either ticked at the side or the person's name underscored: this practice helps ensure correct distribution.

Sometimes the writer may not want the addressee to know that copies have been distributed to other persons—in which case a 'blind carbon copy' note is made. In this situation, the typist will insert a piece of plain paper between the ribbon and the top copy at the printing point. She will then type the letters 'bcc' followed by the names of the other recipients. The bottom copy on which the blind carbon copy note appears should be retained for filing.

Card guide. See **Parts of a typewriter.**

Cardinal numbers. These are the simple numbers 1, 2, 3, (one, two, three) etc., as distinct from ordinal numbers—1st, 2nd, 3rd (first, second, third) etc. The abbreviated forms of ordinal numbers should never be followed by a stop except at the end of a sentence.

Care of the typewriter. To assist with the production of first-class typewritten work it is essential that a typewriter is kept in good working order. There is much that the typist herself can do and she will need a good cleaning kit comprising the following:

1. A soft duster which should be regularly cleaned and replaced.
2. A long-handled, soft-bristled dusting brush.
3. A stiff-bristled, type-face cleaning brush.
4. A bottle of typewriter oil.
5. A small bottle of methylated spirit.

Dust is one of the greatest enemies of the typewriter so it is vital that the typist keeps her typewriter as clean as possible. The following routine is recommended.

1. The typewriter should be covered at the end of each day and whenever it is not in use for a prolonged period.
2. The typist should daily remove the front cover of the frame and carefully brush the dust from all the accessible parts of the typewriter with the long-handled, soft-bristled brush. She should brush away dust from underneath the machine and from the desk.
3. The type faces should be regularly cleaned with the stiff-bristled brush (particularly when the ribbon is new or when stencils have been cut). This should be done carefully with a gentle backward and forward movement: a sideways movement may affect the alignment of the type. The occasional use of a little spirit on the brush will help keep the type faces clean so they produce clean, incisive typewritten work. Alternatively, one can use a spray type-cleaning aerosol, a special roller, or type-clean pieces of plastic. Type-cleaning aerosols are simple and clean to use: some makes are low in toxicity and non-flammable. Putty-like rollers with a handle attached remove dirt when rolled backwards and forwards across the type faces. The special type-clean pieces of plastic are rubbed across the type faces in the same way as the roller: they can be moulded in the hands to present a clean surface after use, and thus may be used many times. If the type faces are regularly cleaned in one of the ways described, it will not be necessary to resort to drastic measures, such as poking with pins or other sharp instruments, which can damage the type.
4. Once a week the typist should remove all dirty, coagulated oil from the carriage rails with a duster. She should then lightly oil a clean section of the duster and gently wipe the carriage rails with it. No other parts of the machine should be oiled by the typist herself.
5. The typist should regularly polish all the plate work and enamel with a soft, clean duster. A little spirit will help remove any ribbon ink, etc., which may have got on to the frame.
6. When erasing, the carriage should be moved to the extreme right or left (using the margin release key) so that rubber particles will not

fall into the type basket, as typewriter erasers contain powdered glass which damages metal.

7. When typing on a single sheet of paper, a backing sheet should always be used to prevent wear and pitting of the platen (see **Platen restorer**). The backing sheet will also help improve the appearance of the typewriting (see **Backing sheets**).

8. When the platen becomes shiny it should be wiped with a cloth moistened with methylated spirit.

9. A typewriter should never be left near a hot radiator as this will dry up the oil: nor should it be left in a position where it may be knocked off the desk by a clumsy passer-by.

10. The typist should never just 'yank' or pull the paper out of her machine: if near the bottom of the paper, she should turn the platen knob, or otherwise use the paper injector/ejector lever or paper release lever.

11. The typewriter desk should be really firm and a non-slip mat on which to stand the typewriter is important. The latter not only helps reduce noise but also softens the reverberations and movement of the typewriter parts—thus assisting to maintain it in smooth and good running order. (See **Mats, typewriter.**)

12. When using an electric typewriter, care should be taken to ensure there are no trailing cables, which could cause harm to both passer-by and typewriter.

13. If a typewriter has to be moved, it should be lifted by the base from the back and *never by any other part*. After use, and when being moved, the carriage should be locked by the special locking device (if the machine has one), or alternatively the margin stops should be moved to the centre of the carriage: this will prevent the carriage from sliding and causing possible damage to the machine.

14. If any part of the typewriter mechanism is not working properly, the typewriter should not be used until a skilled mechanic has repaired the fault. If a typewriter is in frequent use, it should be professionally serviced at least two or three times a year. This is especially necessary in the case of electric typewriters.

15. When an electric typewriter is not going to be used for a period, make sure that it is switched off. Particular care should be taken with machines that do not have a light to indicate they are switched on. This is especially important at the end of the day: a machine left switched on overnight is a serious fire risk, as well as causing unnecessary wear on the motor.

16. If any fault which appears to be connected with the electrical parts occurs with an electric typewriter, *do not* attempt to correct it. Switch off the machine, pull the plug out of the wall socket and call a mechanic. It is dangerous to tamper with electrical equipment, and especially dangerous to probe a machine connected to the mains.

A typewriter is a valuable and indispensable piece of equipment in any office, and if the above points are observed by the typist the working life of her machine will be considerably prolonged, money will be saved, and the typewriter will produce better quality work.

Caret sign. See **Combination characters and special signs.**

Carriage. See **Parts of a typewriter.**

Carriage release lever drills. See **Drills.**

Carriage release levers. See **Parts of a typewriter.**

Carriage return drills. See **Drills.**

Carriage return lever. See **Parts of a Typewriter.**

Catchword. When typed matter consists of more than one page a catchword is sometimes placed at the foot of each page, except the last. A catchword consists of the first word or words on the following page. One line of space is left before typing the catchword: it is preceded by the solidus and ends at the right-hand margin. Catchwords were formerly used as a matter of form in official correspondence, but are now seldom used at all.

Sometimes P.T.O. (or PTO, p.t.o., pto) or Continued (in full or abbreviated) are used instead of a catchword to indicate that the typing continues on another sheet.

In actors' parts in plays, the last word (or words) of the previous speaker is known as a catchword and acts as a cue.

cc (copy circulated to). See **Carbon copying** (*Circulation of copies*).

Cedilla. See **Combination characters and special signs.**

Cent. See **Combination characters and special signs.**

Centring headings. See **Headings.**

Centring—horizontal and vertical (see also **Display**). When the typist is centring or typing any work that involves complicated display, a knowledge of paper sizes and scales is essential. Under **Paper for typewriting** the number of spaces across A4 and A5 paper and the number of vertical lines of typewriting (for both pica and elite pitch) are given.

If the typist experiences difficulty in remembering figures, or if she is typing on a different size of paper (one that is folded, for instance), the process is simple. The paper should be held against the paper bail so that the left-hand edge is at zero, and the number of character spaces across the sheet should be noted. For vertical purposes, there are six lines of typewriting to the inch in single spacing for both pica and elite:

so if you are in any doubt about the correct figure, measure the depth of the paper and multiply the number of inches by six. If an unusual type face is being used, the number of lines to the inch can easily be found by typing on a scrap piece of paper 6–8 words, each beginning on a new line in single spacing; then measure with a ruler. Once these basic facts have been established, it is an easy task for a skilled typist to display her work pleasingly and quickly.

Full instructions for centring main headings over equal left- and right-hand margins are given under **Headings.** If the heading lines are being blocked it will be necessary to centre the longest line only: all other lines will begin at the same point.

If a piece of typewritten display is to be typed on a separate sheet of paper, side margins should be equal; in addition, there should be equal top and bottom margins.

Vertical centring. When centring typewritten matter vertically it is necessary to count the number of line spaces the work will occupy (counting, of course, both type and space). If the line spacing of the display will not be uniform (in a Notice, for example) it is helpful to make a light pencil mark of the spacing to be allowed between the different parts. This should be done *very lightly* with a soft pencil if the figures are to be erased later.

The total number of line spaces the work will occupy should be deducted from the total down the page and the answer divided by two—so that the same space will appear above and below the typing. For example, if a notice has to be typed on A5 landscape (the wider side at the top) and the typewritten matter (including spaces between the lines) covers fifteen lines, this should be deducted from the number of lines down the page (in this case, 35) and the answer divided by two: $35 - 15 = 20$, $20 \div 2 = 10$. Therefore there should be ten line spaces above and below the typewritten matter.

The paper should be inserted into the typewriter so that the top edge appears level with the top edge of the typewriter ribbon; the line space selector set for single spacing and the carriage turned up eleven times. Typing will begin on this eleventh line so that ten clear lines have been left above the typing. The same space will appear below the typing.

Chair, typewriting. Good posture and position at the typewriter are important to the typist (see **Posture and position at typewriter**), and to enable her to work in comfort with the minimum of fatigue a purpose-built typewriter chair should be used—particularly if typing is to be sustained for any length of time.

It should be possible to adjust the height of the typewriter chair and there should be a curved back-support for the typist, to avoid strain on the spine. The seats should be upholstered, with softly-rounded fronts.

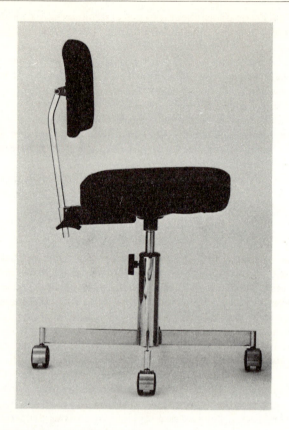

A well-designed typewriter chair

Checking work. See **Proof reading.**

Cheques. Some firms prefer their cheques to be handwritten but others type them. When cheques are typed, a special typewriter with pin-point type is sometimes used: pin-point type is designed so that each character perforates the paper with tiny points and this makes the alteration of sums of money extremely difficult.

If cheques are typed with an ordinary typewriter, it is obviously desirable that an indelible ribbon be used. Figures should always be typed using the decimal point, e.g., £96.00, $6.05, £0.87. This practice differs from handwritten cheques in that with handwriting a hyphen is used to separate the pounds from the pence. When typing the amount in words, the pence may be expressed as figures, unless there are no pounds, e.g., ninety-six pounds only, six pounds 5 (or six pounds 5p), but eighty-seven pence.

Circular letters. See **Letters.**

Civil service letters. See **Letters.**

Clashing of typebars. This is due to faulty touch on the part of the operator and occurs if a key is struck before the previous one has been completely released. The typebars clash and jam near the printing point. When this happens the typebars should be gently separated and released with the fingers. Some machines have a key which, when depressed, will return jammed typebars to their normal position in the type basket.

Cleaning typewriter. See **Care of the typewriter.**

Colon. See **Punctuation marks.**

Column work with column headings (See also **Display**). This is a more complex procedure than typing columns without headings, although the same basic principles apply. Therefore the typist should first master the skill of straightforward column typing before proceeding to this next step. She should also read this section in conjunction with **Column work without column headings.**

(a) *Centring columns to equal left and right margins with column headings wider than the longest word in the column.* The following procedure is recommended.

1. Count the number of characters in each column heading and *lightly* write this in pencil over the column.

2. According to the type of work and the space available, decide how many character spaces are to be left between columns. Lightly write this in pencil in each column space on the copy.

3. Add all these figures together and deduct the total from the number of character spaces across the paper.

4. Divide the answer by two. This is the point where the first column heading should begin and where the left-hand margin stop should be set. Clear any existing tab stops.

5. From the left-hand margin point tap the space bar as many times as there are characters in the first heading. Then tap the space bar according to the number of spaces to be left between columns and set a tab stop. This will be where the second column heading begins.

6. Repeat as in (5) for the second column heading—and so on until all column headings have been dealt with. Right- and left-hand margins will then be equal.

7. Type the first column heading beginning at the left-hand margin point. Press the tab bar/key and type the second column heading—and so on until all the headings have been typed.

8. At least one line space should be left between the column headings and the first line of the columns.

9. The columns should be typed so that each column begins at the same point (unless they contain figures), so that the widest line of the column is centred under the heading. For example, if the width of a column heading is nine characters and the widest item in the column consists of three characters, it will be necessary to tap the space bar three times from the tab stop beginning the column heading to find the point where typing of the column will begin: $9 - 3 = 6$, $6 \div 2 = 3$. This is illustrated in the first column of the example that follows. Once all the column headings have been typed, the left-hand margin and tab stops can be reset at the points where the typing for each column will begin.

STUDENTS ATTENDING FOR ENGLISH

Course No	Monday	Tuesday	Wednesday	Thursday
501	22	18	23	16
502	21	20	19	17
503	20	21	24	16
504	23	21	19	20

(b) *Centring columns to equal left and right margins with column headings narrower than the longest word(s) in the column.* The following procedure is recommended.

1. Count the number of characters in the longest word(s) in each column and *lightly* write this in pencil over the column.

2. According to the type of work and the space available, decide how many character spaces are to be left between each column. Lightly write this in pencil in the column spaces on the copy.

3. Add all these figures together and deduct the total from the number of character spaces across the paper.

4. Divide the answer by two. This is the point where the first column should begin and where the left-hand margin stop should be set. Clear any existing tab stops.

5. From the left-hand margin point tap the space bar as many times as there are characters in the widest line of the first column. Then tap the space bar according to the number of spaces to be left between columns and set a tab stop. This will be where the second column will begin.

6. Repeat as in (5) for the second column—and so on until all columns have been dealt with. Right- and left-hand margins will then be equal.

7. The column headings will need to be typed above the columns and since they will not begin where the left-hand margin stop and tab stops are set, some minor calculations are necessary. Count the number of characters in each heading and lightly pencil these figures over the headings.

8. Centre the main heading (if any), set the line space selector for single spacing and turn up at least twice to the left-hand margin point before typing the column headings.

9. First deduct the number of characters in the first heading from the number of characters in the widest line of the first column. Divide the answer by two and tap the space bar this number of times before typing the heading—which will then appear centred over the typing of the column. Press the tab bar/key to move the carriage to where the second column will begin.

10. Repeat (9) as many times as necessary until all column headings have been typed.

An example follows.

SUSSEX BRANCHES

Town	Address	Tel No
Brighton	44 Crown Court Parade	0273 61204
Eastbourne	26 Hillymead Road	0323 16429
Hastings	41-43 Main Street	0424 17283

(c) *Centring columns to equal left and right margins with some column headings wider and others narrower than the longest word(s) in the column.* The same basic principles as in (a) and (b) above apply, except that the typist must consider each column separately with regard to positioning the column heading in relation to the column width.

This is obviously a more complicated procedure and it should not be attempted until (a) and (b) have been thoroughly mastered.

An illustrative example follows.

39

GOALS SCORED AGAINST LOCAL CLUBS (1976)

Goals	Club	Goals	Club
3	Harriers	1	Longdown
2	Red Aces	3	Spurs
1	Lansdowne	3	Home Park
0	The Wasps	2	Avengers

It will be seen that a wider space has been left between columns (2) and (3) as this is desirable from the point of view of the subject matter.

(*d*) *Column headings consisting of one line and more.* In such a situation the column headings should be centred with each other. The following example will illustrate this.

Course No	Number of Students Enrolled	Number of Students Attending
721	24	19
722	20	16
723	23	17
724	22	18
725	21	16

In the above example, the first column heading lines up with the second line of the second and third columns—so that it is centred to them. Tab stops should be set and column headings positioned in the usual way. The column headings should be typed in their correct sequence, i.e., Course No should *not* be typed first.

When a heading to a column consists of more than one line, *single spacing should be used* as in the above example.

In the following example there are column headings consisting of one, two and three lines. In order to get column two to line up exactly, use of the half spacer is necessary.

COMMERCIAL COURSES

Course	No of Hours of Study	No of Hours for Clerical Duties
Certificate in Office Studies	30	8
Typist/Receptionist	32	9
Secretarial Certificate	33	6
Secretarial Diploma	33	6

(*e*) *More complicated column heading arrangements.* The headings to some tabular work can be complicated in arrangement and the typist should master the basic principles involved so that the work can be carried out speedily and accurately. If sections (*a*) to (*d*) above have been carefully studied and sufficient practice work done, a heading arrangement as in the following example should present few problems.

EXAMINATION RESULTS

Subject	Diploma		Certificate	
	Passed	Failed	Passed	Failed
Audio-typewriting	–	–	5	1
Communication	8	2	15	5
Office Practice	9	1	18	2
Shorthand-typing	3	7	7	7

It will be seen that the heading Diploma is centred over the thirteen spaces from the tab stop set for typing Passed and the end of the column headed Failed (there is one space between each column in this tabulation). Likewise the heading Certificate is centred over the Passed and Failed columns below. One line of space has been left between the top headings Diploma and Certificate and the four headings below: Subject, the heading to the first column, is centred within this space.

For instructions about ruling up, see **Ruling.**

(*f*) *Mixed horizontal and vertical column headings.* Vertical headings require time, patience and skill on the part of the typist and are seldom used. However, occasions may arise when top typists will be required to type them in advanced work and examinations, and the method of typing them should therefore be clearly understood.

An example of a heading with both horizontal and vertical headings follows.

EQUIPMENT ORDERED BY TRAVELLERS

Traveller	Displays	Showcases	Window Lettering	Showcards	Dummy Boxes	Posters	Notes

The body of the tabulation should be typed before the headings are inserted but sufficient space must be left for them. Therefore it is first necessary to determine the depth of space the vertical headings will require. The number of characters (letters and spaces) should be counted in the longest vertical heading and it should be remembered that there are ten characters to the inch with pica pitch and twelve characters to the inch with elite pitch.

In the above example the longest vertical heading is Dummy Boxes (eleven characters in pica pitch). One character space should be allowed before and after the heading, which gives a total of thirteen character spaces—one and three-tenths of an inch. This space should be left between the two horizontal lines within which the headings will be typed.

The paper will need to be inserted into the typewriter sideways for typing the vertical headings—which should all begin at the same point of the scale, as shown, and be centred over their columns. Any horizontal headings should be centred in their boxes and centred to the longest vertical heading. When typing horizontal headings it should be remembered that there are six lines of single space type to the inch for both pica and elite pitch.

(*g*) *Column work with column headings using leader dots.* When typing tabulations it will often be found that the lines of the first column (usually the descriptive one) vary considerably in length: some are short and others double or more in length. In order to improve the appearance of the work and 'square up' the first column, leader dots should be used. In addition, they serve the valuable function of helping to lead the eye correctly to the next column.

A full description of how to type leader dots is given under **Leader dots.** An example follows.

EDUCATION COMMITTEE

Facilities for Recreation, etc

Expenditure on	1976/7 Original Estimate	1976/7 Revised Estimate
	£	£
Play centres..............	10,250	12,000
Playing fields............	86,100	100,000
Swimming baths............	45,000	48,000
Youth centres.............	120,000	130,000
Community centres.........	68,000	70,000
Other community activities	6,500	8,000
Miscellaneous.............	10,500	12,000
TOTAL	£346,350	£380,000

(*h*) *Column typing with column headings using the blocked method of display.* This is easier and quicker than centring the headings to the columns since, once the left-hand margin and tab stops are set, all typing begins at these points.

The typed example given in (*a*) is shown here in blocked style.

STUDENTS ATTENDING FOR ENGLISH

Course No	Monday	Tuesday	Wednesday	Thursday
501	22	18	23	16
502	21	20	19	17
503	20	21	24	16
504	23	21	19	20

If this table were being incorporated in continuous text, the main heading and first column would begin at the left-hand margin point. Apart from this, the same procedure outlined in (*a*), nos. (1), (2), (5–8) would be followed, the main difference being that right- and left-hand margins would not be equal. Point (9) would obviously not apply.

If this blocked table were typed on a separate sheet of paper, points (3) and (4) would be applicable and the table would also be centred vertically (see **Centring—horizontal and vertical**).

The typed example given in (*b*) follows, typed in the blocked style. If incorporated in continuous text the main heading and first column would begin at the left-hand margin point. Apart from this, the same procedure outlined in (*b*), nos. (1), (2), (5), and (6) would be followed.

```
SUSSEX BRANCHES
Town            Address                 Tel No
Brighton        44 Crown Court Parade   0273 61204
Eastbourne      26 Hillymead Road       0323 16429
Hastings        41-43 Main Street       0424 17283
```

If this blocked table were typed on a separate sheet of paper, points (3) and (4) would also be applicable and the table would also be centred vertically (see **Centring—horizontal and vertical**).

The typed example given in (c) follows, typed in the blocked style of layout. The reader will see how the features already illustrated in the previous two typed examples under this section (h) are combined here.

```
GOALS SCORED AGAINST LOCAL CLUBS (1976)

Goals   Club            Goals   Club

3       Harriers        1       Longdown

2       Red Aces        3       Spurs

1       Lansdowne       3       Home Park

0       The Wasps       2       Avengers
```

(i) *Full-page tabulation in the centred style.* A full-page tabulation in the centred style together with recommended typing procedure, is shown on page 45.

When typing a full-page tabulation, a freehand diagram is recommended so that all calculations are clearly set out. With practice, such a diagram can be made in a few minutes and is well worth while. It enables the typist to be satisfied in her mind that her calculations are correct and she can proceed with the typing in an orderly manner: also, if she makes a bad mistake in the middle of typing, she can start again with a minimum of delay.

1. Draw a three-sided rectangle and divide it into as many columns as required by the tabulation. The space on either side should be marked M for the margins (see page 46).

2. Count the characters in the widest item in each column and write this figure in the centre of the column. If the descriptive column is very wide it should be divided to make two lines, or possibly more.

3. Show the number of spaces to be left between each column (this will depend to some extent on the space available and the nature of the work) in a circle to the left of each vertical column line.

HOLIDAYS IN BRITAIN

See the Country in Luxury Coaches

Selected Tours

Area	Days	Tour	Prices from	Hotels
Southern Country Houses	10	SCH 25	£48	Hastings Brighton Southampton
The West Country	14	WC 8	£76	Bath Taunton Exeter Plymouth
The Welsh Scene	10	WS 4	£55	Caernarvon Cardiff
University Highlights	7	VH 3	£40	Oxford Cambridge
Central England	14	CE 15	£70	Derby Coventry Cheltenham Aylesbury
The Lake District	7	LD 5	£48	Keswick Kendal
Scottish Highlights	14	SH 6	£75	Glasgow Oban Edinburgh Perth

Note: if column headings are too wide, abbreviations may be used.

4. Total all these figures and subtract the answer from the number of character spaces across the paper being used.

5. Divide the answer by two for equal margins: this figure should then be written in the margin spaces.

6. Write in at the top of each vertical line the points for the margin (M) and tab (T) settings. Check that the last figure and allowance for the right-hand margin add up to the correct number (in the example given, it is 100).

7. Insert the paper into the typewriter so that the left-hand edge is at zero on the paper bail and clear all existing tab stops.

8. Set the margin and tab stops at the appropriate places, using the figures on the paper bail as a guide.

9. Allow equal space above and below the typing (see **Centring—horizontal and vertical**).

10. Type each full horizontal line at a time, using a ruler on the copy as a line guide. Do *not* type column by column.

All calculations should be clearly shown on the diagram. For method of typing the main centred headings, see **Headings**; and for method of

Column work with column headings

ruling, see **Ruling.** Note that each tab setting marks *the point where the widest item in the column will begin.*

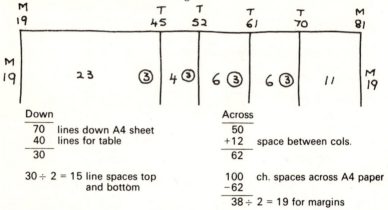

Down
70	lines down A4 sheet
40	lines for table
30	

30 ÷ 2 = 15 line spaces top and bottom

Across
50	
+12	space between cols.
62	

100	ch. spaces across A4 paper
−62	
38 ÷ 2 = 19 for margins	

Diagram for the tabulation of Holidays in Britain

(j) Full-page tabulation in the blocked style. The same tabulation, typed in the blocked method of layout:

HOLIDAYS IN BRITAIN

See the Country in Luxury Coaches

Selected Tours

Area	Days	Tour	Prices from	Hotels
Southern Country Houses	10	SCH 25	£48	Hastings Brighton Southampton
The West Country	14	WC 8	£76	Bath Taunton Exeter Plymouth
The Welsh Scene	10	WS 4	£55	Caernarvon Cardiff
University Highlights	7	VH 3	£40	Oxford Cambridge
Central England	14	CE 15	£70	Derby Coventry Cheltenham Aylesbury
The Lake District	7	LD 5	£48	Keswick Kendal
Scottish Highlights	14	SH 6	£75	Glasgow Oban Edinburgh Perth

Note: Since the figures in the columns headed Days and Tour need not be totalled, it is not necessary for the units to line up.

The recommended procedure for drawing a diagram and making calculations prior to typing is the same as that which follows the centred style of layout under (*i*). As will be seen, the only difference is that all typing begins at the left-hand margin point and at the tab stop positions.

Nothing is centred, which leads to a considerable increase in speed of typing—and many people would consider that the overall general impression is just as pleasing.

Column work without column headings (see also **Display**). Sometimes a typist will be required to type and display simple matter arranged in columns. An equal space should be left between each column. As a general rule three or four spaces are ideal: the columns should not be too spread out since this detracts from the appearance of the work—and can be a positive handicap if the eye has to move across the typing.

Single or double line spacing may be used when typing the columns, depending upon the space available and the nature of the work.

Simple column work of this kind will often be typed on a separate sheet of paper—in which case equal side margins and top and bottom margins should be used (see **Centring—horizontal and vertical**). If the column work must appear within the body of the text and needs to be centred to the typing line, equal side margins make this a simple process. If the blocked method is being used, the first column and the heading (if there is one) will begin at the left-hand margin point.

(*a*) *Centring columns to equal right and left margins.* The following procedure is recommended.

1. Count the number of characters in the longest word(s) in each column and *lightly* write this in pencil over the column.

2. According to the type of work and the space available, decide how many character spaces are to be left between each column. Lightly write this in pencil in the column spaces on the copy.

3. Add all these figures together and deduct the total from the number of character spaces across the paper.

4. Divide the answer by two. This is the point where the first column should begin and where the left-hand margin stop should be set. Clear any existing tab stops.

5. From the left-hand margin point tap the space bar as many times as there are characters in the widest line of the first column. Then tap the space bar according to the number of spaces to be left between columns and set a tab stop. This will be where the second column will begin.

6. Repeat as in (5) for the second column, and so on until all columns have been dealt with. Right- and left-hand margins will then be equal.

7. If the columns have a main heading(s) this should be centred over

the typing, but with equal margins this will present no problem (see **Headings**).

An example follows.

```
          SOME DIFFICULT SPELLINGS

accede        because      catalogue     deceive

accommodate   benign       catastrophe   decision

account       biscuits     category      definite

accuracy      brought      caution       disappoint

autonomy      business     chief         disparage
```

(*b*) *Column typing with the blocked method.* If columns need to be blocked to a predetermined left-hand margin point, the procedure is basically the same except that less calculation is necessary and the space to the right and left of the columns will not be equal. A recommended procedure follows.

1. Count the number of characters in the widest word(s) in each column and *lightly* write this in pencil over the column.

2. According to the type of work and the space available, decide how many character spaces are to be left between each column. Lightly write this in pencil in the column spaces on the copy.

3. From the left-hand margin tap the space bar as many times as there are characters in the widest line of the first column. Then tap the space bar according to the number of spaces to be left between columns and set a tab stop. This will be where the second column will begin.

4. Repeat as in (3) for the second column—and so on until all columns have been dealt with.

5. If the columns have a heading this will begin at the left-hand margin point. See **Headings** for information about heading devices if the heading consists of more than one line.

Combination characters and special signs. A combination character is formed from two single characters—either typed one over the other, or one slightly above or below the other. A special sign uses a key already on the typewriter but employs it for a purpose different from its usual one. When part of the character is higher or lower than the other, care must be taken to see that the platen is returned to its normal position before continuing to type: to facilitate this, use of the half spacer or interliner is recommended rather than the variable line spacer.

Combination characters and special signs increase the number of symbols a typewriter will produce without adding to the number of type bars. The main ones follow.

Name	Example	Method of Formation
Asterisk	✳	Type lower case **x**; then backspace and type a hyphen. The asterisk is the first of the three footnote signs and is raised half a space. Most typewriters now have an asterisk key. (See also **Literary work** (*Footnotes*).)
Brace	{ or }	Use left or right bracket sign, whichever is required, one under the other.
Brackets (square)	⌐ ⌐	Type the solidus, backspace and underscore. When typing the upper horizontal line, the platen must be raised one space.
Caret	∠	Type the solidus, backspace once and type the underscore.
Cedilla	ç	Type lower case **c**, backspace and type a comma *slightly* below the **c**. (See also **Accents**.)
Cent	¢	Type lower case **c**, backspace and type the solidus.
Dagger	‡	Type upper case **I**, backspace and type a hyphen. The dagger is the second footnote sign (see Asterisk, above) and is raised half a space.
Dash	–	A hyphen with a space before and after it.
Decimal Point	13.8	Type the full stop in its normal position.
Degree	54°	Type required figures then a lower case **o** raised half a space.
Diaeresis (umlaut)	Nöel	Type the double quotation sign above the required letter. In English this sign is dying out: at one time it was used in such words as zoölogy and pre-ëminent.
Ditto sign	"	Use double quotation sign.
Division Mark	⌐	Type the right bracket, backspace and use the underscore on the line above.
Division Sign	÷	Type a hyphen, backspace and type a colon.
Dollar	$	Type upper case **S**, backspace and type the solidus.

Combination characters and special signs

Name	Example	Method of Formation
Double Dagger	‡ or ‡	Type two upper case I's, one slightly above the other *or* type upper case I, backspace and type the equals sign *slightly* raised. The double dagger is the third footnote sign (see Asterisk and Dagger above). The double dagger is raised half a space.
Equals Sign	=	Type a hyphen, backspace then type a second hyphen *slightly* above the first one. Most typewriters now have an 'equals' key.
Exclamation Mark	!	Type a single quotation sign, backspace and type a full stop.
Foot Symbol	6'	Type the required figure(s) followed by the single quotation sign.
Fractions (other than those given on keyboard)		See **Mathematical Typing**.
Inches Symbol	9"	Type the required figure(s) followed by the double quotation sign.
Mille	o/oo	Type *slightly* raised lower case **o** followed by a solidus and two lower case **o**'s on the normal typing line.
Minus	6 – 3 = 3	Use the hyphen with a space before and after it. (See also **Mathematical Typing**.)
Minutes	18'	Type the required figure(s) followed by the single quotation sign.
Multiplication Sign	4 x 3 = 12	Use lower case **x** with a space before and after it. (See also **Mathematical Typing**.)
Per Cent Sign	o/o	Type the required figure(s) followed by a slightly raised lower case **o**. Follow this with the solidus and a second lower case **o** on the normal typing line. Most typewriters now have a 'per cent' key.
Seconds	45"	Type the required figure(s) followed by the double quotation sign.
Section Mark	§ or §	Type upper case **S**, backspace and type a second upper case **S** slightly below the first one; *or* follow the same method but use lower case **s** instead.

Name	Example	Method of Formation
Semi-colon	;	Type a colon, backspace and type a comma. Most typewriters now have a semi-colon key.

Common word drills. See **Drills.**

Common words. See **Word frequency: its significance in typewriting.**

Compliments slips. Compliments slips are usually printed on A6 (half A5) paper and are sent with leaflets, etc., where no specific message is required. They begin with the words WITH THE COMPLIMENTS OF followed by the name of the firm (or a particular officer of the firm) and its address.

If compliments slips are rarely required, they may be typed, displayed on A6 paper.

Some firms which find A4 too large for their correspondence requirements, and A5 too small, use two-thirds of an A4 sheet for letter purposes and the bottom one-third for a compliment slip. See p. 189 for an illustration.

Composing machines. See **Special purpose typewriters.**

Contents page(s). See **Literary work.**

Copyholders (see also **Posture and position at typewriter**). Copyholders situated behind the typewriter are not recommended as they remove the copy too far from the eyes: they also tend to make the typist strain forward in a tense position which causes fatigue. The ideal position for the copy is immediately in front of the worker as she types, and copyholders have been developed with this principle in mind. The fixing of such elaborate copyholders should be rigid enough to prevent vibration and rattle.

It is not advisable to use a metal copyholder that consists of a stand placed on an upright rod and metal base because the copy will vibrate and the copyholder rattle—both of which are distracting and tiring to the typist.

The copy should be in a gently sloping position—*not* placed flat on the desk, since this causes eye strain. There should be as little as possible effort involved in reading the copy, merely a slight turn of the head.

It is generally agreed that the best type of copyholder consists of a gently-sloping block with a narrow ledge at the base for the foot of the copy to rest against.

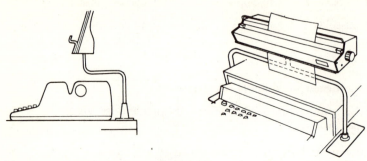

Two types of copyholder. One is fixed at the rear of the typewriter and the other bridges the carriage

Copying machines. See **Photocopying.**

Correcting errors (see also **Carbon copying, Ink duplicating, Spirit duplicating** and **Offset lithography duplicating**). All typists, no matter how skilful they may be, occasionally make errors that have to be corrected; therefore mastery of the different methods of correction is important for the production of first-class typewritten work. A page of otherwise good typing can be completely marred by a few poorly made corrections. Correction takes time so it is worth learning the different methods and correct techniques and persevering until corrections can be made so well that the alterations are barely, if at all, visible. Lazy typists often type over their errors or -x them out: such people, however, rarely obtain good secretarial or clerical jobs—and, of course, such disdain is heavily penalized in typewriting examinations.

Erasing. The most common method of correcting typewriting errors is by use of a rubber eraser. In the early stages of typing instruction, students are not allowed to correct: this is because the teacher can learn much from the type of error being made and its frequency, and give help accordingly. However, once students begin production work (letters usually being the first exercise of this kind) they are usually told to correct any errors as they go along, in order to help them into the habit of producing good, mailable copy. Many students do not master sufficiently well the important technique of erasing. Neat and swift erasing is a skilled operation requiring specific teaching on the part of the teacher and careful practice by the students.

Students should possess both a soft and hard eraser, which should always be kept scrupulously clean. There are several different kinds on the market but possibly the best is the pencil type that has soft rubber at one end and hard rubber at the other end (two in one—therefore often called a 'twin' eraser). One advantage of the pencil type of eraser over the other shapes (circular, hexagonal, wedge-shaped, etc.) is that it is easier for the typist to rub only on the actual error. This is important for really good erasing and many typists rub away on a much larger area of paper than that occupied by the error. It is possible to purchase celluloid or plastic shields (with various shapes and sizes cut out of them) to assist the typist here. However, if she skilfully uses a 'twin' eraser these are not necessary: in fact they can be a hindrance and time-waster and result in smudging of the copy.

Electric erasers are available which have a revolving rubber tip. They are comparatively expensive for normal office use but generally found in drawing offices.

After lifting the paper bail and turning the platen so that the mistake lies on the erasure table (the sloping metal bar situated immediately behind the platen), the surface ink of the error should be carefully removed with the soft end of the eraser using a gentle, circular motion. As far as possible, only the side of the eraser tip (which should be blunt) should come into contact with the paper: fingers should be kept well away to avoid finger marks and smudging. Care should be taken to avoid the part obliteration of neighbouring letters or characters. The typewriter carriage should first be moved, using the margin release key, to the extreme right- or left-hand position (whichever is nearer to the error) to prevent eraser particles from falling down into the type basket —one of the worst enemies of the typewriter. For the same reason, when erasure of the correction is completed, the typist should firmly blow or brush the rubber dust away from the typewriter.

After the surface ink has been removed with a soft eraser, the typist should then use a hard eraser to remove the remainder of the ink. Special care should be taken here for if the rubbing is too vigorous, either unnecessary damage to the paper or an actual hole will result. For a really good correction the typist should finally place a piece of paper over the erased spot and rub it with her thumbnail to smooth down the paper fibres that have been disturbed. When typing in the correction, care should be taken (with manual typewriters) to ensure that the keys are struck with the same pressure as for the rest of the typing on the page.

If you have to make a correction when nearing the bottom of the paper, turn back to the top of the paper instead of turning on. The correction can be made by bringing the paper over the top of the machine (so that the error lies on the erasure table): a carbon copy is less likely to slip with this method.

It is much easier to correct work while it is still in the typewriter, so the typist should get into the habit of checking a page of typing before removing it from the machine. If you need to make a correction after the paper has been taken from the typewriter, great care must be taken to ensure perfect alignment (by using the paper-release lever, variable line spacer, and line indicators). Accurate registration is secured by bringing a thin letter (e.g., **i** or **l**) exactly above the printing point, then using the variable line spacer to get the typing line level with the line indicators (See **Parts of a typewriter** (*Line indicators*)). Until you are perfectly familiar with a particular typewriter it is a good idea to check the position and alignment by disengaging the ribbon (using the stencil switch), and very lightly tapping the first letter to see how it will appear.

Other kinds of correctors. On the market there are various other correcting products which can be used instead of an eraser. Descriptions of the main ones follow.

Opaquing liquid. The most common form is applied from a bottle by means of a small brush that is attached to the top of the bottle, like a nail varnish brush. One can also buy a specially-designed 'correction pen'. Pens are comparatively more expensive than bottled opaquing fluid but are especially useful for pin-point corrections: in addition, they are convenient for carrying about in a handbag or pocket. The liquid is dispersed from a small opening in the tip of the pen through a valve that opens when pressure is applied to the point (or sometimes when the pen is shaken). Thus, with these correcting fluids the error is painted over and, when dry, the correction is made. Care must be taken to use the liquid sparingly or the dry blob will stand above the surface of the paper. It is important to wait until the fluid is completely dry before typing over the correction, otherwise the typist will merely end up with a mess. Some of these liquids are described as 'liquid paper' and it is stated that they penetrate into the paper without build-up or flaking.

Many people find the liquid correctors too obvious for general use but often use them when typescript is to be photocopied or electronically stencilled.

Correction paper. One can purchase specially-prepared strips of paper (available in a variety of types and colours to accord with the paper and type of work) whereby the typist types over the error through one of these strips and then, after removing the strip, types in the correction. Care has to be taken to see that the same spot on the correction strip is not used more than once or the error will not be satisfactorily obliterated and, in addition, the colour of the strip must match that of the paper exactly or the correction will be very noticeable. If the paper on which such corrections are made is frequently handled or folded, the coating powder tends to wear off, revealing the error and thus giving the impression of an overtype.

Correction ribbons. Typewriter ribbons are available which cover up errors in a similar way to correction paper. The lower track of the ribbon is impregnated with a white compound and when this is brought into operation the error can be overlaid with a white powder and the correction made with the inked part of the ribbon.

Pressure-sensitive letters. It is possible to buy 'patches' (pressure-sensitive letters) based on the transfer system: these are widely used by designers. They are supplied in sheets of the most commonly used type faces. Individual letters, complete with a white backing, can be placed over an error and pressed on, covering the error and putting the correct letter in place in one operation. These are particularly useful when making corrections after the paper has been removed from the type-writer.

All the correcting methods described under the heading *Other kinds of correctors* will deal with the *top copy only*: carbon copies are best handled in the usual way with an eraser (see **Carbon copying**).

In most public typewriting examinations, corrections are not penalized if they are well made and barely visible—but this is seldom the case with methods other than erasing. There is, perhaps, no satisfactory substitute for good erasing, and the use of other methods is advocated chiefly if speed of production of a top copy is the main factor or, in some cases, when preparing masters for reproduction.

Half-space correcting. Sometimes a wrong word may be typed that has only one character more, or less, than the correct word. If the typist realizes the error immediately she can, of course, correct in the usual way: however, she may not notice it until considerably later. By using what is known as half-space correcting, such a mistake can be corrected so that it is not necessary to retype a whole page or large part of one. After the correction there will be either half a space or one and a half spaces on either side of the correction depending on whether a character is being added or subtracted. Some typewriters (particularly electrics) have a special key for half-space correcting to make it possible for a character to be typed exactly half way between the set units of the escapement; but if a typewriter is not equipped in this way it is still possible (except with electric typewriters) to correct satisfactorily by the half-space method. There are several ways of doing this but the easiest and most reliable way is as follows.

For instance, if it is necessary to correct the word 'had' to 'have' the incorrect word should first be erased and the carriage moved to the position where the second letter had been typed. The backspace key should be held right down, the first letter typed and then the backspace key released. Then one space should be tapped, the backspace key held down again while the second letter is typed, then the backspace key released. Each subsequent letter should be dealt with in the same way.

If it necessary to reverse the procedure and, say, correct 'have' to 'had', the same method should be followed—except that the typist should start by moving the carriage to where the third letter had been typed.

If half-space correcting is practised for a few minutes it will be found a simple and effective means of correction. The spacing before and after the word is always different from the standard one space but the difference is scarcely noticeable—and enlightened typewriting examiners recognize the occasional need for half-space correcting, and if it is well done they do not penalize.

Correcting on papers fastened together. If an error is discovered on a sheet of typescript that is fastened to others at the top, it is possible to correct it without separating all the sheets of paper. After the error has been erased, a sheet of plain paper should be inserted into the typewriter in the normal way: it should be turned up about an inch and a half above the line indicators. Then the bottom of the sheet for correction should be inserted between the paper in the machine and the *front* of the platen and the platen turned backwards to the point where the correction is to be made. As soon as the feed rollers under the platen grip the paper to be corrected the plain paper can be removed. The paper should then be adjusted to the right position for correction.

The correction of errors requires time, skill and patience. The fewer the errors made the less time will be wasted and the less will patience be tried. In all typewriting work, therefore, the typist should aim at *speed combined with accuracy* and should not type beyond the speed at which she can type with a high degree of accuracy. The typist should remember that correction is really a waste of valuable time—and it is not for nothing that most typewriting speed championships deduct ten words for every error made.

Correcting on papers fastened together. See **Correcting errors.**

Correction paper. See **Correcting errors.**

Correction ribbons. See **Correcting errors.**

Correction signs. See **Typewriter and manuscript signs.**

Credit note. See **Invoices.**

Cylinder. See **Parts of a typewriter.**

Dagger. See **Combination signs and special characters.**

Dash. See **Punctuation marks.**

Date. See **Letters.**

Dead keys. See **Accents.**

Debit note. See **Invoices.**

Decimal point. In typewriting the decimal point is indicated by using the full stop (lightly struck so it will not pierce the paper). When handwriting one normally raises the decimal point but for typewriting purposes it is typed on the normal line of typing, as in this example.

The gross weight is 65.75 kg but the net weight is only 52.45 kg.

Always show the required number of decimal places by using zero, if necessary. Examples follow.

Two decimal places: 74.60 not 74.6

Three decimal places: type 27.750 not 27.75

Decorations. See **Titles, decorations, qualifications, forms of address, etc.**

Degree mark. See **Combination signs and special characters.**

Demonstration. Demonstration and imitation play an important part throughout our lives. All young children possess a natural instinct to imitate after watching other children or people do particular things. At first the imitation is unwitting and they learn by trial and error. As a child's intellect develops, however, he becomes less and less satisfied with trying to succeed in doing a particular thing without guidance. He asks to be *shown* how to accomplish a particular movement or series of movements. For instance, when he first learns to dress himself, the operation of doing up buttons or tying shoe laces seems difficult—and many demonstrations and attempts are necessary before the performance becomes automatic. This, of course, is *deliberate imitation*—which speeds up the learning process and reduces the number of trials and errors.

In the learning of any complex skilled movement, demonstration by an expert (with accompanying trial and error, and success) plays an important part. No one, no matter how clever he may be, can satisfactorily acquire a difficult skill before observing an expert performing it and giving guidance.

Many apparently simple operations are, in fact, quite complicated. Most of us carry out complex movements—such as driving a car, or typing—and tend to forget that the acquisition of those skills was initially difficult and painstaking.

It is often said that many people can *do* things expertly but cannot *teach* them. This is because they cannot attune their minds to those of the learners and do not realize that the art of demonstration is a very important part of the skills teacher's attributes. A good skills teacher should, of course, be an expert practitioner. In addition, she should practise demonstration of the particular features of her art, analyse each movement she will have to teach, and practise verbal description of it.

We all differ to some extent in our ability to do certain things. With regard to skills, the visiles learn more by watching a movement, and the motiles learn more by 'getting the feel' of it. Some motiles actually need at times to experience a movement mentally and to be put through the motions of a task (without actually doing it) before they can perform it.

In the teaching situation, skill students should be encouraged occasionally to describe their own actions, both orally and in writing, and should be given assistance in acquiring the necessary vocabulary. This is a valuable exercise in several ways: it improves their English ability, both spoken and written, and helps them to realize the need for presenting descriptions in logical order. All these skills will, of course, be of great value to the students, and when the need arises for them to demonstrate and explain a movement, or series of movements, to someone else, they will have a good idea how to go about it successfully.

Certain features of skill teaching are common to the teaching of most other skills. For instance, it is always necessary to explain what is going to be demonstrated so the students know what to look for: the teacher should always explain *why* a certain process is preferred to others. Clarity of presentation is of prime importance (this is why the teacher needs to practise not only the demonstration itself, but also the verbal description of it), and the teacher should ensure that the demonstration is clearly visible to all the students. Unless these fundamental preliminaries are observed, the demonstration may well be a failure, with the concept of what is being attempted becoming lost in confusion and a fog of words.

In typewriting lessons, if the class is small the teacher may prefer to use a demonstration stand that she can wheel round the classroom, and so effectively repeat her demonstration and description as many times as necessary. Other teachers prefer to sit at a typewriter and teach a particular manipulation to small groups at a time while the rest of the class is usefully engaged in some silent task. In addition, if one has the facilities, the teacher may on some occasions prefer to use a film loop (a short piece of film with its end joined to its beginning so that the particular sequence of movements can be repeated as often as required). Some colleges are now using closed-circuit television for typewriting demonstrations. Whatever the method of demonstration, the teacher should begin by ensuring that the materials and apparatus she is going to use are entirely satisfactory: for instance, if using a film loop, nothing can be more disastrous than finding at the last moment that the projector will not work properly.

It is important that the learners first watch the skilled practitioner performing the *whole* of the skill they are about to learn: the separate movements they are to master should be fused into a rapid, harmonious whole so that they have the incentive of a good model at which to aim. The teacher should demonstrate the complete skill several times to ensure that the students have mastered the impression of the whole.

Next the teacher should break down the whole into its constituent parts. A good practice here is for the teacher to summarize verbally the movements she will demonstrate, at the same time writing them on the chalkboard or overhead projector, point by point, and numbering them in their correct sequence. Later, when the students are working on their own, this visual summary can be referred to, if necessary. The teacher should then demonstrate each movement slowly and separately and at the same time explain what she is doing—but using a minimum of words. This part of the demonstration should be repeated several times since it will be difficult for most students to grasp all the points from a single demonstration. The number of repetitions will depend on the complexity of the manipulation and the ability of the students.

The teacher should follow up this breaking down of the whole movement into parts by repetition of the complete skilled movement—in which all the individual movements are blended into a rapid, single whole. The students should never be allowed to lose sight of their ultimate aim.

Next the teacher should invite questions so that any queries or misapprehensions can be cleared up. In addition, she should ask specific questions to ensure that the points to be aimed at are clearly understood. When satisfied on this point, the teacher should get the class or group to imitate her separate movements at a *controlled speed*, but for a short time only. She should watch the learners' performance very carefully and look out for any incorrect movements so that they can be rectified before becoming firmly fixed, when they prove very difficult to correct.

If necessary, the teacher should demonstrate the movements again, calling attention to any general weakness she has noticed. The students should then proceed to practice drill—working on their own at their own speed, with the teacher redemonstrating to individuals or selected groups according to need.

The whole process may be briefly summarized as follows. First demonstrate with speed and expertise to establish a goal for the learners; then slowly analyse the skill into its component parts. Follow this by synthesizing the parts into the whole rapidly; be short and clear in verbal description. Make sure that everyone sees and understands. This basic process applies to the demonstration of most manipulative actions.

Few educationalists condemn demonstration as a teaching method—except in the case of Art and creative subjects. Advocates of demonstration maintain that without it students waste time because, left to their own devices, they develop bad habits that later have to be unlearned (a very difficult process): they also lack the incentive of a good model. It is obviously desirable to teach from the beginning the methods that the experts agree are the best.

Demonstration in teaching use of the shift keys. The foregoing points will be illustrated by a suggested procedure for teaching use of the shift keys.

1. Check that the typewriter (or other means of demonstration) is satisfactory and positioned so that the whole class can clearly see what is being done.

2. Give a skilled demonstration of using shift keys, typing, for instance, a line of words all beginning with a capital letter—so the students can note the fluency they aim eventually to attain. Ensure that these words are written on the chalkboard or overhead projector before the lesson begins.

3. Demonstrate again, this time slowly, analysing each part of the whole movement and describing it briefly in words:

   (a) temporary removal of hand from above the home keys and depression of appropriate shift key with the little finger;
   (b) striking of appropriate letter with the other hand;
   (c) release of shift key and return of hand above the home keys.

Repeat this several times, calling out 'one, two, three' as the different movements are made. Stress the importance of the three-step method until the skill is mastered. Lack of co-ordination of the movements will result (with manual typewriters) in the upper case letters being out of alignment.

4. Repeat the demonstration of the skilled movement, pointing out that the three separate movements are eventually merged into one flowing whole.

5. Invite and ask questions.

6. Get the class to imitate the teacher at a *controlled speed* and under the direction of the teacher as she calls out 'one, two, three'—again typing the words displayed on the chalkboard or overhead projector.

7. Redemonstrate as in (3) if necessary, drawing attention to particular faults you have observed.

8. Give the class practice drill, setting a typing exercise containing a large number of words beginning with a capital letter. Watch each pupil

carefully and demonstrate again to individuals or selected groups as necessary.

Diaeresis (umlaut). See **Combination characters and special signs.**

Disengaging ribbon. This is done by moving the ribbon position indicator to the white marker. When the ribbon is disengaged the type-bars come into direct contact with the paper. The ribbon should always be disengaged when typing stencils: it is also advisable to disengage the ribbon—in order to check position and alignment—before typing in the first letter of a correction after erasing. (See also *Double carbon paper* under **Carbon copying**).

Display. Any typewritten displayed work involves skilful use of paper space and a feeling for pleasing and artistic arrangement. 'Display' does not imply that the work must be centred. First-class displayed matter can be produced by use of both the centred and blocked method of layout. The style chosen will depend on various factors including the nature of the work, the preference of the writer and, possibly, the speed with which the work is required.

Some typists of an artistic temperament have a natural ability for display work. However, most typists, with practice and a sound knowledge of typewriting 'theory' (heading devices, paper sizes and scales, etc.) and good usage, can develop display skill.

Many sections in this work deal with display of one kind or another. Even the typing of a business letter, a memo, or minutes of a meeting, for instance, requires display ability. However, the most searching test of display skill is in the production of tabular matter.

First-class production of tabular matter requires complete mastery of the ability to select the most appropriate size of paper and use it in a balanced and artistic way, with speed. The reader should, in particular, carefully study and apply the information given in the following sections:

Headings; Centring—horizontal and vertical; Column work without headings; Column work with headings; Ruling.

The section **Column work with headings** includes ten sub-sections which are graded according to difficulty: beginning with simple tabulated matter with headings and progressing through all the necessary stages to production of a full-page tabulation in 'both the centred and blocked styles.

Ditto marks. See **Combination characters and special signs.**

Division mark. See **Combination characters and special signs.**

Division of words at line ends (see also **Bell, warning**). A skilled typist will ensure that she keeps as even a right-hand margin as possible. As a time-saver, many experienced operators never divide words at the end of lines. The complicated and sometimes baffling 'rules' for line-end division are thus avoided, yet the right-hand margin can appear quite acceptable. Where line-end division is employed, it should be *kept to a minimum* and a typist should not divide on more than two consecutive lines. When a word is divided a hyphen should be used at the end of the line, not at the beginning of the following line.

Generally accepted rules for word division follow.

1. The pronunciation of a word is the most important factor to consider and several of the following rules are covered by this point. In general, the typist should divide between syllables. This will be clear if she says a word aloud and notes the way it falls into natural syllables, e.g., pic-ture, lan-tern, flex-ible. Words should be divided at these natural points.

2. Words that begin with a prefix should be divided after the prefix, e.g., con-dition, trans-fer: conversely, words that end with a suffix should be divided before the suffix, e.g., harm-less, knowledge-able.

3. When double consonants occur in the middle of a word, divide between them, e.g., neces-sary, inter-rupted. However, if a root word ends in a double consonant the division should be made after the root word, e.g., miss-ing, tell-ing.

4. When three consonants come together in the middle of a word, divide before or after the consonants that are pronounced together, e.g., crum-bling, bank-ruptcy.

5. Words that already contain a hyphen should be divided at the point of the hyphen and never split a second time, e.g., self-reliant, pre-eminent.

6. Composite words should be divided into their original parts, e.g., school-master, mantel-piece.

Words should not be divided in the following cases.

1. Words of one syllable and their plurals should not be divided (with the exception of chil-dren).

2. The last word of a paragraph or page should not be divided.

3. Numbers and sets of figures should not be divided, e.g., £200.50½, 14 × 3 m.

4. Abbreviations should not be divided, e.g., OHMS, UNESCO.

5. A person's name should not be divided. For instance, Mr should not be separated from Brown nor should Mrs W. be separated from her surname, Smith. Likewise the typist should avoid separating degrees and honorary letters from a person's name.

6. Proper nouns are best not divided, e.g., Manchester, Josephine.

7. One or two letters should never stand alone either at the beginning or end of a line.

Dollar sign. See **Combination characters and special signs.**

Double dagger. See **Combination characters and special signs.**

Double letter drills. See **Drills.**

Drafts (see also **Margins**). A draft is the first or any subsequent version of a document (which may be in manuscript or typed form) where revision or amendment is anticipated. In typed form, such a draft should be prepared in double or treble spacing, on inferior quality A4 paper, with wide side margins where alterations can be written, if necessary. The word DRAFT should appear prominently at the top, preferably underlined in red.

Alternatively, if a typist wishes to display matter on a stencil or other reprographic master, she may decide to type a draft first to see how it will fit on to the size of paper required—and from the draft decide upon any desirable alterations. In this case the draft will be typed in the spacing required for the final version.

Drawband. See **Parts of a typewriter.**

Drills. The word 'drill' is perhaps an unfortunate one since it tends to have unpleasant connotations. However, in mastering the skill of typewriting, drills play an important part.

A drill should be a short, intensive and timed typewriting effort with the main aim of improving some particular aspect of keyboard or typewriting technique. Drills are important in typewriting training since they focus attention on specific important aspects of the total skill. They also provide for the intelligent repetition of mental/physical acts until habit has made the acts second nature and they can be performed without conscious effort.

Thus drills should be short (lasting only a few minutes) and varied and have a particular aim that the students should *understand*. It is absolutely vital that the need for repetition is understood: meaningless repetition is of no educational value. The story is told of a young boy who could not master the perfect tense of the verb 'to go'. His teacher, without due explanation, ordered him to write 'I have gone' one hundred times after school. Having done this, the boy left the teacher a note saying 'Teacher, I have finished and have went home'! The same basic principle can be applied to typewriting students who carry out drills without really understanding the *purpose* of what they are doing. Thus, each typewriting drill must have a particular aim and the student must feel a need to improve and master the technique—and achieve a feeling of *satisfaction* when she has successfully accomplished it.

Although the drill period within a lesson should be short and timed, it is not necessary that the students should always perform the same drill: some can be practising for double letter control, others can be working on location drills, and so on, according to need.

Some teachers use a series of drills based on a cyclic plan so that the various points of technique and weakness are dealt with in rotation. With this scheme all aspects of typewriting are dealt with systematically and the students concentrate on one thing at a time.

An important part of the teacher's skill lies in being able to explain and demonstrate good techniques and spot quickly students' weaknesses —so they can be put to work on appropriate drills.

Drills can be divided into three main classes: keyboard drills, technique drills, and remedial drills. Remedial drills are dealt with under **Errors, their cause and remedy.** In addition, finger exercises can be beneficial.

Finger exercises. Finger exercises should be performed for only a minute or so at a time. They serve a dual purpose: they help strengthen the finger muscles and prepare the fingers before beginning to type and, in addition, can have a relaxing effect when the muscles are fatigued after prolonged typing. Here are some suggested exercises.

1. Alternately wring the hands tightly, then shake the loosened fingers from the wrists.

2. Spread the fingers as much as possible. Then spread each finger as wide as possible, working on each finger separately.

3. Repeatedly bring the tips of the fingers to the palms without bending the knuckles of the first joints.

4. Spread the fingers of both hands and hold them outspread for a few moments: then relax the fingers and lightly form a fist.

Keyboard drills. These are designed to improve the student's speed and accuracy in mastering the keyboard. Many teachers begin a lesson with a 'warming-up drill': this is a useful way to fill in the time when students are settling in their places, the register is being marked, etc. Warming-up drills are, of course, a form of keyboard drill, and three suggestions follow. The teacher should stress the need for speed and accuracy.

1. *Alphabetic drill.* This recalls all the letter reaches. The class starts by typing one line of each of the following:

abc abc abc abc abc abc abc abc abc abc abc abc abc abc abc abc abc
abcd abcd abcd abcd abcd abcd abcd abcd abcd abcd abcd abcd abcd
abcde abcde abcde abcde abcde abcde abcde abcde abcde abcde abcde

The class continues in this way, adding one letter at a time until the whole alphabet has been covered.

2. *Alphabetic sentences.* The teacher writes a sentence containing all the letters of the alphabet on the chalkboard or overhead projector. The class copies this repeatedly for a few minutes. Again, practice on all the letter reaches is achieved. See **Alphabetic sentences.**

3. *The expert's rhythm drill.* In this drill there is an absence of reaches except movement of the index fingers to the letters **g** and **h**. The students can concentrate on maintaining correct hand position over the home keys and striking the keys with a sharp, staccato touch. Here is the drill, which must be repeated.

a;sldkfjghfjdksla; a;sldkfjghfjdksla; a;sldkfjghfjdksla;

4. *Location drills.* These always concentrate on a home key position and include other letters and characters struck with the same finger—usually starting and finishing with the home key, as in the following examples.

ded lol ded lol ded lol ded lol ded lol ded lol ded lol ded lol ded lol
dedcd lol.l dedcd lol.l dedcd lol.l dedcd lol.l dedcd lol.l dedcd lol.l

The drills can be performed for each finger and extended to include all the characters struck with each finger. Location drills help establish an association between the key(s) to be mastered and the controlling finger and home key.

5. *Common word drills.* The typist should aim to build up an 'automatic' typing vocabulary as quickly as possible. The importance of the 700 common words and their derivatives is dealt with under **Word frequency, its significance in typing**—together with suggestions which could form the basis of drills on these words.

6. *Phrase drills.* A list of common phrases can be set out on the chalkboard or overhead projector. They should be copied using the centre of the paper, the left-hand margin stop being set at an appropriate position. This kind of drill, as in the following example, gives the students repetitive practice in typing common phrases and at the same time acts as a carriage return drill.

> and thank you for your letter of
> and we have received the goods that
> reply at the earliest possible date
> and you will be very glad to know

7. *Double letter drills.* Particularly with manual typewriters, students

often experience difficulty typing repeated letters evenly. Occasional drills dealing with this weakness can be used, as here.

gallop carrot gallop carrot gallop carrot gallop carrot gallop carrot gallop less woo less woo less woo less woo less woo less woo less woo less woo offer kipper offer kipper offer kipper offer kipper offer kipper offer kipper

8. *Figure drills.* These can start with a home key and continue with the figure struck with the same finger. As with letter location drills, these drills help establish association between the figures and the controlling home keys.

d3d j7j d3d j7j d3d j7j d3d j7j d3d j7j d3d j7j d3d j7j d3d j7j d3d j7j
f4f h6h f4f h6h f4f h6h f4f h6h f4f h6h f4f h6h f4f h6h f4f h6h f4f h6h
g5g k8k g5g k8k g5g k8k g5g k8k g5g k8k g5g k8k g5g k8k g5g k8k

9. *One-finger word drills.* These are words that usually slow up typing, but practice on them can help speed up typing.

hunt papa hunt papa hunt papa hunt papa hunt papa hunt papa hunt
hut sow hut sow hut sow hut sow hut sow hut sow hut sow hut sow

10. *One-hand drills.* These drills give practice on words typed with one hand—again slow to type.

add moon add moon add moon add moon add moon add moon add
aft hip aft hip aft hip aft hip aft hip aft hip aft hip aft hip aft hip
address pun address pun address pun address pun address pun address

As in the above examples, it is best to use alternate hands.

11. *Prefix and suffix drills.* Drills containing frequently used prefixes and suffixes are obviously speed building.

confirm contact confirm contact confirm contact confirm contact confirm inspire inept inspire inept inspire inept inspire inept inspire inept submarine submit submarine submit submarine submit submarine command commence command commence command commence waiting housing waiting housing waiting housing waiting housing temper jumper temper jumper temper jumper temper jumper temper ceaseless shameless ceaseless shameless ceaseless shameless ceaseless hardship friendship hardship friendship hardship friendship fundamental instrumental fundamental instrumental fundamental

12. *Words commonly mis-spelt.* Although there is a generally accepted list of words that are commonly mis-spelt, most teachers, in addition, compile their own lists based on their students' work. Repeated practice on these words can help the students master the correct spelling.

13. *Alternate hand drills.* Words which use the two hands alternately are comparatively quick to type. Nevertheless, occasional drills on such words help boost the students' confidence and speed.

make with make with make with make with make with make with make
girl name girl name girl name girl name girl name girl name girl name
when half when half when half when half when half when half when half
wish city wish city wish city wish city wish city wish city wish city wish

Technique drills. In addition to having keyboard drills, it is important that students are also given drills on the various manipulations connected with Typewriting—to improve speed and performance. Such drills include the following.

Assembly of papers and their insertion and removal from the typewriter
Setting margins and using the margin release key
Setting and use of tabulator
Use of shift keys
Use of carriage release lever
Carriage return
Use of space bar
Use of backspacer
Use of line space selector

1. *Paper-handling and margin-setting drills* (see also **Inserting paper into typewriter** and **Removing paper from typewriter**). Many typists display a complete lack of urgency when assembling their papers and inserting and removing them from the typewriter— although they are quick in other aspects of typewriting. Drills can play an important part here in developing the right mental attitude.

From the first lesson the importance should be stressed of positioning the paper guide so that, for normal typing, the left-hand edge of the paper(s) is at zero on the paper scales. Stationery requirements should be kept on the left of the typewriter and copy material on the right-hand side.

Many different paper-handling drills can be devised and the following is merely one suggestion.

a. The class should assemble paper and backing sheet and insert them correctly into the typewriter with the paper grips well positioned.

b. Set margin stops and type three lines of a keyboard drill.

c. Remove the paper from the typewriter as quickly as possible (using the paper ejector lever, if there is one, otherwise the paper release lever).

d. Perform and repeat (a)–(c) as many times as possible in five minutes.

2. *Margin release key drills.* This key should be used as little as possible. However, there are instances when its use is necessary—such as enumerating paragraphs in the left-hand margin; typing the first line of each hanging paragraph; and for line-end division of words. Occasional drills on the margin release key should be given to encourage speedy and skilful use of the key, using a minimum amount of finger movement and interruption in the flow of typing.

3. *Tabulator drills.* A useful drill to speed up use of the tabulator key/bar is to require the class to type columns of words, working *across the page* as quickly as possible, to pre-set tabulator positions. Again, this should be timed over four or five minutes, the students typing as many accurate lines as possible in the given time.

4. *Shift key drills.* Correct shift key operation is particularly important when using manual typewriters. Faulty timing will result in a raised upper case letter or character. A useful drill is for the class to type repeatedly, for a given time, a paragraph containing a large number of upper case letters and characters. Alternatively, they could repeat a line such as the following.

Accra Bath Canterbury Dublin Elgin Freetown Geneva Hull

Other lines, based on the same principle, can be prepared by the teacher so that every upper case letter and character is covered.

5. *Carriage release lever drills.* A useful drill here is to combine practice in the use of the carriage return lever with underscoring. The students should type as many times as possible in a given time a line such as the following.

He read The Daily News Extra every day for a month.

6. *Carriage return drills.* It is important with manual typewriters that the carriage should be returned as quickly and skilfully as possible (see *Carriage return lever* under **Parts of a typewriter** for correct method of return). With electric typewriters, carriage return is achieved merely by depression of a special key.

Drills can help considerably in speeding up and improving carriage return: if manual carriage return is not well carried out, an uneven left-hand margin can result.

A good drill here is for the teacher to write on the chalkboard or overhead projector a list of words or phrases, one per line. The class should copy these as many times as possible in two or three minutes, returning the carriage as quickly as possible, and aiming to keep an exactly even left-hand margin.

7. *Space bar drills.* The space bar should always be struck with the

right-hand thumb, as quickly and lightly as possible. A useful drill is to combine practice in use of the space bar with typing the alphabet. The aim should be to type the letters and spaces as quickly as possible, taking care that the letters are not run together and the space bar not struck more than once. An example follows.

a b c d e f g h i j k l m n o p q r s t u v w x y z a b c d e f g h i j k l m n o

The typing of the alphabet should be repeated in this way for two or three minutes.

8. *Backspace key drills.* The backspace key should be used as little as possible since its excessive use can result in damage to the typewriter. On manual machines, considerable pressure has to be used to operate this key and it is therefore best done with either the strong index finger or the second finger. Nevertheless, the movement should be performed as quickly as possible.

A useful backspace drill is to use a sentence in which all short words should be underscored after backspacing the required number of times. An example follows.

Now is the time for all good men to come to the aid of the party.

The backspace key can also be used in timed drills for centring short headings.

9. *Line space selector drills.* See *Line space selector* under **Parts of a typewriter** for a description of this mechanism. A useful drill is to write up five columns of words and instruct the students to type them, column by column, changing the line spacing for each column. The example that follows combines line-spacing practice with the typing of words using alternate hands.

1	$1\frac{1}{2}$	2	$2\frac{1}{2}$	3
girl	when	hang	maps	clay
bush	dock			
land		none	half	
hand	vine			tone
	lake	they		
			cork	
		firm		dusk
			turn	
				fish

Dropped head. See **Literary work.**

Dual pitch typewriter. See **Special purpose typewriters.**

Dual unit typewriter. See **Special purpose typewriters.**

Duplicating. See **Reprography processes.**

Dvorak keyboard. See **Arrangement of the keyboard.**

Ejector/injector lever. See **Parts of a typewriter** (*Paper injector/ ejector*).

Electric typewriters. (See also **Parts of a typewriter.**) Commercial offices are increasingly using electric typewriters—yet many students leave school or college to take up office jobs having been trained solely on manuals. A survey held in 1972 showed that less than ten per cent of typewriters in educational use were electric machines, although the advantages to be gained from the students learning typewriting using *both* types are considerable.

Miss Rosemary Harris, the founder Principal of the Langham Secretarial College in London, carried out experiments over a number of years which produced results showing that students who used electric typewriters either exclusively in the first term of a one-year course or on a dual-training basis throughout the one year (using electric and manual typewriters in alternate lessons) produced higher speeds and greater accuracy on manual typewriters than students trained solely on manual machines. Thus, using both kinds of typewriter not only better prepared the students for office work, but speeds on manual machines (and most offices still use at least some of these) were increased as a result of the experience on electric typewriters. In general, similar experiments carried out in America by a number of investigators (F. Winger and L. J. Fedor, to name but two) point to the same conclusions as Miss Harris's experiments. It must be mentioned, however, that two American investigators, Antonette di Loreto and H. L. Adams, found no significant differences in the performance of students trained on electric as well as manual machines.

Since, on the whole, there seems much to be gained from secretarial students acquiring experience on electric typewriters, one might well ask why there are so few electric machines in use in schools and colleges. In many cases the simple answer is expense (both initial and for repairs and maintenance) but another factor is that some teachers of long standing who have no personal experience of using electric machines are reluctant to learn the new techniques and implications of electric typewriters—and as a result do not press sufficiently hard for their purchase and installation.

There is little doubt that many people who have been trained exclusively on manuals and have typed solely on them for a long period of time, experience a fear and antipathy at the thought of changing to electric typewriters. This applies particularly to housewives who wish to return to secretarial work after a long absence. In practice, however, such fears usually prove groundless and it is generally found that adjustment to electrics does not constitute a major office problem and most skilled manual operators can satisfactorily adjust their techniques in a few hours of typing.

Differences in technique

1. Key striking on both manual and electric typewriters is a *ballistic* motion but the vital difference here is that electrics require considerably less force then manuals. Because the keys of an electric typewriter need only a slight 'dab' for an impression to be made, precision of movement of the fingers becomes very important.

2. In the early stages of instruction on manual machines, students are often told to keep their fingers on the home row: such an instruction to students on electric typewriters would obviously have disastrous results. This is perhaps the most serious obstacle to proficient manual operators changing to electric machines. The habit of resting their fingers on the home keys (and especially on the two guide keys, **a** and **;**) has become so ingrained that considerable difficulty is experienced in ensuring that keys are touched only when those keys are required for typing. It is, of course, important that all skilled typists maintain the central position of the hands at the keyboard—but the fingers should hover lightly *above* the home keys.

3. The angle of the keyboard is greater on a manual than on an electric typewriter: in fact, the keyboard angle of an electric machine is approximately twelve degrees compared with an angle of approximately thirty degrees on a manual. This considerable difference in angle obviously requires differences in hand position and curvature of the fingers. When typing on the less steeply banked electric keyboard, the hands are held much flatter and the fingers less curved than when using a manual keyboard—and there are certain other corresponding slight differences in the position of the wrists and forearms. Because the required force is less and the position of the hands flatter for electric typing, some people talk of 'playing' when referring to key striking. This, however, is very misleading since there is no holding or pressing of the keys: the keys are hit with a staccato touch just as with manual typing, and the only difference is one of *force*.

4. When using a manual typewriter, correct and skilled manipulation of the carriage return lever is very important from the point of view of speed, and this manipulation has to be carefully learnt and practised

by users of manual machines. However, on an electric typewriter, the operator merely has to lightly strike the carriage return *key*—so that it is no longer an important arm and hand motion but merely a key depression. This, of course, means that carriage return on an electric typewriter is easier to learn; but very skilled manual operators can, in fact, return the carriage more quickly than electric typists since the electrical carriage return movement cannot be speeded up beyond a certain point. This is an important consideration for high-speed and champion typists.

5. There are other less important technique differences between manual and electric typewriters. Electric machines have repeat action keys which, if kept depressed, will continue typing the same letter or character. The number of repeat action keys varies from machine to machine but the most usual ones are the underscore, hyphen, full stop, and letter **x** (for -xing out unwanted words in drafts, etc.). In addition, on most electric models the space bar, backspace key and carriage return key will continue to operate rapidly if kept depressed. The tabulator key, when operated, does not have to be held down as with manual typewriters.

Do typists using electric machines produce more output? Much has been made of the fact that less force is required to type on an electric typewriter than on a manual one and it is often stressed that electric typists experience less fatigue than manual typists—and as a result can produce a greater output. Leonard West, the American expert on typing, denies this idea and believes that it is an aspect that is overplayed in advertising propaganda—which tends to depict the electric typist going off glowingly to her evening date, full of energy, while her manual counterpart is so worn out that she can hardly drag herself home to bed! West believes the difference expended in energy between the two (even in the carriage return) is so slight, provided the manual is in good working order, as to be insignificant. West states: 'Is one more fatigued after wielding a meat fork for a few minutes than after wielding a lighter dessert fork for the same number of minutes? One suspects a good deal of brainwashing in the marketing of electric machines. The electric typist who reports feeling less tired than after manual typing may be reporting how she has been led to think she ought to feel, with no evidence in the form of measured performance data.'

The American, W. H. Enneis, examined the question of electric versus manual typewriters with particular reference to subjective reports of greater fatigue and less output on the part of manual typists. He anticipated that manual typists would produce less output, particularly in tasks which one might suppose required greater physical effort (envelope addressing, the completion of form letters, etc.). However, he had to reject this hypothesis since his findings showed that daily output did not differ on manuals and electrics: in fact *manual output during the last hour of the day exceeded electric output.*

Typewriting as a job of work comes low on the list of tasks so far as expended energy is concerned. It is probable that fatigue arises not so much from the amount of physical energy actually used in typing as from incorrect posture and mental fatigue due to the fact that typewriting is a complex skill in which constant co-ordination of the mind and fingers is required.

Advantages of Electric Typewriters. Electric typewriters are undoubtedly superior to manuals in several important respects and it is a pity that salesmen often overstress the fatigue factor at the expense of more important features. Some of the advantages of electrics over manuals are listed below.

1. Electric typewriters produce copy of uniform density of impression, regardless of the typist's touch. Such evenly shaded copy is a rare product of the manual typewriter, where the force with which the key is struck is a significant factor.

2. The density of the printing can be regulated on an electric typewriter by means of an impression control switch—thus making it possible to type more carbon copies than on a manual typewriter. Up to twenty copies can be taken at one typing, depending on the weight of of the paper and carbons being used.

3. Various touch faults that are common with manual typists are eliminated in electric typing, e.g., capital letters out of alignment, dropped lower case characters.

4. The electrically-controlled type impressions provide a sharp, even striking of the keys so that it is easier to produce good-quality stencils and masters for other reprographic processes.

5. Some electric typewriters have proportional spacing, i.e., the width of space needed for the different letters varies with the size of the letter (see **Proportional spacing**). For example, the letters **i, l,** and **j** occupy less space than, say, **m** or **w**—as in letterpress printing. Proportional spacing improves the general appearance of typed matter and makes it easier to read. Satisfactory correction of errors, however, is extremely difficult, unless the mistake is noticed immediately it is made.

6. With some of the more expensive and sophisticated electric models (see **Special purpose typewriters**) a variety of different type faces is available which are easily interchangeable; also, the typewritten work can be justified to give an exactly even right-hand margin.

When one considers the above list, it is hardly surprising that more and more commercial offices are purchasing electric typewriters. In a way, and probably partly due to advertising pressures, an electric typewriter has become a status symbol and many people will not take office appointments unless they are assured that they will be able to use an expensive electric typewriter. In advertisements for secretarial positions, one frequently sees the availability of prestige electric machines mentioned—no doubt as a bait.

No matter what the reasons may be, the sales of electric typewriters to offices are rapidly increasing so, since many young people who are training as secretaries will probably be required to use electric as well as manual typewriters in their future employment, it is obviously desirable that they should have experience on both types in their school or college training. If this is not possible, the next best thing is to be aware of the differences between the two types of machine and understand the differences involved in typewriting techniques. Such understanding will at least lessen the fear of having to change from one kind of machine to another.

Elite. See **Pitch.**

Ellipsis. See **Omission of words.**

Emphasizing words. If one wishes to indicate in typescript that a word or words should be emphasized, the most common method is to underscore. A second method to give *greater* emphasis within the same piece of work is to use capital letters for the whole of the section that requires further emphasis. In addition, if one is using a bichrome ribbon, the second colour can be brought into use—but, of course, this would only be effective on a top copy. It would be necessary to insert strips of appropriately-coloured carbon paper (with the carbon-coated surface immediately facing the carbon copies) for the second colour to appear on the carbon copies. For this reason the method is seldom adopted when more than a single copy is required. The second colour would not, of course, show up in photocopying.

If the typist is using a typewriter with an easily-changed typeface head, and has at her disposal a variety of typefaces, she can change the typeface being used in order to achieve emphasis.

Note: Underscoring in typescript indicates to the printer that the matter should be printed in italics. A word or words underlined with a wavy line tell him that <u>bold</u> characters are required, as in the word 'Note'.

End of paper. The typist should always leave approximately 25 mm (1 in.) of space at the foot of a sheet of typing. There are several ways of ensuring this.

1. Make a light horizontal pencil mark the correct distance from the

foot of the paper in the left-hand margin. As the typist approaches the end of the paper this line will be immediately visible to her when she returns the carriage to start a new line. She can then remove the paper when that line has been typed, and start a fresh sheet of paper. The light pencil mark can then be easily erased. This is a widely-used method.

2. Sometimes a bold horizontal line is drawn across the backing sheet at the point where the typing should finish. However, unless thin paper is being used, this line is often not immediately visible and can be overlooked. The method is not effective when carbon copies are being taken or when good-quality paper is being used.

3. It is possible to obtain backing sheets (wider than A4 paper) that are marked off in lines of typewriting and inches along the right-hand edge. These help ensure a uniform bottom margin to the paper—but closer attention by the typist is required than in the method described under (1).

4. Alternatively, some typists like to use a plain backing sheet that is slightly wider than the paper, and draw a thick horizontal line on the backing sheet at the appropriate point in the right-hand margin (the left-hand edges of the paper(s) and backing sheet should always line up).

5. Many typewriters have a last line indicator on the paper support at the rear of the carriage. These differ in operation and if the typist decides to use this device she should consult the instruction booklet for the typewriter concerned.

Endorsement. See **Bills of quantities** and **Legal typing** and **Specifications.**

English, knowledge of. Any typist, no matter how skilled she may be at typing, finds it a slow, laborious process to type in a language she does not understand. The better her understanding of the language, the more rapid and accurate will be her typing in it. This basic principle applies equally well to the English language. The better a typist's command of her own language, the more this will help her overall efficiency as a typist.

In particular, a typist should be good at spelling and have a good command of words, particularly homophones. If at all in doubt about the spelling of a word she should consult a dictionary, which should always be ready to hand when typing. It is a good idea for the typist to make a list of words that she finds difficult, and when she gets spare time to practice typing them: they should be deleted from her list only when she has fully mastered them.

A good knowledge of punctuation, grammar, and sentence construction is also important to the typist. Although copying well-written and well-punctuated English *can* assist the typist—but only if she intelligently studies the material typed—punctuation, grammar, sentence construction and good style should receive particular attention in English classes.

It is important that the typist *understands* what she is typing—particularly when typing from a manuscript draft—so if there is any doubt here, she should quickly read through the work before beginning to type and boldly mark anything that might otherwise not be immediately clear as she types.

If a typist aspires to become a secretary or personal assistant, she should be able to compose good letters, reports, etc.,—either on her own or from brief dictated notes.

Enumerating sections, paragraphs and pages (see also **Roman numerals**). If a document is a complicated one with numerous sections and sub-divisions, a clearly-followed code should be used to distinguish their order of importance. In this context the following are used:

Large roman numerals
Uppercase letters
Arabic figures
Lower case letters
Small roman numerals

The above need not all be used, nor necessarily in the order given—the number of symbols and the form used will depend on the nature of the work, the number of sub-divisions necessary, and the preferences of the writer or typist. However, a system, once adopted, should be used consistently throughout a piece of work.

In many typewriting tasks only one or two methods of enumeration are required: in this situation most typists prefer to use arabic figures and/or lower case letters. If only one type of sub-division is necessary, typists often use lower case letters, since they obviate the problem of lining up the units of arabic figures once ten is reached.

Some examples of numbered and lettered paragraphs follow. They should be studied as a whole.

1 This is a numbered paragraph using arabic figures. The numbers 1, 2, 3, and so on may be typed (as in this example) without a following stop, with three spaces before the left-hand margin of the paragraph which can be blocked or indented. If a stop follows the figure (or if it is enclosed in brackets) two or three spaces should be left before beginning the paragraph.

The left-hand margin stop should be set for the paragraphs and the margin release key used for moving the carriage back for typing the figures. A tabular stop should be set for the figure position and, if indented paragraphs are used, a second tabular stop should be set for the indentation.

2. This is another example of a numbered paragraph. Again, the figure may or may not be followed by a stop or enclosed in brackets—as described in the preceding example. With this type of numbered paragraph the figures do not stand out so prominently as in the last example, since they are not set outside the body of the paragraph.

a   This is a lettered paragraph. If the letter stands on its own, as in this example, it should be followed by three spaces before typing of the paragraph begins. The letter may be followed by a stop or enclosed in brackets. The same principles outlined in the first example apply here, too.

(b) This is another example of a lettered paragraph. As in the second example, the letter does not stand out prominently since it is not set outside the body of the paragraph. Although brackets may be used to enclose figures or letters in enumerated paragraphs, many typists avoid them because they obviously take longer to type than the other methods.

Multi-number system of enumeration. An illustration of this method of enumeration is included under **Blocked layout.** It will be seen that each main section is given a consecutive number: this is followed by a number which represents a sub-heading—and all paragraphs within each sub-heading are separately numbered. Each number is followed by a stop, whether or not open punctuation is being used.

Many organizations use this method for reports, minutes, and other documents for ease of referencing.

Numbering pages (see also *Pagination* under **Literary work**). When a letter, report or other typewritten document runs into more than one page, the sheets must be numbered for two main reasons. Firstly, if the pages get out of order they can be quickly reassembled correctly. Secondly, numbering makes reference to a particular page and paragraph an easy matter. If the document is to be bound in some way, the pages are numbered to facilitate referencing, indexing, and so on.

The first typewritten page of a letter, report, and many other documents is not usually numbered: only subsequent ones are. Arabic figures should be used: the number can stand alone, be followed by a stop, be enclosed in brackets, or have a hyphen or dash on either side of it. Consistency of style here—as with most typewriting matter—should be followed within a single piece of work.

Likewise, positioning of the numbers should be consistent on each page. The figures are usually placed at the top of pages, in the centre, if only one side of each sheet is used: alternatively, they may appear at the bottom centre of each sheet, or at the top at the right-hand margin position. If *both* sides of paper are used and the sheets are to be bound in some way, the numbers often appear at the top left-hand margin position for the second and each subsequent even-numbered page, and and at the top right-hand margin position for the third and every following uneven-numbered page. Alternatively, all numbers can be centred at the top or bottom of each sheet.

Whether numbers are placed at the top or bottom of pages, there should be a uniform space between the top or bottom edge of the paper and the figures. Since it is customary to leave six line spaces at the top of each continuation sheet, a good practice is to type the number on the third line down from the top of the page, with the text beginning on the seventh line. It is similarly customary to leave six line spaces at the foot of each sheet so, if the numbers are to be placed at the bottom, a useful practice is to make a light horizontal pencil mark in the left-hand margin at the point where the typewriting text should finish and type the number on the third line down from that point, in order to maintain uniformity of position.

Envelopes. A wide variety of sizes of envelopes is still used (especially for personal correspondence), although a transition to the International Paper Sizes (IPS) is rapidly taking place. IPS envelopes are designed to take A sizes of paper (see **Paper for typewriting**) either unfolded or folded. IPS envelopes are known by the letter B or C followed by a number. The sizes of the most commonly used IPS range follow.

C4	229×324 mm (approx	9	$\times$	$12\frac{3}{4}$ in.)	Takes A4 unfolded.
C5	162×229 mm (	,,	$6\frac{3}{8}$	$\times$	9 in.)	Takes A4 folded once or A5 unfolded.
C6	114×162 mm (	,,	$4\frac{1}{2}$	$\times$	$6\frac{3}{8}$ in.)	Takes A5 folded once or A4 folded twice.
C5/6 (DL)	110×220 mm (	,,	$4\frac{1}{4}$	$\times$	$8\frac{5}{8}$ in.)	Takes A4 folded equally into three or A5 folded once.
C7/6	81×162 mm (	,,	$3\frac{1}{4}$	$\times$	$6\frac{3}{8}$ in.)	Takes A5 folded twice. Little used at present because it is too similar to the English commercial size ($6 \times 3\frac{1}{2}$ in.).

The size C5/6 is commonly known as DL which stands for 'DIN lange' (see **Paper for typewriting**).

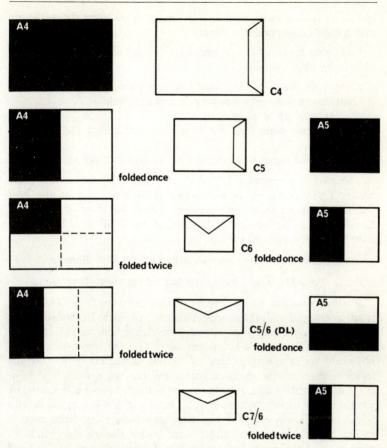

Chart demonstrating the sizes of IPS envelopes in relation to the A sizes of paper

The most common non-IPS envelopes are:

Commercial	152 × 89 mm	(6 × 3½ in.)
Square	133 × 108 mm	(5¼ × 4¼ in.)
Foolscap	229 × 102 mm	(9 × 4 in.)
Draft	267 × 114 mm	(10½ × 4½ in.)

Typewriter envelopes. Special typewriter envelopes are available in banker style (see page 80) which have a narrow, straight-edged sealing flap: this enables the typist to obtain a better finish to her work since she does not have to type over an uneven surface. Envelopes are available in a variety of paper qualities—e.g., bond, parchment, cream

Envelopes

and azure laid or wove, manilla—and many firms select the quality to match their correspondence paper.

Post Office Preferred sizes of envelopes. To fall within the POP range of sizes envelopes should be:

1. minimum size—140 mm long × 90 mm wide (approx. $5\frac{1}{2}$ × $3\frac{1}{2}$ in.)
maximum size—235 mm long × 120 mm wide
(approx. $9\frac{1}{4}$ × $4\frac{3}{4}$ in.);
2. oblong in shape with the longer side at least 1.414 times the shorter side;
3. made from paper weighing at least 63 grammes per square metre.

The two most popular IPS sizes (C6 and DL) fall within these limits. The modern electronic sorting equipment used by the Post Office is designed to accept envelopes within the above-stated limit. Envelopes that are smaller or larger than the POP sizes have to be sorted by other, slower methods.

Banker envelopes. These have their flap on the long dimension.

Pocket envelopes. These have their flap on the short dimension.

Window envelopes. These have a panel cut from the front. This panel is either covered with transparent paper or left open: in the latter case the envelopes are known as aperture envelopes and are not classified within the POP range. Window envelopes save the typist time as it is obviously not necessary to type an address on the envelope since the inside address on the enclosed letter, invoice, etc., is used. The position for typing the name and address on the headed paper is indicated by a ruled box or merely by dots or short right angles. Correct and careful folding is obviously essential when window envelopes are being used to ensure that the name and address are visible though the 'window': some printed stationery has one or two 'fold' marks on the left-hand edge of the paper.

Envelope typing. Envelopes should be inserted into the typewriter at the left-hand side of the platen with the left-hand edge of the envelope resting against the paper guide, which should be in its normal position to correspond with O on the paper bail. With banker envelopes the flap should be downwards and facing the typist as the envelope is inserted into the typewriter: with pocket envelopes the flap should be at the left-hand side. The right-hand paper grip should be moved so that it will grip the right-hand side of the envelope—this is particularly important if there is to be a long run of envelope typing. The left-hand paper grip should not require moving since it will be in its normal position for gripping paper.

The name and address should always be typed parallel to the wider side of the envelope, with each part of the address on a separate line. It is of assistance to the postal authorities if the name of the town is typed in capital letters. Except in the case of a few large cities (named in the Post Office Guide) the county should be typed as well. The postcode should *always be typed last*, preferably on a separate line and it should not be punctuated or underscored. There should be one space between the two parts of the postcode and if the postcode is typed on the same line as the town or county there should be 2–6 spaces in front of the postcode.

If it is necessary to indicate that the letter is personal, urgent, confidential, registered, recorded delivery, etc., this should be typed *above* the name of the addressee and separated from it by one line of space. The quickest method is to type this information in closed capitals but it is sometimes typed with initial capital(s) and underscored. By Hand should by typed at the top right-hand corner of the envelope so that it will not be stamped in error—or if it *is* subsequently decided to post the letter instead, the By Hand instruction will be covered by the stamps.

Envelopes look best if typed so that the name and address is approximately centred horizontally and vertically: this should be estimated, not measured in any way. However, it must be remembered that there should always be at least 38 mm ($1\frac{1}{2}$ in.) of space above the typewritten matter to accommodate the postage stamps and postmark.

The quickest way to type envelopes is to use the blocked method and open punctuation (with single or one-and-a-half line spacing—the latter making the address more legible) so that the left-hand margin stop can be set at the point where each line will begin. Some firms, however, prefer the indented, fully-punctuated method. For large envelopes, double spacing, with the lines either blocked or each one indented three spaces, is more suitable. See under **Titles and forms of address** for information about typing names on envelopes.

Here are some examples of envelope addressing.

```
CONFIDENTIAL              Personal

Mrs M Kennedy             Mr. J. H. Hunter,
27 Lancaster Road         93 Parkside Avenue,
BOLTON                       SALTASH,
BL4 9EL                         Cornwall    PL12 6SZ


FOR THE ATTENTION OF      Urgent
MR A BROWN
                          Mrs M Maple,
Messrs Jones & Latimer    49 Cranworth Gardens,
44-46 Longside Road       SOUTHAMPTON,
LONDON    WC2B 6AS        SQ4 6GB
```

Rapid envelope and card typing. To save time when typing a large number of envelopes or cards, the following procedure is recommended. Place the untyped envelopes (or cards) on the left-hand side of the typewriter in a neat pile with the flaps all the same way. Insert into the typewriter an envelope or card and bring it into typing position. Then insert another envelope or card behind the platen so that it is resting on the paper table. When the first envelope or card has been typed, use the platen knob and the left hand to twirl it out of the typewriter: this motion will, at the same time, bring further forward the envelope or card that was resting against the paper table. The typed envelope or card should be taken with the right hand and placed face downwards on the right-hand side of the typewriter. When the next envelope or card has been brought forward into the correct typing position, still using the platen knob and left hand, another envelope or card can be placed behind the platen—and so on until all the required envelopes and cards have been typed. If the paper guide is correctly positioned and the left-hand margin stop set for the beginning of each line, this method will greatly speed up the typing of large quantities of envelopes or cards.

Equals sign. See **Combination characters and special signs** and **Mathematical typing.**

Erasing. See **Correcting errors.**

Error charts. See **Errors, their cause and remedy.**

Errors, their cause and remedy (see also **Drills**). Until skill is acquired, beginners in Typewriting will inevitably make errors. The cause of errors is often difficult to establish and even well-trained and highly-experienced typists make mistakes where it is difficult to pinpoint the reasons for them.

Errors are often the result of lack of attention; indifference and lack of interest in the work; ignorance or imperfect mastery of a particular reach or technique; or simply 'mood'—we all have those days when we repeatedly make errors for no apparent reason.

In the early learning stages it is necessary that proper checks are made and records of errors kept—and appropriate remedial drills set. As far as possible the onus for this should be placed on the students themselves. Motivated learners will be eager to improve their skill and *want* to overcome their faults. Therefore, from an early stage the students should correct their own typewritten work, neatly encircling each error— preferably with a red biro for clarity. Even so, the teacher should systematically check the corrections of a few students in each lesson—to encourage them to be as meticulous as possible in spotting their errors and also to note any mistakes that the learners may not be fully aware of themselves (such as incorrect spacing with punctuation marks).

The teacher should stress to the class that they should not produce correct typewritten work at the expense of using bad techniques. At the beginning of typewriting training it is important that good habits and techniques are built up since these are the only sure foundations for high speed and skill.

Keyboard errors and their remedy. Obviously, the mere encircling of all errors by the students will not in itself lead to improvement. Records of the errors must be kept so that teachers can detect letters and other characters that *repeatedly* cause trouble, and give suitable remedial drills during the drill period in a lesson.

Thus, in the early lessons students should keep a record of their keyboard errors. The teacher should provide each member of the class with an alphabetical check list and ask the students to put a cross under each letter every time it is incorrectly typed. These check lists should be kept in the students' folders and completed two or three times a week after set periods of four or five minutes of typing. Persistent errors that need corrective action will show up in this time. It would be too time consuming to expect every error in every lesson to be noted on the chart—and this would achieve no more than the method recommended.

Each letter or character that a student frequently types incorrectly should be given special attention. Different drills should be devised for each letter and character—which should appear in words or connected matter. Suggestions for the letters **a** and **b** follow.

Letter a
again apathy actual again apathy actual again apathy actual again apathy
abate attract amiable abate attract amiable abate attract amiable abate
ajar avail academy ajar avail academy ajar avail academy ajar avail
ahead accommodation away ahead accommodation away ahead

An acknowledgement of the actual letter was necessary.
A quaint bazaar on the large plaza was a great attraction.
In case the train is late, make alternative arrangements.

Letter b
baby barber habitable baby barber habitable baby barber habitable baby
bubble abbot cobbler bubble abbot cobbler bubble abbot cobbler
absorbent abbey busby absorbent abbey busby absorbent abbey busby
rhubarb babble barbaric rhubarb babble barbaric rhubarb babble

Because of his bad beginning, the baby became difficult.
The baker's bank balance showed that business was bad.
The bag broke and the bright beads scattered before the beggar.

Date	a	b	c	d	e	f	g	h	i	j	k	l	m	n	o	p	q	r	s	t	u	v	w	x	y	z	.	,	;	:	?

Name _____

Class _____

Suggested keyboard analysis chart

Other errors to be checked by the students. In addition to keyboard mistakes there are various other types of error that the student should check and record herself.

	Date										
Faulty timing of shift key											
Spacing errors											
Touch errors—crowding, under-typed, out of alignment											
Centring errors											
Omissions from copy											
Additions to copy											
Transpositions											
Substitutes for copy											
Overtyping											
-xing out work											
Visible corrections											
Very uneven right-hand margin											
Faulty left-hand margin											

Name _____

Class _____

Suggested list and chart layout

It is suggested that each student completes such a check list two or three times a week after a specific, timed period of typewriting—again inserting a cross for each error made. Occasional errors of a particular type are natural, but persistent repetition of the same mistake needs attention.

Technique errors to be checked by the teacher. There will, of course, be certain techniques which the teacher herself should regularly check with classes of beginners, until she is confident that good habits are well established. The teacher should keep a check list for each student— which can be based on the layout above. These forms should be kept alphabetically in a ring binder, with all the forms for each class together. A list of technique points to be checked follows, although it will, of course, vary to some extent according to the level of the students.

Inserting paper incorrectly
Removing paper incorrectly
Returning carriage incorrectly
Bad posture
Incorrect fingering
Excessive looking at fingers
Excessive looking at typewritten work
Incorrect use of space bar
Faulty use of shift key and shift lock

With classes of beginners, such checks should be regularly made at least three times a week—although the teacher should obviously try to make a student unaware that she is being watched.

As will be seen, proper recording, analysis, and treatment of typewriting errors requires considerable work and patience on the part of both teacher and student. Although a certain remedy may be effective with one pupil, it may prove quite ineffective with another, in which case suitable alternatives should be sought.

Despite the fact that much work and patient application is necessary, most teachers agree that the keeping of proper records and the use of drills lead, in general, to improvement in overall performance.

A list of typewriting errors with suggested cause and remedy follows. In studying it, however, the reader should bear in mind all the problems associated with error analysis and treatment.

Errors and suggested corrective action (see also **Drills**).

Error and Cause

Remedy

1. Letter or character frequently typed incorrectly; also wrong hand but correct finger— **e** for **i**, **f** for **j**, etc. Due to inadequate association and practice in initial learning stages.

Location Drills to establish the correct hand and finger and association with other letters which the finger controls.

2. Keys jamming at printing point. Due to striking a further letter before releasing the first one.

More deliberate and even timing of key strikes.

3. Faulty touch (with manual machines). Crowding, shadowing and undertyping of letters: due to faulty key striking.

As for (2) above.

4. Capital letters and other upper case characters out of alignment. Due to faulty use of the shift key.

Shift Key Drills.

5. Irregular left-hand margin—with manual machines due to failure to return carriage to its fullest extent. With electric type-writers, this error is usually the the result of a machine defect.

Carriage Return Drills.

6. Inconsistent indentation for paragraphs. Due to tapping the space bar instead of setting a tab stop—or faulty use of the tab key/bar.

Ensure the tabulator is being used. Tabulator Drills.

7. Omitting letters, i.e., tht for that or a d for and, etc. Due to not striking the keys with sufficient force (with manual machines) or not touching the key at all with electrics.

If a particular letter causes difficulty give appropriate letter drills (see under *Keyboard errors and their remedy*). Otherwise as for (2) above.

8. Transposition of letters or words is usually due to lack of concentration. Use of similar but wrong word—were for where, etc. Due to lack of concentration on copy or faulty command of the language. Omitting a line or phrase by picking up a repeated word at the wrong place. Due to eyes not remaining on copy or lack of concentration.

Concentration drills that require close attention to the copy. An example is a changing line such as the following.

ai ail fail fails failed failing

Alternatively, type an exercise containing difficult words that necessitate close attention to the copy.

Other faults, such as bad line-end division of words and display faults can be remedied by a more thorough knowledge of typewriting 'theory' and good usage.

Escapement. See **Parts of a typewriter.**

Examination hints. When you sit a typewriting examination you will have spent many months of hard work preparing for it, and there is much that you yourself can do to help ensure success.

Keep a method workbook. If you have been well taught you will have had a considerable amount of practice on all kinds of test, at the appropriate standard, that you are likely to meet in the examination. You should always pay particular attention to any corrections your teacher may make on your work—and if you do not understand any of them you should not hesitate in asking her to explain them. During your training, keep a notebook listing particular errors you make and improved methods of tackling any particular type of exercise which causes you difficulty. Keep this up to date (with the information under specific headings—Letters, Memos, Manuscript Work, Tabulations, etc.) and consult it regularly to prevent repetition of a particular error and to improve and speed up your typewritten work. Only cross an item out of your notebook when you are absolutely sure you have mastered it.

Work on past papers. If you can go into the examination room with a sense of confidence, knowing what to expect and knowing that you will be able to complete the test—or most of it—in the permitted time, this will help you to avoid 'examination nerves' which could have a disastrous effect upon your performance.

You should have carefully studied and worked through as many past papers as possible of the examination you are taking before you sit it. Always read carefully the general instructions as these vary little, if at all, from examination to examination—and familiarity with them will be an obvious help in the examination. Work through several past papers under examinaton conditions (without referring to any book) and carefully time yourself to make sure you can satisfactorily complete an adequate part of the paper in the allotted time.

Necessary materials not provided at the examination. Make sure you are familiar with the list of items that you should take with you to the examination—good typewriter eraser, pencil, black ballpoint pen, ruler, carbon paper, blank paper for practice prior to the commencement of the examination, etc. Assemble these in a folder a day or two before the examination or, in the stress of the moment, you may forget all about them.

Arrival at the examination room. Try to ensure that you arrive at least twenty minutes before the examination begins so you can adjust the height of your chair and practice on the typewriter you will be using. Not only will this preliminary practice help to familiarize you with the typewriter but it will bring to light any mechanical defect so you can immediately point this out to the invigilator and, if possible, be given an alternative machine. This practice will also help to calm your nerves so that when the examination actually begins you will be in the right frame of mind from the very start.

Completion of entry form. If it is necessary to complete an entry form at the examination, make sure that you fill in all the required particulars correctly and legibly. If you pass the examination, your certificate will be made out in the name you provide so take particular care when writing your name, especially if it is an unusual one.

General points before beginning to type. Glance through the whole examination paper before beginning to type. You may work the exercises in any order and although you should not just type all the easy ones (which usually carry fewest marks) it is a good idea to start the examination with one or two pieces of work that you know will present you with little difficulty, since this will help to build up your confidence. If you start with one of the more difficult tests and get bogged down in it, this could fluster you and ruin your chances of overall success.

Always read through—and make sure you follow—any particular instructions before beginning to type an exercise. Remember that the examination paper is *yours* so do not hesitate to mark boldly in red such points as the insertion of ballooned matter, enclosure(s) for letters, date on letter, transposed matter, etc. Familiarity with the subject matter and an *understanding* of what you are typing are considerable aids to success: these can be gained from a quick reading through of each test before beginning to type.

Remember to type your examination number or name (whichever is required) at the top of each sheet of paper and begin each exercise on a new piece of paper, clean on both sides. Allocate your time sensibly and aim to complete as much of the examination as possible. Each exercise will be given a certain number of marks so although you should work steadily and carefully, correcting errors as you go along and reading through and correcting any other errors before removing the paper from the typewriter, *do not* repeat an exercise if you notice only one or two errors that you cannot correct. Remember—if you do not attempt an exercise you cannot obtain any of the marks allocated to it, whereas an exercise with only one or two errors will probably be awarded a considerable proportion of its marks.

Defect in typewriter. If a fault develops in your typewriter after the beginning of the examination, inform the invigilator immediately. She will give you another machine if possible; otherwise she will make a note of the defect so the examiner can take this into consideration when marking your papers.

Spoilt work. If you begin an exercise, make a bad error and start again, make sure you draw a line right across the discarded work so the examiner does not mark it in error. Place cancelled work at the back of your folder together with unused paper.

Manuscript exercises. Many people experience difficulty reading other people's writing—and the handwriting in some examinations, particularly at advanced level, is often far from clear. As with other tests, read a manuscript exercise right through before typing and pay particular attention to the meaning if you have difficulty in deciphering the handwriting. Often a word that is not clear at first makes sense when you become more familiar with the subject matter and the writing, and see the same word in a different context—where the context helps you to determine its meaning.

If a word is illegibly written, or an unusual one, it is often written in capital letters in the margin, enclosed in a 'balloon', to assist you with the spelling.

Do not copy abbreviations, except the generally used ones such as i.e. and e.g.

Headings. You should remember that if a heading is treble underlined this indicates that it should be typed in spaced capitals with three spaces between each word. If it is underlined twice, this requires closed capitals; and if underlined once it should be typed as given and underscored. These points are often not spelt out and you are expected to understand the method of underlining. Remember that a heading should never be double underscored and if you are typing the body of the matter in double spacing you should leave at least one additional line of space between the heading and beginning of the text.

If a heading has to be centred and there are no specific instructions about margins, use equal margins for ease and quickness. Simply move the carriage so the printing point is at the centre of the paper and backspace once for every two characters (including spaces) before beginning to type.

Continuation sheets. If a particular exercise is a long one and double spacing is required, make a light pencil mark one inch from the bottom of the paper in the left-hand margin so you will not type too far down the paper and thus unnecessarily lose marks. You should leave one inch at the foot of each sheet of paper if using a continuation sheet and the same amount of space above the typing on any continuation sheets. Do not forget to number continuation sheets (on the third line down from the top of the paper, commencing the actual text on the seventh line): if it is a letter, make sure you head the second sheet correctly.

It is a good idea to strike through in red on the examination paper the last word you typed on a page so that when you start a new sheet you will not waste time trying to find your place in the copy.

Layout. If there are no particular instructions and you are not certain how best to set out an exercise, follow the layout of the copy. If any matter is to be inset you should indent it equally from both margins if using indented paragraphs. Adjust your margin stops accordingly—and do not forget to alter them when reverting to the original typing line.

Correction of errors. As already stated, you should carefully correct all errors you notice as you go along. Remember—corrections are time consuming so do not rush; type at a speed you can control. Before removing a sheet of paper from the typewriter always read it through as you may find some additional errors that you were unaware of as you were typing. As you will know, it is much easier to make good corrections while the paper is still in the typewriter.

In examinations always correct by means of an eraser, as other methods of correcting rarely produce really satisfactory results. If your corrections are well made and barely visible, you will not lose marks. The best kind of typewriter eraser is the pencil type that has soft rubber at one end and hard rubber at the other end. With an eraser of this kind it is easy to rub only on the incorrect letter(s), so that the surrounding letters are not partly obliterated. Use the soft end first to remove the surplus ink, then the hard end to remove the remainder of the ink. Rub gently with a light, circular motion—otherwise you may end up with a hole in the paper. **Never overtype or -x out mistakes** or you will be heavily penalized each time you do it.

Tabular work. Remember that work of this kind usually consists of about eighty per cent calculations and twenty per cent typing. It is important that a tabulation is well displayed on the paper so take care with your calculations and check them before you begin typing. It is well worth while clearly setting out a diagram of the work on a spare sheet of paper, marking clearly the number of spaces required for the longest item in each column, the number of spaces you are allowing between columns (which should be equal) and the width of the margins (which should likewise be equal). Make a note of the points at which you will set your margin and tab stops, and the number of line spaces that will be left above and below the actual typing. It is helpful to do this, especially if you make a bad mistake and wish to start the exercise again; the clear setting out of your figures will enable you to begin again with a minimum of delay.

Consistency. Unless there are specific instructions, any recognized method of display, consistently used, will be accepted by the examiner.

You should also be consistent within a single piece of work regarding such matters as the method of typing numbers, the date, percentages, and so on. For instance, if you type '8 per cent' you should not, later in the same exercise, type '10%'. You should also be consistent in your spacing after punctuation marks. Remember that one space after a full stop is not acceptable.

Use all the time. If you finish typing all the exercises before the time is up, resist the temptation to hand in your papers and leave the examination room. Carefully read through all your work again, paying particular attention to points such as special instructions, insertion of ballooned additions at the correct place, and checking you have not omitted some lines of an exercise by picking up a repeated word at the wrong point.

If you discover a bad error and have the time, it will pay you to retype the exercise. Mark in the correction(s) on your *typed* version (particularly if it was copied from complicated manuscript) and type from this. You will find it much quicker than typing the whole exercise again from the examination paper.

Exclamation mark. See **Combination characters and special signs** and **Punctuation marks.**

Expert's rhythm drill. See **Drills.**

Extra typewriter characters. These are the various characters provided on the standard typewriter keyboard, in addition to the alphabet, punctuation and figure characters. They consist of the following list: where use of the character is dealt with under another section(s), this is stated.

*	Asterisk	See **Combination characters** and *Footnotes* under **Literary work.**
"	Double Quotation Marks	See **Combination characters** and **Punctuation marks.**
/	Solidus	See **Combination characters** and below.
@	'At the price of'	See below.
£	Pound (sterling)	See **Money, typing of.**
—	Underscore	See **Underscoring** and **Combination characters.**
&	Ampersand	See below.
'	Single Quotation Mark	See **Combination Characters** and **Punctuation marks.**
(	Left-hand bracket	See **Combination characters** and **Punctuation marks.**

)	Right-hand bracket	See **Combination characters** and **Punctuation marks.**
+	Plus sign	See **Mathematical typing.**
=	Equals sign	See **Combination characters** and **Mathematical typing.**
-	Hyphen	See **Combination characters, Mathematical typing,** and **Punctuation marks.**
%	Per cent sign	See **Combination characters** and below.

1. / (*Solidus*). In addition to the uses given under **Combination characters,** the solidus is used in the following ways.

(a) As an alternative to the hyphen to represent 'to' in numbers, e.g., 70/75.
(b) In sloping fractions—see **Fractions.**
(c) In references, e.g., RWK/ms (see **Letters**).

2. @ (*at the price of*). This is used only in the typing of invoices, estimates, etc., e.g., 146 typewriting chairs @ £18.50.

3. & (*Ampersand*). This is an abbreviation for the word 'and' and is used in the following cases.

(a) In the names of firms, e.g., Messrs Turner & Wilson.
(b) In certain abbreviations, e.g., E & OE (errors and omissions excepted), C & F (cost and freight).
(c) In addresses, e.g., 24 & 25 Mount Road.

The ampersand is never used to represent the word 'and' in continuous prose unless the above occur in the body of the text.

4. % (*per cent*). This sign is used to represent 'per cent' in conjunction with *figures*. No space is left between the figure and symbol, e.g., 6%, 98%.

Fair copy. See **Legal work** and **Literary work.**

Faulty touch. See **Errors, their cause and remedy.**

Feed rollers. See **Parts of a typewriter.**

Figure drills. See **Drills.**

Film scripts. Film scripts are a highly specialized form of typewriting and comparatively few typists will ever be required to type them.
The layout varies very considerably from studio to studio. It is impossible to state any hard and fast rules for layout except that *all styles allow a generous mass of white space* for the technical staff to make

notes. Such space is obviously necessary since the director and his assistants will, during the shooting of the film, undoubtedly make changes with regard to camera angles and shots, and the way a scene is performed.

Each scene is numbered consecutively throughout the film, with a description of its location and time of day. The scenes are not necessarily shot consecutively. Often all the scenes in which a particular actor appears are shot consecutively: obviously to save money and prevent him from having to be present during the shooting of the whole film. In addition, if a number of scenes require to be filmed on a particular location, they are all performed together. The director usually shoots each scene several times—both in close up and at distance—and the selected portions of film are joined later.

Once the film script has been typed on A4 paper the required number of copies for the cast and technicians are photocopied or duplicated.

Since each studio has its own 'house style', the typist will be required to follow this. A competent typist will soon be able to master the conventions required.

Finger exercises. See **Drills.**

Fingering methods. There are two generally recognized methods of fingering—straight (sometimes called the vertical method) and standard (sometimes known as the horizontal method).

With straight fingering the keyboard is regarded as being divided into so many oblique but straight vertical rows of keys, each finger keeping to its vertical row(s).

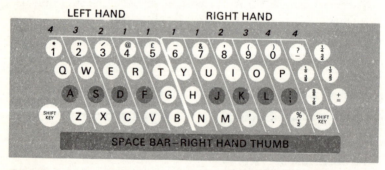

Straight fingering. The correct fingering is indicated by numbers

Standard fingering differs from the straight method in that the keys in the bottom row are divided so that the key for each finger falls to the left of the key above it.

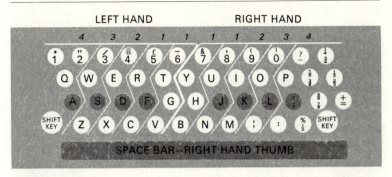

Standard fingering. The correct fingering is indicated by numbers

Most keyboard mastery textbooks adopt one or the other of these two fingering methods, although the order in which the keys are introduced varies considerably. Teachers often find it easier to teach according to the method they have learnt themselves, and choose their textbook accordingly.

Students should never be compelled to change from one method of fingering to the other once it has been mastered. It cannot be said that one of the methods is superior to the other and really first-class typists have been produced by both methods.

Fit. See **Literary work.**

Folding paper. Careless and incorrect methods of folding paper too many times so that a large part of the envelope is unfilled should be avoided. Poor folding of paper spoils the appearance of work and creates a bad impression in the mind of the recipient. (See diagram on p. 96.)

Foot symbol. See **Combination characters and special signs.**

Footnotes. See **Literary work.**

Foreign words and phrases, typing of. In the English language there are many foreign words and phrases in use for which there is no exact English equivalent. Some of these are in such general use that we are often unaware of their foreign origin and the fact that they have not been anglicized—e.g., carte blanche, interim, pro tem, sub poena.

At one time it was considered necessary in typing to distinguish 'foreign' words and phrases in some way. Often they were underscored (and printed in italics) or placed inside single or double quotation marks. It is becoming increasingly the tendency to make no distinction at all in the typing and printing of foreign words and phrases. The following example would appear perfectly normal and correct to most people.

'His loutish behaviour merely betrayed his lack of savoir faire and inconsideration for other people's feelings.'

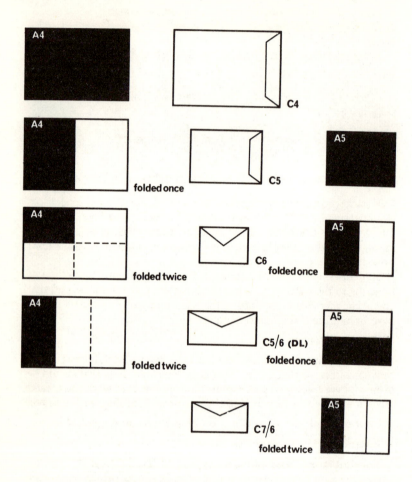

Diagram showing the correct ways of folding sizes of paper for insertion into different types of envelopes

Form letters. See **Letters.**

Forms of address. See **Titles, decorations, qualifications, forms of address, etc.**

Fractions. The typewriter keyboard is fitted with special keys for the most commonly-used fractions. If others are needed they have to be typed using either the solidus or underscore.

1. *Fractions provided on keyboard.* These are $\frac{1}{4}$, $\frac{3}{4}$, $\frac{1}{8}$, $\frac{3}{8}$, $\frac{5}{8}$, $\frac{7}{8}$, $\frac{1}{3}$, $\frac{2}{3}$ and $\frac{1}{2}$. It will be seen that the shift key has to be used when typing some of them.

No space should be left between the whole number and the fraction, e.g., $10\frac{1}{2}$, $4\frac{1}{3}$.

2. *Sloping fractions.* When fractions are typed using the solidus key they are known as sloping fractions, the solidus being used to separate the numerator from the denominator. With sloping fractions a space must be left between the unit figure of the whole number and the first figure of the fraction. Examples are 4 3/5, 26 15/16. An alternative but less frequently-used method is to type a stop instead of the space, as in 4.3/5, 26.15/16.

3. *Underscore fractions.* The second method of typing fractions not provided on the keyboard is to use the underscore, as in $4\frac{3}{5}$ and $26\frac{15}{16}$. When the whole number has been typed the paper should be raised half a space (using the half spacer) before the numerator is typed. The numerator should be underscored then the backspace key used before turning the paper down two half spaces and typing the denominator.

As will be seen, fractions made up using the solidus and underscore are cumbersome and their use obviously limited. Where such fractions are used, all other fractions (apart from those provided on the keyboard) *in the same work* should be formed by the same method. It is not satisfactory to mix sloping and underscore fractions.

If a typist has to type a considerable amount of mathematical work that contains fractions, she should use a typewriter with a special mathematical keyboard. See **Mathematical typing.**

Frontispiece. See **Literary work.**

Guide keys. See **Home keys.**

Half space correcting. See **Correcting errors.**

Half-spacer. See *Platen turning knobs* under **Parts of a typewriter.**

Half title. See **Literary work.**

Hanging paragraphs. See **Paragraphs.**

Headings (see also **Display**). A variety of types of heading is used in typewriting and each kind can be used to advantage in skilfully-displayed work.

1. *Heading devices.* Prominence should be given to the important aspects in a main heading consisting of more than one line, by skilful

use of the various heading devices—spaced capitals, closed capitals, initial capitals, and underscoring. Note how, in the following example, the various key items stand out. Note also that there is no punctuation at the end of lines in main headings.

T R U S T   M U L T I R E N T A L

FOR LOW-COST COLOUR TV

From Only £7.20 Down

When typing from manuscript or corrected typescript, three lines under a heading indicate to the typist that spaced capitals should be used; a heading underlined twice should be typed in closed capitals, and a heading with initial capitals that is underlined once should be underscored. Sometimes instructions to this effect are included on the copy but in some examinations, particularly advanced ones, the typist is expected to know this system. If a heading that is double or treble underlined is to be underscored, an instruction should be added.

If spaced capitals are being typed there should be one space between each letter in each word and three spaces between each word. There may be one or two spaces between words when using closed capitals in a heading (but consistency is essential) and when typing in lower case with initial capitals there should be one space between words. The preceding example illustrates these points.

Headings and line spacing. The line spacing between different lines in a main heading can vary according to the nature of the heading and the work. The lines should not be too spaced out or they will lose their impact: not should they be cramped. It is here that the artistic skill of the typist comes into play. In the example already illustrated, $1\frac{1}{2}$ line spaces were left between the first and second lines and one line space between the second and third lines.

There should always be at least six line spaces between the top of the paper and the first line of a main heading. Normally, however, the heading begins a few lines lower down: this is known as a dropped head.

If the text following a heading, or series of headings, is to be typed in double spacing (i.e., one line space between lines of type) there should be at least two line spaces between the last line of the heading and the beginning of the text—to give a balanced appearance to the work. Hard and fast rules cannot be stated since a decision should be based on the requirements of a particular piece of work, but a main heading, whether of one or several lines, should always receive due prominence.

2. *Centred headings.* These should be centred over the typewriting

line. If side margins are equal this is a simple matter, but if the left-hand margin is wider than the right-hand one, the process is slightly more complicated.

(a) *Centring over equal margins.* Check that the left-hand edge of the paper is at zero on the paper bail and note the number of character spaces across the width of the paper (e.g., A4 paper with elite type—100). Move the carriage by means of the carriage release lever until the printing point is at the centre of the paper (50 in the above example) and backspace once for every two characters (letters and spaces) in the heading. If the heading consists of an uneven number of character spaces it does not matter whether you backspace for the odd letter or not, provided you are consistent. If the heading consists of more than one line, each heading can be dealt with in this way.

Alternatively, count the number of characters (letters and spaces) in the heading. Deduct this figure from the character spaces across the paper: divide the answer by two and move the carriage so that the printing point is beneath this figure on the paper bail. Begin typing the centred heading at this point. If the heading consists of more than one line, the same procedure can be used for each line. An example follows.

SPECIAL OFFERS

IN LEATHERWEAR

FOR LADIES AND MEN

Line 1. The heading SPECIAL OFFERS comprises 14 characters. On A4 paper, using elite type, there are 100 character spaces across the width of the paper. 100 − 14 = 86, 86 ÷ 2 = 43. Begin typing at point 43 on the paper bail with the left-hand edge of the paper at zero.

Line 2. The heading IN LEATHERWEAR consists of exactly the same number of characters as the first line; therefore typing will begin at the same point on the paper scale.

Line 3. FOR LADIES AND MEN comprises 18 characters. 100 − 18 = 82, 82 ÷ 2 = 41. Begin typing at point 41 on the paper scale.

When centring a heading of several lines over equal margins, many typists prefer the following method. Count the number of characters in each line and centre the first line according to the method just described. Centre all remaining lines *according to their length in relation to the first line.* In the example given, the third line consists of 18 characters: this is 4 characters wider than the first line. Divide this figure (4) by 2 which gives an answer of 2. Since the line is *wider* than the first one, backspace twice from the point where the first line began. There will then be 2 additional letters either side of the first heading. If the line were *shorter* than the first one, the calculations would be the same except that you would tap in the appropriate number of spaces from the point where the first line began. For instance, if the third line were FOR LADIES (instead of FOR LADIES AND MEN), there are 10 characters in this line and the relative difference with the first line is 4 characters. Since the line is *shorter* tap in half this figure (2) from the point where the first line began (point 43 on the paper bail). The headings would then appear as follows.

SPECIAL OFFERS

IN LEATHERWEAR

FOR LADIES

In the examples given, the lines all consist of an even number of characters. If the character count gives an uneven figure, either add on or subtract one each time to make the figure even—but be consistent here.

(b) *Centring over unequal margins.* See that the left-hand edge of the paper is at zero on the paper bail. Add together the degrees on the scale at which the margins are set and divide the answer by two to find the centre point of the typing line. Backspace once for every two characters (letters and spaces) in the heading. For example, if margins are 15 and 90 (on A4 paper), add these figures together, which gives 105; divide by 2 which gives 52 (or 53)—the central point of the typing line.

If the heading consists of more than one line, it is a simple matter, once the first line is centred correctly, to centre the others by the relativity method described in the last paragraph under (a).

3. *Blocked headings.* Increasingly, main headings are not being centred (which takes time and skill), but blocked instead. This means that all lines of a heading begin at the left-hand margin point and the same basic principles outlined under *Heading devices* apply. An example of a blocked heading follows.

T H E   W H I T E   H A R T   H O T E L

BRIGHTON, Sussex

Luncheon Menu

4. Shoulder Headings

This is an example of a shoulder heading. This style is often used for sub-headings in a piece of typewritten work that has a main heading—which may consist of one or more lines. The main heading may be centred or blocked and typed as already outlined in this section.

A shoulder heading begins at the left-hand margin point and may be typed with initial capitals (as in this example) or closed capitals. Shoulder headings are usually underscored, but this is not essential. Shoulder headings should not be followed by a full stop and there should be one line of space between the heading and the beginning of the text. After shoulder headings the paragraphs may be indented—as in this example—or blocked.

5. Paragraph Headings.   This is a paragraph heading and it will be seen that the text begins on the same line as the heading. Paragraph headings may be typed in a variety of ways. They can be in lower case with initial capitals, as in this example, or in closed capitals. Paragraph headings are usually underscored, particularly if initial capitals are used, to give the heading prominence. They may or may not be followed by a full stop; if a full stop is used, it should be followed by two or three spaces before the text begins.

Paragraph headings are usually blocked, beginning at the left-hand margin point, as in this example, but they may also be indented, beginning five or six spaces to the right of the left-hand margin. Consistency on this point within a single piece of work is important.

6. MARGINAL OR SIDE HEADINGS
This is an example of a marginal or side heading—the terms are synonymous. A marginal heading is typed to the right of the left-hand margin and there should be at least one character space between the longest line in the marginal heading (or series of marginal headings) and the text—so that the text appears all in line.

Paragraphs following marginal headings may be blocked, as in this example, or indented. The left-hand margin stop should be set where the lines of the text will begin and the margin release key used for moving the carriage back when a marginal heading needs to be typed. All lines of a marginal heading should begin at the same point of the scale and a tab stop should be set for this purpose. If indented paragraphs are used, a second tab stop should be set for the indentation.

Marginal headings are usually typed in closed capitals (as in this example), although they are sometimes typed in lower case with initial capitals, with or without underscoring. Use of closed capitals without underscoring gives marginal headings prominence and is the quickest and most satisfactory way of typing them.

Headlines. See **Literary work.**

History of the typewriter. In the nineteenth century two inventions that Man had been working on for hundreds of years made great strides forward. One was the system of shorthand invented by Sir Isaac Pitman and the other was the production of a commercially viable typewriter that could type faster than one could write longhand.

Evidence of Man's desire to increase the speed at which his thoughts and speech could be recorded goes back to the earliest civilizations. A form of shorthand writing was certainly used by the Greeks in the fourth century BC and from that time until the present day numerous shorthand systems have been devised. However, the publication of *Stenographic Sound-Hand* by Isaac Pitman in 1837 introduced to the world the shorthand system that has achieved the widest universal use and acclaim.

Another idea to reduce the labour of handwriting was to develop a machine that would type. Printing was adopted in Europe in the mid-fifteenth century—after an 800-year development in the Far East. Until then, every document had to be laboriously written out by hand. Printing, of course, helped bring about a great advance in Man's development, but still he evinced a desire to produce a machine that would 'print' for him individually. The first recorded evidence of this is a patent granted by Queen Anne in 1714 to a Henry Mill for 'an artificial machine or method for the impressing or transcribing of letters singly or progressively one after another, as in writing whereby all writings whatsoever may be engrossed in paper or parchment so neat and exact as not to be distinguished from print . . .'

Following Mill's invention, a number of primitive mechanisms were produced and it is interesting to note that many of the early 'typewriters' were designed to help blind people read and write—speed of operation being a very secondary consideration: the type produced by such machines was, of course, embossed and led eventually to the production of Braille's system in 1829.

All the early typewriters fall into one of about a dozen categories, according to how the type was actually impressed upon the paper. The technicalities of the different types is complex and anyone interested in the working mechanisms of early typewriters should visit the Science Museum in Kensington where there is a good collection of early typewriters. It is possible here to mention but a few of the important developments in typewriter construction.

In 1833 an important contribution was made by Xavier Progin, a printer from Marseilles: he produced the first machine of the *downstrike* class which had a circular type-basket with type bars striking down to a common printing point. Progin claimed that his machine would write 'almost as fast as a pen'—so like most of the early type-writers, it was slow and cumbersome in operation. Another contribution of importance was provided by an Italian, Guiseppe Ravizza, who from 1830 to 1885 produced seventeen different models, all first examples of the *up-strike* class: Ravizza was also the inventor of the ribbon inking system.

One serious drawback of many early typewriters was that the width of the typewriting paper was limited to about four inches because the paper had to be placed in a cylindrical wire-mesh basket.

The Hammond Ideal (1884). Note the piano-like keys and cylindrical wire-mesh basket which limited the width of the paper

It was in America in the second half of the nineteenth century that important work was done by a group of men which led to the first commercial production of typewriters. In 1866 Christopher Latham Sholes and Carlos Glidden were working together on the development of a machine for numbering consecutively the pages of books. They became interested in further developing their invention to produce a machine that would type letters as well as figures; and a third man, Samuel Soulé, joined them in their venture. They produced several working models and gained the interest and support of James Densmore, a businessman with great enthusiasm for the new idea. Sholes, perhaps the most brilliant of the working trio, was of a shy and retiring disposition and would possibly not have persisted in his sometimes depressing attempts but for Densmore's constructive criticism and drive.

A pre-1900 Remington advertisement

By 1872 a sufficiently successful machine had been developed for the group to try to find a manufacturer. E. Remington & Sons, the small arms manufacturers, were approached. Remingtons had given over part of their armaments factory to the production of such things as sewing machines, and were thus well equipped for the development of mechanism such as is required in typewriter construction. Remingtons were at first dubious about this new proposal but eventually, in March 1873, a contract was signed for the manufacture of typewriters and the first typewriter was despatched from the Remington factory early in 1874. Shown on page 104 is an advertisement from this period.

It is interesting to note that both Sholes and Glidden had been compositors and were not interested in arranging the keyboard for rapid typing using all the fingers. In fact touch typing as we know it did not develop until considerably later: the earliest typists were all 'sight' operators and used two, three, or as many fingers as they thought fit (see **Touch typewriting**). In developing their various models, Sholes and Glidden encountered serious clashing of the type-bars even at moderate speeds. Therefore they juggled the letters around and, quite deliberately, positioned the most frequently used keys to *slow down the operator* and thus prevent the typebars from colliding and sticking at the printing point. The result was the universal keyboard which we all know today—the arrangement of which has been severely criticized from the point of view of speed of operation (see **Arrangement of keyboard**).

At first the Remington Company found it a hard task to interest the public in their newly-manufactured typewriters and when the typewriter made its first serious public appearance at the Centennial Exposition in 1876, it attracted little attention. Early sales were slow, even though the potential speed of the typewriters far surpassed the speed of the pen.

One disadvantage of the earliest Remington typewriters was that the operator could not see what had been typed without lifting the carriage by means of a handle (see illustration on p. 106 of Lillian Sholes typing on one of her father's early models). Thus the machine introduced by E. E. Horton in 1883 represented a great step forward in that it was the first typewriter of the type-bar class to secure fully visible typing.

Early recipients of typed letters thought they were printed and the story is told of a Kentucky mountaineer who returned a typewritten letter he had received with the indignant note: 'You don't need to print no letters for me. I kin read writin.'

Early objection to typescript letters was general: many people preferred the copperplate business handwriting of the day and felt that receipt of a typed communication was, in some way, insulting. However, Queen Victoria had a typewriter and used it frequently. This helped break down the initial prejudices against typewritten work.

Lillian Sholes typing on one of her father's early models

In the first quarter of the twentieth century a general standardization of typewriter design took place and all the leading makes became equipped with standard controls such as margin stops, tabulators, and ribbon colour control. Improvements in mechanism and design have continued right up to the present day and many visitors to the Business Efficiency Exhibitions, when surveying the range of typewriters, are surprised to know that the first typewriter was manufactured and sold just over a hundred years ago.

Electric typewriters were first introduced in the 1930s. The IBM golf ball machine is basically an ingenious modification of the early type-wheel design: it differs from all other machines in that the carriage remains stationary while the type-ball head moves along the platen. The Hammond Ideal typewriter, illustrated on page 103, is the ancestor of the Varityper—the sole successful survivor of the swinging-sector class of typewriters.

Present-day sophistications and developments of the typewriter are numerous and some of the more important ones are described under **Special purpose typewriters.**

When Queen Anne granted the patent to Henry Mill in 1714 she could hardly have envisaged the momentous future of 'writing machines'. Without doubt the typewriter, in conjunction with the use of shorthand, was a factor in the emancipation of women. And it is difficult to imagine today's world of commerce and industry functioning smoothly without assistance from the ubiquitous typewriter to deal with all the necessary background paper work.

Despite the chequered start of manufactured typewriters, an astute minority foresaw the potential of typewriters and in the early 1880s young ladies were first shown how to type. Dire consequences were predicted for the revolutionary idea of young women typing in offices and many considered the female mind and constitution too frail to survive such rigours! But soon offices came to realize the advantages of using typewriters rather than the pen for most of their paper work, and a demand for typists arose which has increased in momentum right up to the present day.

Home keys. These are the eight keys on the middle row of letters which act as guides for the rest of the keys in 'touch' typing.

LEFT HAND   RIGHT HAND

The little finger of the left hand should be positioned lightly above the letter **a** and the little finger of the right hand above the **colon/semicolon** key. These two keys are often known as the 'guide keys' since from them the other three fingers of each hand naturally fall into their correct position.

During the keyboard learning stage the fingers should remain in this central position over the keyboard and be trained to make the correct movements to the other keys. Each finger should move independently of the others and should immediately return to its correct home key after striking a different letter or character. Only when high typewriting speeds are reached will this central hand position be abandoned during typing. Even then, whenever there is a pause in typing, the expert typist will find that her fingers naturally revert to the home key position.

Hook in. See **Literary work.**

Horizontal centring. See **Centring—horizontal and vertical.**

Hyphen. See **Punctuation marks.**

Inches sign. See **Combination characters and special signs.**

Income and expenditure account (also known as **Receipts and payments account**). This type of account is used by non-trading and non-profit making concerns (such as clubs and charitable societies) to record the cash received and paid out during a given period of time. It also states the amount of cash in hand, this clearly being the difference between the two, taking into account the cash in hand at the beginning of the period in question.

An income and expenditure account is divided into two sides like a balance sheet. One side records details of income received during a stated period and the other side shows the expenses incurred. The amount by which income has exceeded expenditure is shown on the expenditure side (this will obviously be the cash in hand)— so that the two sides add up to the same total.

Income and expenditure accounts are usually simple in nature and can normally be contained on a single sheet of A4 paper (with the longer side at the top). The principles for typing them are the same as for typing a balance sheet on a single sheet of paper (see **Balance sheets**). Frequently, a red line is ruled down the middle of the paper to divide expenditure from income.

Inconsistent indentation. See **Errors, their cause and remedy.**

Indented paragraphs. See **Paragraphs.**

Inferior (lowered) characters (see also **Superior (raised) characters**). Inferior characters are lowered half a space below the normal typing line. The half-space mechanism, interliner or variable line spacer are used for this purpose. Inferior characters are used in chemical expressions and formulae, e.g., H_2SO_4.

Information. See **Reference, sources of.**

Injector/ejector lever. See **Parts of a typewriter** (*Paper injector/ ejector lever*).

Ink duplicating. (See also **Reprography processes.**) With this method of reproduction an ink duplicating machine is necessary. The master is cut by drawing or writing (with a special stylus) or by typing on a stencil.

A stencil is joined to a backing sheet. The backing sheet is attached to a special heading which consists of a number of perforations of various shapes and sizes: these enable the completed stencil to be attached to the drum of the duplicator. Different makes of duplicator have headings of a different design, so it is advisable to obtain the correct type of stencil. Some stencils, however, have a heading which will fit more than one type of machine. Sometimes the stencil and backing sheet is interleaved with a sheet of greaseproof paper, which should be removed before the master is cut. In addition, stencils are usually interleaved with a sheet of 'once-only' carbon paper: sometimes this is attached to the backing sheet with the carbon-coated side facing the stencil. This carbon paper facilitates reading of the stencil as it is being typed. If desired, a second sheet of carbon paper can be inserted, the carbon-coated side facing the backing sheet: this will produce a copy of the typed matter on the backing sheet—an aid to the rapid reading and checking of what has been typed so that undetected errors or required alterations can be made before the copies are run off.

The upper side of a stencil contains a number of figures and lines. The figures down each side indicate the number of line spaces and the scales at the top and bottom are marked for both pica and elite type. A broken line runs down the vertical centre of the master: this line is useful for centring headings, etc., if equal margins are used. In addition, various sizes of paper (A6, A5, A4, etc.) are given, and the typist should not type outside the lines for the size of paper she requires.

When one writes or types on the stencil, the fibrous tissues are cut so that when the stencil is fitted to the drum of the duplicator, ink can penetrate the perforations and enable the characters to be reproduced in their exact form.

Various grades of stencil are available from the economy grade (which will produce up to 1,000 copies) to the cellulose-coated types which, if well-cut and well-handled, will produce up to 10,000 copies.

It is possible to produce copies consisting of more than one colour. However, a separate master must be cut for each colour and each colour requires a separate run through the machine. Before changing the ink colour, a machine needs very thorough cleaning. This chore is made easier if a complete change of cylinder can be made.

The frequent cutting of stencils tends to clog the type faces with fibrous tissues. The use of high-quality stencils reduces such type-filling to a minimum. Nevertheless, some typists prefer to place a sheet of plastic film over the stencil when typing—as this prevents the type faces becoming clogged. This is particularly useful if many stencils are being typed since the typist does not have to keep stopping to clean the type: it also prevents the centres of certain letters (e.g., **o**, **d**, **p**, and **b**) being cut right out. The plastic material is thin but resilient and it does

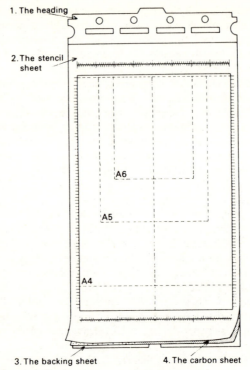

1. The heading

2. The stencil sheet

A6

A5

A4

3. The backing sheet

4. The carbon sheet

Diagram of a stencil

not prevent the type cutting through the stencils. It is possible to obtain stencils with this special coating incorporated.

Points to observe when typing stencils

1. The backing sheet should not be removed.

2. One or two sheets of once-only carbon paper can be used as already described.

3. The type ribbon should be disengaged by moving the ribbon switch to the stencil position (usually white).

4. The type faces should be clean and in good condition.

5. A soft or medium-surface platen is best for stencil cutting, as compared with a hard platen, for the typing of numerous carbon copies. Some typewriters can be fitted with interchangeable platens so that it is an easy matter to fit a substitute platen if necessary. With stencil cutting the platen should be smooth enough to allow the backing sheet to absorb any unevenness.

6. With a manual typewriter the typist should use a sharp (but not

heavy), even touch. Any unevenness in striking the keys will show clearly on the copies. If too heavy a touch is used the centres of certain letters (**o** in particular) are likely to be cut out. If this happens, the centre should be carefully replaced with a pin or moistened finger. Otherwise an ugly, black blob will appear on the copies.

7. When the stencil has been inserted into the typewriter, the top horizontal line should be aligned with the paper bail and line indicators. If adjustment is necessary, the paper release lever should be used.

8. When typing the stencil, care should be taken in setting the margin stops to ensure that type does not extend beyond any of the lines given for the size of paper required.

Correction of errors on stencils. A typist should correct any errors she notices as she goes along, using the special correcting fluid that is available. This fluid is supplied in small bottles fitted with a screw cap to which a small brush is attached. It is obtainable in red or white.

First the stencil should be raised so the error rests on the erasure table. The paper bail should be lifted and the portion of stencil to be corrected should be raised slightly by inserting a pencil or similar object between the stencil and carbon paper beneath—to prevent the two sticking together. The error should then be painted over with the correcting fluid and a few seconds allowed for it to dry (the typist can check through what she has already typed while the fluid is drying). The pencil, etc., should then be removed, the paper bail replaced, and the platen turned back to the correct position for typing the correction. Slight additional pressure should be used when typing over correcting fluid to ensure that the extra thickness will be adequately penetrated.

If a full line or a heading needs to be deleted and the space is not required for additional typing, the quickest method is to use a strip of gummed paper (such strips are usually supplied in boxes of stencils).

When an extensive correction has to be made, this should be done by 'grafting'. The stencil should be removed from the typewriter and that portion of the stencil containing the error should be carefully cut out with a small sharp blade, the stencil alone resting on a hard surface while this is done. Part of another stencil, slightly larger than the patch cut out, should then be inserted in its place and secured in position by painting correcting fluid all round its edge. Care must be taken to obtain correct alignment before typing in the correction.

With all stencil corrections the typist should make sure that she does not obliterate any part that has been correctly typed.

Since a large number of copies will probably be made from a single stencil, it is vital that it should be carefully checked. No stencil should be removed from the typewriter before being checked (preferably by a second person) and any corrections made.

If one is cutting a stencil from a manuscript draft, it should first be read through completely so that everything is clear before typing begins. If the stencil involves considerable display, it will often be worth while typing a draft first on plain paper: this will probably result in a better master and obviate having to start again with wastage of expensive materials.

Ruling on a stencil should be done by use of a stylus and ruler, the stencil resting on a hard base-plate. Ruling is assisted by the provision of horizontal and vertical lines on the stencil face. It is a good practice first to lightly rule the four outside lines with an HB pencil before fully cutting them with a stylus: this will help ensure neat corners.

A stylus is always used for the insertion of a signature on a circular letter, etc.

If the stencils need to be kept for future use, they should be cleaned with spirit and either kept flat in special absorbent stencil folders or hung on metal rods: a copy of the typed matter should be attached so its contents will be readily apparent. Stencils 'kept standing' in this way should be numbered and listed under various headings—so they can be easily located when required.

Apart from typing on to stencils, there are other methods of making stencil masters. Electronic stencil makers can copy photos, drawings and printed or typed texts, ready for duplicating. There are also photocopying methods of producing stencil masters from such originals.

Inserting paper into typewriter (see **Adjustment of paper**). The following procedure (which should be studied in conjunction with **Parts of a typewriter and their uses**) should be adopted when inserting paper, envelopes, etc., into the typewriter.

1. Ensure that the paper guide is set at zero on the paper scales—to secure uniform margins on successive sheets of paper.
2. Grip the papers, with or without backing sheet (see **Backing sheets**), in the left hand and drop them behind the platen until the bottom edges rest evenly against the feed rollers. If carbon paper(s) is being used, see **Carbon copying** (*Correct insertion into the typewriter*) for a description of the correct method of assembling the papers.
3. If the typewriter is fitted with a paper injector/ejector lever, this should be used with the right hand to rapidly move on the paper to the position required for starting to type: otherwise turn the right-hand platen knob with the right hand.
4. Make sure the paper is straight by aligning it with the paper bail. If it is crooked, the paper release lever should be used so it can be straightened.
5. Move the left- and right-hand paper grips (if necessary) to ensure the paper is held firmly against the platen.

6. Set the margin stops (also a tabular stop if indented paragraphs are to be used) and line space selector at the required positions, and begin typing.

Inset matter. This, as the name implies, is information that is typed within continuous prose so that it stands out for some particular reason. It is usually typed in single spacing and separated from the text by a line space above and below it. Inset matter may consist of a series of items that are numbered or lettered, or preceded by paragraph headings: in such cases each enumerated item will be separated by a line of space. Inset matter may be typed in the blocked, indented, or hanging style of paragraph (see **Paragraphs**).

If indented paragraphs are used, inset matter is sometimes centred so that there is equal space on either side of the longest line of the inset and the normal typing line above and below. This is illustrated in the indented letter (No. 3) under **Letters** (*Business letters*). Alternatively, the inset matter can begin at the tab stop set for the paragraph indentation (illustrated in *Business letters* No. 2B) and end so that there are at least five or six character spaces between the end of the inset and the right-hand margin position. The right-hand margin stop should be adjusted for this purpose and moved back to its permanent position when typing of the inset is completed.

When the blocked method of layout is being used, the 'inset' matter can begin at the left-hand margin position (see *Business letters*, No. 1).

The last two methods described above are obviously the quickest to type, since no elaborate calculations are involved.

Although the examples mentioned and illustrated under **Letters** show information that consists of separate lines, inset matter may be continuous prose—a quotation for example. The start of each paragraph of a quotation is preceded by quotation marks but there are quotation marks at the end of the *last paragraph only*.

Instruction booklet for typewriter. Typewriter manufacturers publish an instruction booklet for each different model of machine they produce, and supply a copy with each new typewriter. If this becomes lost, a replacement copy can usually be obtained upon request.

An instruction booklet illustrates and describes the mechanism of the different parts of the typewriter, how to fix a new ribbon, etc., and the typist should carefully study it if she is not already familiar with the particular machine that she must use.

Interliner. See **Parts of a typewriter.**

Invitations. Invitations to weddings, twenty-first birthday parties, business functions, etc., are usually sent out in the form of displayed printed cards. A typist may be required to type the copy for invitations for the printer and should therefore be familiar with their form and wording. In addition, if the number of invited guests is small, a typist may have to type an original and photocopy or duplicate the required number.

Invitations are usually formal in tone and expressed in the third person. No salutation, complimentary close or signature is required and the invited guest's name is usually handwritten by the sender to give a personal touch. A typed example follows.

```
        Mr and Mrs J Johnson
    request the pleasure of the company of
            . . . . . . . . . . . . . . . . . . . .
    at the marriage of their daughter, Jane
            to Mr Francis Flanders
        at St Mary's Church, Watford
        on Saturday 24 March at 12 noon
    and afterwards at the County Hotel
        RSVP
        34 Wood Lane
        WATFORD
        WD1 2NW
```

The style of reply should be based on the form of the invitation and if it is formal and in the third person, the reply should be similarly expressed. The reply should include full details of the function as given on the invitation. If an invitation is being refused, it is polite to give a reason. A reply to an invitation may be typed on a card or on A5 paper and a typical example of layout and wording follows.

```
28 Coldharbour Lane
Bushey
WATFORD

Miss Mary Brown thanks Mr and Mrs Johnson for
their kind invitation to the wedding of their
daughter, Jane, to Mr Francis Flanders at
St Mary's Church, Watford at noon on 24 March
and afterwards at the County Hotel, and has
much pleasure in accepting.
```

If an invitation is to a husband and wife, a secretary will be asked to reply on behalf of them both. In this case she should send a carbon copy of the reply to the wife.

Sometimes a secretary will have to find out, by telephoning, the type of dress to be worn at a social occasion: usually, however, invitations to formal occasions have printed on the cards 'dinner jackets', etc., so that everyone knows what he or she is expected to wear.

Invoices. An invoice is a document sent to the purchaser of goods by the seller. It gives full details of the goods sold. Invoices are usually typed on specially printed forms (A4 or A5—the latter with the wider side at the top). The layout and ruling vary considerably but they are basically of two types:

1. Forms listing a single day's purchases.
2. Forms despatched once a month, listing all the items and details purchased throughout that month.

The printed information on invoices (see note under **Letters—** *Business letters*) includes:

1. Name, address, etc., of seller
2. Invoice number
3. Ruled columns and boxes
4. Terms of payment

The letters E & OE (errors and omissions excepted) are usually printed on invoice forms. This indicates that the seller reserves the right to correct any errors that subsequently come to light.

Particulars which are typewritten include:

1. Name and address of purchaser
2. Date of purchase
3. Quantity of goods supplied
4. Description of goods
5. Unit prices
6. VAT
7. Total prices
8. Discount
9. Carriage or postage charges
10. Method of despatch

Most invoice forms contain a ruled box, etc., for insertion of the purchaser's name and address so that window envelopes can be used (see **Envelopes**).

Margin and tabular stops. The left-hand margin stop should be set at the point where the typing of the first column will commence. Tab stops should be set for each following column. At least one character space should be left between each vertical line and the beginning or end of the typewritten matter. On some invoice forms a vertical line is inserted to separate the pounds from the pence in money total columns. On others this information is inserted in a single column and the typist needs to head the column with the £ sign and use the decimal point to divide the pounds from the pence (see **Money, typing of**).

Spacing. Single or double spacing is used between items according to the length of the invoice and the space available.

Carbon copies. Small firms usually take one carbon copy only for their records. In large firms, however, the typist may be required to take several carbon copies for different purposes. The top copy is usually sent to the customer and carbon copies made for other departments or needs, e.g., Accounts Department, Advice Note, Delivery Note.

When several carbon copies are required, firms often use a continuous stationery typewriter. With these typewriters the paper is fed in from a continuous roll and can be torn off in sets (by means of perforations) when the typing is complete. With some machines, as one set of documents is completed, the carbon paper is automatically fed into the next set by the use of a lever. Use of a continuous stationery typewriter considerably increases the speed and efficiency of the typist. Another method of producing several copies is to use NCR (no carbon required) paper (see separate entry under **NCR paper**).

Note: Pro Forma Invoices, Debit and Credit Notes are set out in a similar manner to invoices. With credit notes the printed (and sometimes the typewritten) particulars are usually in red for distinction.

Export invoices. Firms which export goods abroad use a special export invoice form which contains, in addition to the particulars already mentioned, the name of the vessel, etc., on which the goods are to be sent, details of cargo marks and cargo charges.

Consular invoices. When exported goods are subject to import duty in the country of destination, a special consular invoice form is used. This contains a declaration to the effect that the details and prices quoted are true and correct and that the goods are of British manufacture and origin. Such an invoice bears a consular stamp.

An increasing amount of accounting work is being done by mechanized accounting machines. In firms where computerized or mechanized accounting systems are used, financial forms, including invoices, provide spaces for the inclusion of a variety of codes, special purpose columns, etc.,—all necessary for data processing.

Irregular left-hand margin. See **Errors, their cause and remedy** and **Margins**.

Italics. See **Emphasizing words** and **Underscoring**.

Itineraries. It is often necessary for a secretary to make all the required arrangements for her employer if he is to be out of the office on business—sometimes for only a day but also, perhaps, for several days or more. She will need to book his accommodation and travel arrangements well in advance, organize the necessary papers and files, and plan an appointments schedule in consultation with him.

An itinerary should be clearly typed in column form and give precise details of dates, arrival and departure times of trains, planes, etc.; hotel accommodation booked, names, addresses and telephone numbers of people to be seen, etc., including times. It should contain full details of the programme for any particular trip so that her boss knows exactly where he should be at any given time (within reason!).

If the itinerary is short—covering, for instance, only one day—it is best typed on thin card of a convenient size (e.g. a postcard) so it can be kept in a wallet. However, if the business trip is a long one and the information lengthy, the itinerary can be typed on A4 paper, since it will probably be kept in a file.

An example of a typed itinerary follows.

```
Four-day Sales Promotion Tour
(Mr J A Bond)

Monday 12 October      0940 hrs    Leave Euston for Northampton
                       1230 hrs    Lunch at Victoria Hotel with Mr G Dunn
                       1400 hrs    Sales Conference in Regal Suite at Victoria
                                   Hotel

                       Accommodation booked at Churchill Hotel

Tuesday 13 October     0900 hrs    Leave Northampton for Birmingham
                       1145 hrs    Meeting followed by lunch with Mr G Clarke
                                   of Mercury Products in his office (24 Fenton
                                   Street, Birmingham)
                       1500 hrs    Meeting with Mr P Holden of Bland & Wechsler
                                   Limited (93 West Street, Birmingham)
                       2200 hrs    Leave Birmingham for Glasgow

Wednesday 14 October   1030 hrs    All-day meeting of Scottish dealers at
                                   Lansdowne Hotel

                       Accommodation booked at Regent Palace Hotel

Thursday 15 October    1030 hrs    Meeting followed by lunch with Mr G Halls at
                                   Swan Hotel
                       1400 hrs    Sales Conference in Franklin Room at Swan
                                   Hotel
                       2100 hrs    Flight from Glasgow to Heathrow (book in at
                                   airport by 2000 hrs)
```

Justified right-hand margin. It will be seen that in printing, all complete lines begin and end at exactly the same point. In typewritten work a uniform left-hand margin is easily secured by means of the left-hand margin stop and correct manipulation of the carriage-return lever. However, a completely even, or 'justified', right-hand margin is not possible with most typewriters—unless the space between the words is adjusted to ensure that the lines all end at the same point. For this purpose a draft must, of course, be typed. When retyping, the first line should be the required length and the spaces between words should be suitably adjusted on subsequent lines so that they end flush with the first line. Obviously, such a procedure is very time consuming and could only be recommended for the production of originals for high-class work.

It is much easier to justify the right-hand margin on a typewriter that has proportional spacing (see **Proportional spacing**), and the result is more pleasing to the eye since the different letters occupy different space, according to their size and width: also, there are sometimes two space bars, one giving a movement of two units and the other, three units.

Typewriters are obtainable which have a special device for 'justifying'. They equalize the space between every word when the draft has been typed and the required number of spaces to be added to each line is known. Such a device is known as an Automatic Right-Margin Justifying Device. (See also **Special purpose typewriters.**)

Keyboard. See **Parts of a typewriter**

Keyboard arrangement. See **Arrangement of the keyboard**.

Keyboard drills. See **Drills.**

Keyboard errors and their remedy. See **Errors, their cause and remedy.**

Last line indicator. See **Parts of a typewriter.**

Leader dots (see also **Column work with column headings** (g)). The main purpose of leader dots is to help lead the eye from one point to another on the same line when there is a considerable space between the typewritten matter.

Leader dots are frequently used in the first column of tabular statements when this column (often the descriptive one) varies considerably in length. If some items in the descriptive column are much longer than the others, it is advisable to extend the longer lines to a second, and in some cases a third, line: when this is done, leader dots should be used only on the last line of the item.

Apart from assisting the reading, leader dots help give the typewritten work a more balanced and pleasing appearance since they 'square up' a column of typewriting which would otherwise have a ragged and irregular appearance. For this reason the leader dots should all end at the same point—which should be approximately in line with the longest item in the column (if continuous dots are used, they can line up exactly).

At least one space must always be left between the last word and the first leader dot and between the last leader dot and the following word or vertical line (if ruling is used). The full stop key is used for leader dots; therefore the dots should be typed evenly and lightly or they will pierce the paper and spoil the appearance of the work.

The recommended methods of typing leader dots are as follows:

1. Two dots followed by three spaces   ..   ..
2. Three dots followed by two spaces   ... ...
3. Regularly spaced dots, e.g., one dot
followed by four spaces   .   .   .   .   .
4. Continuous dots   ....

When typing leader dots in groups, they must be typed uniformly underneath each other and the typist should never commence with part of a group—the carriage should be moved to the position where the first complete group will begin. In the first three methods described and illustrated above, it will be seen that the groups are in multiples of five. This makes it easy to find the position where the first group of dots should begin if the typist always begins her grouping at any point five on the scale of the paper bail (25, 30, 35, etc.). Leader dots should *always* be inserted on each line as the complete line is typed: if the practice of typing in groups of five (or continuous dots) is adopted, this should present no difficulty.

When using leader dots between two columns of typewritten inset matter, a lengthy series of dots should be avoided—or the main purpose of using them (i.e., guiding the eye from one item to the next on the same line) will be partly defeated.

Learning to type. Anyone who wishes to learn to type should do so preferably under the tuition of a qualified teacher and at least with the aid of a good typewriting instruction book. Having purchased a typewriter, one should resist the temptation to use it without expert advice. Many people start to type using only two or three fingers: they build up a reasonable and limited speed and often regret doing this because, using the wrong techniques, their skill can only develop to a certain point. Of necessity, their eyes must be constantly darting from the copy to the keyboard and typescript—with resulting fatigue and loss of speed.

It stands to reason that a typist needs to have a central position at the keyboard for the placing of her hands if she is ever to become a high-speed 'touch' typist. Each finger, through repetition and practice, can be trained to move up or down and in the right direction from the home keys to the required character. It takes time and patience, but the effort is worthwhile since one is building a sound foundation for the development of speed and skill.

In addition, the techniques for manipulating various parts of the typewriter have been critically examined for many years, and teachers instruct their pupils in the generally considered best ways of using the various typewriter devices. For instance, with manual typewriters 'correct' return of the carriage is important to skill development. The carriage return lever should be struck firmly and sharply with the index finger of the left hand: the hand should be flat, palm down, and the carriage should be 'thrown' back with just enough force to ensure that it reaches the left-hand margin stop. Many self-taught typists tend to grasp the carriage return lever between the thumb and fingers and 'draw' it back.

Habits once formed are very difficult to break, and for this reason teachers prefer to have students with no typewriting experience rather than people who have taught themselves and developed bad habits.

In the early stages of typewriting training students are bound to make mistakes, but what matters most is that they are laying the foundation of sound typewriting skill by *doing things the right way*.

There are many points a learner needs to be taught, apart from those already outlined. She needs to understand the importance of good posture and position at the typewriter, how and when to erase, the importance of developing speed and accuracy side by side—to mention but a few.

Therefore, a would-be beginner in Typewriting should enrol for instruction under a qualified teacher. If this is not possible, she should obtain a good typewriting instruction book (designed for self-instruction) and carefully study it as she proceeds through the course.

Legal typing. Many typists are never required to type legal work. Nevertheless, it is a useful part of a typist's training if she learns something about the particular features of typing legal documents and understands the meaning of some of the commonly used legal terms and phrases. Most typewriting textbooks for intermediate and advanced students include a certain amount of legal typing and some examining bodies require the typing of legal exercises.

Legal typing requires a long-carriage typewriter since draft or brief paper is frequently used. Normally, however, in school or college typing practice, legal work is typed on A4 paper.

Although many of the conventions of legal typing are common throughout the legal profession, one should remember that, as with other typing, practice in certain matters varies from firm to firm. A typist entering a legal office should always follow the particular style of her employers. She will be shown typed examples of any document she is asked to type and will be able to use these as a guide until she is perfectly familiar with the particular preferences and conventions of her employers. Even so, it will be of assistance to her if she has already had practice in legal typing at school or college, since many of the particular features of legal typing are widely used.

There are various stages in the typing of legal documents.

1. *The draft.* This is often typed in treble spacing and should be clearly headed DRAFT on the endorsement. Wide margins are used to take any subsequent alterations and insertions. Drafts are often made purely for office use so that the document can be considered further before the final copy (the engrossment) is made. In some cases a very rough draft is first typed for the solicitor's own use, and then the rough draft is retyped for submission to the solicitor acting for the other party, if appropriate. In other cases the engrossment is typed direct from short-hand, an audio recording, or a rough draft when it is not necessary to submit the document to the solicitor on the other side.

Sometimes three copies of the draft are required—but this depends on the nature of the document. When three copies are needed, the second carbon is retained by the solicitor and the top copy and first carbon sent to the solicitor acting for the other party. If no amendments are required, the top copy is returned marked 'approved as drawn', and the first carbon is retained for reference purposes. However, if alterations or additions are required, these are made, in red, on the top copy and marked up on the retained copy. The solicitor who compiled the document marks up his copy with the amendments. If further alterations are required, the top copy travels between the two solicitors and each marks up his copy with the amendments that have been made. This 'to and fro' procedure can go on for some considerable time. A different colour is used for each set of amendments so that the order of the changes can be traced, if necessary.

2. *The clean draft or fair copy.* If a clean draft or fair copy is required, care should be taken to ensure that all amendments are correctly included. However, a fair copy is often not made and, unless the amendments are voluminous or difficult to read, the engrossment is typed direct from the agreed draft.

3. *The engrossment.* The engrossment is the final copy of the document, typed in the agreed form, and will be signed by the interested parties. The word 'engrossment' means 'large writing' and originates from the time when the final copy was always written by a professional writer (using 'copperplate' handwriting) who was known as an engrosser.

With certain types of legal document there is a second copy, called the counterpart. The original is signed or executed by one party and the counterpart is signed or executed by the other party and then the parts are exchanged. There may be more than one signatory to each part of the document.

An engrossment is usually typed in double or one-and-a-half spacing and no abbreviations or alterations are permitted. Figures, including dates, are typed as words—with the exception of property numbers, the dates of Acts of Parliament, and numbered paragraphs. It is not usual to type postal codes in engrossments: instead it is usual to see, for example, 'Hornsey in the London Borough of Haringey' rather than 'Hornsey, London N8 8LS'. If alterations are required after the engrossment is typed, they have to be initialled or signed by the interested parties.

Engrossments are usually typed with a black record ribbon, which will not fade. Both sides of the paper (usually double sheets of brief or draft parchment-type paper) are used and a left-hand margin of 35 mm ($1\frac{1}{2}$ in.) is used on the first page and every following odd-numbered page. The right-hand margin is 10 mm ($\frac{1}{2}$ in.). On the second and every subsequent even-numbered page, the wide margin appears on the right side of the paper and the narrower one on the left. This practice allows for a 'stitching margin', since all the sheets are bound together in some way: usually, green silk or narrow tape is used for this purpose. Many legal offices, however, use specially-ruled paper, and the typist is required to type within the confines of the ruling.

Engrossments require very accurate typing since corrections are not permitted: if the typist makes an error, she should retype her work. Traces of alteration could result in litigation.

Punctuation marks are usually omitted from legal documents since their use can often result in a doubtful meaning—or the meaning can sometimes be altered by the insertion of additional punctuation. If a legal document includes numbered clauses which do not finish at the end of a line, the remainder of the line is ruled up with ink (or sometimes filled in with typed hyphens)—as is every other incomplete line in the body of the document—up to the right-hand margin, which should be made exactly even by this means. Where pre-ruled sheets are used, the hyphens or line is taken right up to the vertical line. This practice makes additions to a document after signature impossible.

The beginning of a new sentence is indicated by space in front of the first word—which begins with a capital letter or is typed in closed capitals.

Division of words at the end of lines should be avoided when typing engrossments. Many legal offices make it a rule that line-end division of words should not be used.

Legal documents require the capitalization of certain words to ensure that certain portions stand out. It is impossible to state hard and fast rules here since practice on this point varies according to the preferences and traditions of a particular firm. However, the first words of a legal document usually state its nature and these are normally typed in spaced capitals, e.g., T H I S A G R E E M E N T : the word 'between' is likewise frequently typed in spaced capitals. The names of the interested parties, when first mentioned, are usually typed in closed capitals, as are the first word or words of each clause or recital.

The pages of engrossments are not normally numbered. In order to keep them in the correct order, the typist should mark the top corner lightly in pencil so that, when sewn up, the numbers do not show.

If copies of an engrossment are typed, the word COPY should precede the description of the document in the endorsement and the word Signed should be typed in brackets in front of the name of the signatory (or signatories), which should also be typed. However, if copies of an engrossment are required, they are now usually photocopied.

Many legal documents are completed by typing the Testimonium and Attestation Clause (in Scottish law, the two are combined in what is known as a Testing Clause).

Testimonium clause. A testimonium clause varies in wording, but here is an example.

```
IN WITNESS whereof the parties hereto have
hereunto set their hands and seals this ninth
day of January one thousand nine hundred and
seventy-six before the witness hereto
subscribing.
```

Attestation Clause. An example of an attestation clause follows.

```
SIGNED SEALED AND DELIVERED)
by the within-named JOHN      }  (John Brown signs
BROWN in the presence of:  )      here)      (L.S.)

(witness' signature,          )
address and occupation or     }
description appear here)     )
```

If a document is being executed under the Common Seal of a Limited Company, care must be taken to ensure that it is possible to affix the Seal. If the document has to be sealed on any even-numbered page 'THE COMMON SEAL of ....LIMITED' etc., should appear on the right-hand side of the page, thus:

```
            (THE COMMON SEAL of................
(L.S.)      {LIMITED was hereunto affixed in the
            (presence of:

                                       Director

                                       Secretary
```

Some legal documents in common use that use standard wording are obtainable from law stationers in printed form so that only the blanks for specific details have to be filled in.

The endorsement. The endorsement is typed so that it appears on the top of the folded document: the left-hand edge of the endorsement consists purely of folds, all open pages being on the right. If the document consists of more than one sheet, the endorsement must appear on the back page of the last sheet. The sheets should be folded (and

```
DATED                                          1976



                    MR. DAVID JONES
                       - to -

                  MR. RAYMOND JOHNSON




                    A S S I G N M E N T

         of leasehold property situate at and known
         as 22 The Crescent in the City of Cardiff
```

A typed endorsement

creased) so that the lower edges meet the upper ones: then the paper should be doubled in the same way a second time, when the lower crease will consist entirely of folds. The side then uppermost should be used for typing the endorsement. An easy way to master this is to memorize 'bottom to top, bottom to top; then the top of the endorsement is on the left-hand side'.

When A4 or foolscap paper is being used, the completed engrossment should be folded (and creased) in two, from left to right, and the endorsement typed on the side then uppermost: again, the fold—or folds if more than one page is used—will appear on the left-hand side of the endorsement with the open page (or pages) all appearing on the right.

If, because of bulk, the whole engrossment cannot be inserted into the typewriter for typing the endorsement, only the necessary sheet should be put into the machine—care being taken to ensure that the typing appears in the correct position and in the right direction.

Although the endorsement is typed at the draft and fair copy stage, the date is left blank until the signing of the engrossment.

The endorsement contains the following information: (1) the date (2) the names of the interested parties (3) description of the type of document (4) the name and address of the solicitor on draft or copy Wills, Conveyances or similar documents, but not on originals. In litigation matters the name and address of the solicitor always appears and should be followed by 'Solicitors for the Defendant' or 'Solicitors for the Plaintiff as the case may be.

For further information on legal work, see *A Secretary's Guide to the Legal Office* by Annette K. Parry (Pitman).

Some other legal terms and brief definitions

Abstract of title. A summary of the documents and facts constituting the title to real estate, going back for a minimum period of fifteen years: it contains copies or abstracts of the documents in a specialized shortened form.

Affidavit. A written declaration given on oath before a Commissioner for Oaths, a duly authorized Solicitor or a Notary Public.

Agreement. Any document in writing signed by two or more persons agreeing to do a specific thing.

Assignment. A document in which the transfer of rights or property is made.

Attestation. Attestation is the act of witnessing a signature to a document. It is immaterial whether or not the witness knows anything about the contents of the document in question but the addition of his/ her signature, address, and occupation or description is essential.

Brief. This document is prepared by a Solicitor for the use of Counsel in Court, and contains full details of the Client's case.

Conveyance. The document by which the legal ownership of land or property is transferred from the Vendor to the Purchaser.

Deed. Any document that is executed under seal (see below).

Defendant. The sued party in a legal case. In some actions, the Defendant is the Respondent.

Document under hand. A document in writing signed by the interested parties but not bearing a seal, e.g., tenancy agreements for periods of three years or less, Wills.

Document under seal. A deed (see above). This type of document is not only signed by the parties concerned, but bears their seals as well. The sealing is done by placing the finger on the seal (locus sigilli) and saying 'I deliver this as my act and deed'. The deed is then signed. The sealing and signing are attested by a witness who signs to this effect and then adds his/her address and occupation or description. Limited Companies and Corporations use a much larger seal (known as a Common Seal) than the one in general use: the signing and sealing is done by appropriate individual members of the organization.

Execute. To execute a document means to sign and seal it in the case of a deed, or to sign it in the case of a document under hand.

Lease. A contract in writing for a period of three years or more, under seal, whereby one person agrees to let land or premises to another person for a specified period at a fixed rent. Leases for three years or less are usually under hand documents and are called Tenancy Agreements.

The *lessor* is the person who grants the lease and the *lessee* is granted the lease.

Locus Sigilli. A Latin term, meaning 'the place of the seal'. If the document is under seal, it is customary to type L.S., usually to the right of where each party will sign, and where the seal will appear. L.S. is enclosed in typed brackets or a drawn circle.

Plantiff. The party who commences litigation and sues another party.

Probate. This is the procedure by which a Will is put into effect when a Testator/Testatrix (see under Will) dies, and is called 'proving a Will'. The Executors deliver to the Probate Registry the original Will, together with an account of the estate, an Oath that they will duly administer the estate, and the fee payable. The Probate Registry issues, in exchange, a photostat copy of the Will, bound up with an order of the Court under its seal, stating that the Will has been duly proved by the Executors. This document is known as a probate.

Statement of claim. The formal document used in a legal action which sets out fully the facts on which the Plaintiff relies to support his case.

Will. A document which sets out the wishes of a person concerning the distribution of his/her property and wealth and administration of his/her estate after his/her death. The person making the Will is known as the *Testator* (male) or *Testatrix* (female): the *Executor* (male) or *Excutrix* (female) is the person appointed by the Testator/Testatrix to execute his/her Will.

A holograph Will is one which is written entirely in handwriting by the Testator or Testatrix.

Letter-heads. Business letters are typed on specially printed letter-heads which provide detailed information about the organization and include some or all of the following.

1. Name and address of the organization
2. Telephone number
3. Nature of business
4. Telex number
5. Telegraphic address
6. Company number
7. Names of directors

In addition, to comply with E.E.C. legislation, which came into force on 1 January 1973, letter headings are required to show:

(a) Registration number (i.e., the number appearing on the company's Certificate of Incorporation).
(b) Place of registration.
(c) The words 'Limited Liability' in the case of a limited company exempt from the obligation to use the word 'Limited' as part of its name.
(d) Reference to paid-up capital when reference is made to the amount of share capital.

Business letter-heads are printed in a variety of styles and colours. Often the letter-head is printed all in black but sometimes a different colour is used, or a combination of black and a second colour (blue, red, and orange being popular). In addition, some firms have the printed information embossed, for prestige purposes.

W. HEFFER & SONS LTD
Booksellers & Publishers
3 - 4 PETTY CURY
CAMBRIDGE, ENGLAND
Telephone: 58351 ∾ *Telegrams: Heffer, Cambridge*

DEPARTMENTAL REFERENCE

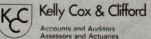

Kelly Cox & Clifford

Accounts and Auditors
Assessors and Actuaries

Registered address	14 Regent Walk London WC2B 5PB
Telephone	01-405 69712
Company Number	50690C England

11 November 1976

Pitman Publishing Limited

Registered Address:
39 Parker Street, London WC2B 5PB

Telephone: 01-242 1655
Night Service: 01-242 5750

Company No: 215457 England

Some examples of letter-heads

The first example illustrated is completely centred and somewhat ornate in style. This letter-head would be most suitable to the indented style of letter layout.

The second example is designed so that the printed information occupies a minimum of space. A line runs horizontally across the paper the full width of the printed particulars. This line could well be used by the typist to establish her margin positions which, in this particular case, would provide equal margins. This letter-head could be successfully used for any style of letter layout.

In the third example the typist would set her left-hand margin in line with the left-hand margin of the printed heading: all the other information is blocked. This letter-head is well designed for a blocked or semi-blocked style of letter form.

One side only of the paper is used when typing the top copy of a letter. If a letter runs to a second, and additional pages, plain paper (of the same colour and quality as the letter-head) is used. Each 'continuation sheet' must be numbered and headed (see *Business letters* under **Letters**).

Letters. These will be dealt with under the headings *Business letters, Circular letters, Civil Service letters, Form letters* and *Personal letters*.

Business letters. Business letters are typed on A5, A4 or two-thirds A4 paper (see page 189) according to the length of the letter. The layout varies considerably from firm to firm: some of the most widely used styles are illustrated at the end of this section.

Open punctuation. 'Open punctuation' is being used increasingly, especially in conjunction with the fully-blocked and semi-blocked styles. As will be seen in the letter examples illustrating this form of punctuation, only the body of a letter is punctuated in the normal way, punctuation marks being omitted above and below the body of the letter—with only a few minor exceptions. For instance, if the town and county are typed on the same line, they are often separated by a comma as an alternative to leaving extra space. Also, if a letter concludes with a postscript this is, of course, continuous prose and is therefore normally punctuated.

Many forward looking offices prefer the blocked style (with open punctuation) because it is faster to type, and yet presents a neat and pleasing appearance. Others, however, use the traditional indented style, while yet others prefer a modification or combination of these styles.

The main parts of a business letter follow. They should be studied in conjunction with the illustrated letter styles.

1. *Printed heading* (see also **Letter-heads**). Business letters are usually typed on paper that has a printed heading which states the name and address of the firm, its registered office and its telephone number. In addition, the printed heading may include some or all of the following, according to the size and preferences of the firm: telex number, telegraphic address, company number, nature of business, names of directors.

2. *Reference(s)*. If the printed letter-head contains a special position for the reference(s), this should be used. The illustrated letter styles show other possible positions. The reference usually consists of the upper case initials of the person who dictated the letter, followed by the initials of the typist (the latter sometimes in lower case); it may also indicate the department of the firm and a file number. A reference is never followed by a full stop. If the letter is replying to a communication containing a reference, this should be given: it is courteous to give the reference of the other firm first. The different parts of a reference may be separated by the solidus but a quicker, more modern method is to use full stops instead.

3. *Date*. The recommended order is day, month, year, as in 18 January 1976. The date may be typed in a wide variety of forms and the month may be abbreviated. It is not acceptable all in words nor, in general, all in figures because of the obvious confusion that could arise, as in some countries, including the U.S.A., it is standard practice to put the month first, e.g., January 18 1976. Some firms, however, particularly international ones, use an all-numerical method. It is easy to remember (and avoids confusion) since it proceeds from the general to the particular, i.e., it begins with the year, followed by the month and then the day. Examples are: 1976 01 12 (12 January 1976) and 1975 10 21 (21 October 1975).

4. *Inside name and address* (see *Envelope typing* under **Envelopes** for guidance about postcode display, etc.). This is included to ensure that each letter is inserted in its correct envelope; also to enable the carbon copy to be filed correctly. The ampersand (&) may be used here, also the abbreviations Co., Ltd, etc. Single spacing is used, with all lines beginning at the left-hand margin point. It was once the practice, with

the indented style, to indent each line five or six spaces: however, this is now rarely the case.

The inside name and address is usually typed at the head of the letter, although some firms place it at the end. If the letter requires a continuation sheet, it is better to type the inside name and address at the head of the letter, otherwise the first sheet will not be immediately identifiable if a number of papers get out of order for some reason. If a window envelope is to be used, the name and address will be typed at the head of the letter and will have to be carefully positioned within clearly defined marks (see *Window envelopes* under **Envelopes**).

5. *Attention line.* If the letter is addressed to a firm (in which case the salutation will be Dear Sirs) but the writer wants it to be dealt with by a particular person, this is indicated in one of the following ways:

```
For the attention of Mr. J. Smith

FOR THE ATTENTION OF MR J SMITH

ATTENTION OF MR J SMITH

ATTENTION: MR J SMITH
```

The use of closed capitals without underscoring, as in the last three examples, is quicker than the first method which requires underscoring to make the information stand out sufficiently well. Confidential, Personal, etc., are likewise typed in closed capitals without underscoring; or in lower case with an initial capital and underscored.

Information of this nature is typed below the inside name and address and above the salutation. However, if window envelopes are used (see **Envelopes**), care must be taken to see that nothing appears below the postcode on the envelope, and therefore, in order to comply with Post Office regulations, the attention line should appear above the inside name and address.

6. *Salutation.* The words of greeting that open a letter are known as the salutation. Examples of the most common forms are: Dear Sir, Dear Sirs, Dear Madam, Dear Mr. Jones, Dear Mrs Turner.

7. *Subject headings.* Sometimes a letter contains a heading which indicates the main subject of the letter. This is typed below the salutation in one of the following ways:

Purchase of 85 Goldsmith Gardens, Eastbourne

PURCHASE OF 85 GOLDSMITH GARDENS, EASTBOURNE

The second method is obviously the quicker to type. A subject heading does not end with a full stop unless the last word is abbreviated and the typist is using the method of typing stops after abbreviations.

A single letter may deal with a number of subjects, each requiring its own heading. These may be typed as paragraph headings (where the text starts on the same line as the heading), as shoulder headings (where each heading occupies a separate line), or with each subject centred (see **Paragraph headings**). In such a case, a carbon copy or photo-copy may have to be made—for filing purposes—for each subject heading.

8. *Body of the letter*. This contains the subject matter of the letter and it is divided into paragraphs. The paragraphs may be indented or blocked. The body of the letter is usually typed in single spacing with a line of space between each paragraph. However, if the letter is short, double or one-and-a-half spacing is sometimes used.

The body of the letter should not contain abbreviations, except generally accepted ones such as i.e. and e.g. The ampersand (&) should not be used unless the name of a firm (e.g., Messrs Jones & Smith) or numbers (e.g., 29 & 41 London Road) are being quoted.

9. *Complimentary close*. This is typed below the text of the letter in one of the ways illustrated in the following letter styles. The most common forms are: Yours faithfully, Yours truly, and Yours sincerely—the first word only beginning with a capital letter.

If the salutation is Dear Sir or Dear Madam, the complimentary close is usually the more formal Yours faithfully or Yours truly. However, if the letter begins with the more personal Dear Mr. Jones or Dear Mrs Brown, the complimentary close is often the less formal Yours sincerely.

If the name of the firm is given after the complimentary close, it is typed either on the next line or after one line of space in closed capitals.

10. *Signature*. This is handwritten, although sometimes a rubber stamp facsimile impression of the writer's signature is used. Four or five line spaces should be left between the complimentary close and the designation to allow enough space for the signature. Often the name of

the signatory is typed below the signature (which is frequently barely legible!) and this is followed by his designation on the next line.

If the person who has dictated the letter is not able to sign it, it is usually signed by some other authorized person. This is often indicated by typing the letters pp (abbreviation for the Latin *per procurationem*: on behalf of) in front of the name of the dictator of the letter, followed by the signature and designation of the authorized person. Another method is to type 'Personally dictated by B M Smith and signed in his absence by Miss J Waters, his Secretary'.

11. *Enclosures*. Enclosures are indicated in a number of ways. Sometimes the word Enclosure is typed in full at the foot of the letter, but this wastes time. More often it is abbreviated to Enc, enc, or ENC. If there is more than one enclosure, often simply the plural of the preceding examples is used—Encs, encs, ENCS—but sometimes the number of enclosures is stated, e.g., Encs 3, encs 2, ENCS 4. Some firms state the nature of enclosures, e.g., enc invoice.

Another method of showing enclosures is to type a marginal mark (which may be a solidus, two or three hyphens or dots) in the left-hand margin each time an enclosure is mentioned. This helps the typist to ensure that all the required enclosures are inserted in the envelope before despatch. A less-commonly used method is to use stick-on enclosure labels. These are usually printed in a bright colour in two perforated sections and numbered: one section is affixed to the top of the letter and the other to the appropriate enclosure.

All enclosures should be securely attached to the letter or document they accompany to avoid the risk of their not being removed from the envelope by the recipient—and perhaps accidentally thrown away. When an enclosure is smaller in size than the letter (a cheque for instance) it should be attached *above* the letter. Conversely, an enclosure larger in size than the letter should be attached *under* it.

12. *Postscript*. This is typed last and is preceded by P.S. Sometimes it contains matter that the dictator has accidentally omitted, but often it is used deliberately to draw attention to a particular point. The signatory usually initials a postscript.

13. *Circulation of copies*. See *Circulation of carbon copies* under **Carbon copying.**

Examples of the most widely used letter styles follow.

1. A fully-blocked letter on A5 paper.

```
Your ref   PF/ew
Our ref    Pur/1873

24 May 19--

Messrs J & P Fountain
25-27 Crown Court Road
PAISLEY, Scotland
PA2 6AF

FOR THE ATTENTION OF MR P FOUNTAIN

Dear Sirs

SPECIAL OFFER CARPETING

I enclose our cheque in settlement of your last account.
Please quote your lowest prices for the following advertised
special offer carpeting: -

100 m x 4 m wool carpeting, Star Quality
100 m x 3 m carpeting, 80% wool, 20% nylon
 50 m x 4 m Supreme Cord carpeting

Kindly send samples and sales literature.  When writing,please
confirm that you can deliver within 4 weeks of receipt of order.

Yours faithfully
QUALITY CARPETS LIMITED


D Brown
Purchasing Manager

enc
```

Note the following points:

1. Everything begins at the left-hand margin, including the inset matter.

2. Open punctuation. No punctuation marks above and below the body of the letter except between PAISLEY and Scotland.

3. The reference(s) is sometimes typed at the foot of the letter.

2A. The same letter in a semi-blocked style.

```
                              Your ref  PF/ew
                              Our ref   Pur/1873

                              24 May 19--

Messrs J & P Fountain
25-27 Crown Court Road
PAISLEY, Scotland
PA2 6AF

FOR THE ATTENTION OF MR P FOUNTAIN

Dear Sirs

SPECIAL OFFER CARPETING

I enclose our cheque in settlement of your last account.
Please quote your lowest prices for the following advertised
special offer carpeting:-

100 m x 4 m wool carpeting, Star Quality
100 m x 3 m carpeting, 80% wool, 20% nylon
 50 m x 4 m Supreme Cord carpeting

Kindly send samples and sales literature.  When writing, please
confirm that you can deliver within 4 weeks of receipt of order.

                              Yours faithfully
                              QUALITY CARPETS LIMITED



                              D Brown
                              Purchasing Manager

enc
```

Note the following points:

1. Everything begins either at the left-hand margin point or at a tabular stop set approximately half way across the typing line. This avoids 'crowding' at the left-hand margin point so that various items stand out more clearly—an obvious advantage to the reader and filist: this effect is achieved with scarcely any loss of the typist's time.

2. Open punctuation as in Example 1.

Letters

2B. The same letter in a different semi-blocked style.

```
Your ref  PF/ew
Our ref   Pur/1873                              24 May 19--

Messrs J & P Fountain
25-27 Crown Court Road
PAISLEY, Scotland
PA2 6AF

FOR THE ATTENTION OF MR P FOUNTAIN

Dear Sirs

        SPECIAL OFFER CARPETING

        I enclose our cheque in settlement of your last account.
Please quote your lowest prices for the following advertised
special offer carpeting:-

        100 m x 4 m wool carpeting, Star Quality
        100 m x 3 m carpeting, 80% wool, 20% nylon
         50 m x 4 m Supreme Cord carpeting

        Kindly send samples and sales literature.  When writing,
please confirm that you can deliver within 4 weeks of receipt
of order.

                        Yours faithfully
                        QUALITY CARPETS LIMITED



                        D Brown
                        Purchasing Manager

Enc 1
```

Note the following points:

1. Date typed on same line as second reference and finishing flush with the right-hand margin.

2. Indented paragraphs with the inset matter and the subject heading beginning at the tabular point set for indenting the paragraphs.

3. Signature block. Each line begins at a tabular point set approximately half way across the typing line.

4. Open punctuation.

3. The same letter in the traditional displayed style.

Your ref: PF/EW
Our ref: Pur/1873   24th May, 19--

Messrs. J. & P. Fountain,
25-27 Crown Court Road,
PAISLEY, Scotland,
PA2 6AF

For the Attention of Mr. P. Fountain

Dear Sirs,

<u>Special Offer Carpeting</u>

    I enclose our cheque in settlement of your last account.
Please quote your lowest prices for the following advertised
special offer carpeting:-

        100 m x 4 m wool carpeting, Star Quality
        100 m x 3 m carpeting, 80% wool, 20% nylon
        50 m x 4 m Supreme Cord carpeting

    Kindly send samples and sales literature. When writ-
ing, please confirm that you can deliver within 4 weeks of
receipt of order.

Yours faithfully,
QUALITY CARPETS LIMITED

D. Brown
Purchasing Manager

Enc.

Note these points:
1. Whole letter fully punctuated, common with the indented style.
2. Date opposite second reference, finishing flush right.
3. Indented paragraphs.
4. Inset matter indented equally from both margins.
5. Display of signature block.
6. Attention line and subject heading typed in lower case with initial capitals and underscored. Subject heading centred to the typing line.

The foregoing examples are by no means exhaustive and are intended only as a guide to some of the most commonly used styles. An examination of a variety of letters sent out by a number of firms would no doubt show certain deviations. No one can say that one method only is 'correct'. The main criterion should be that the letters are well typed and consistently displayed within a single firm or department.

The number of line spaces between the different parts of a letter can vary according to its length in relation to the size of paper. However, it is speedier and better practice if the typist always uses the same number of line spaces between parts and varies her margins unless she is restricted in margin setting by the letter-head.

When centring is required, it is quicker to use equal margins since one should always centre to the width of the typing line. When margins are equal, it is a simple matter to move the carriage so that the printing point is at the centre of the paper, and then to backspace once for every two characters or spaces in the line to be centred. See **Headings** for centring over unequal margins.

As already mentioned, a number of variations are possible with all the styles illustrated, and the typist should always follow the preferences of her employers. She should remember that the letters sent out by her firm are, in a way, an ambassador and advertisement, and she should therefore ensure that they are well displayed and typed and consistent in style according to her employers' wishes.

Continuation sheets. If a letter consists of more than one page of typing, the second and subsequent pages are called continuation sheets. The typist should get the whole letter on one page if possible: therefore it is preferable to use A4 paper rather than A5 with a continuation sheet. If a continuation sheet is necessary the typist should try to ensure that it contains at least three lines of type in addition to the signature block. P.T.O. and Contd need not be used, nor should the typist use a catchword (see **Catchword**): these are a waste of time and add nothing to clarity.

The paper for continuation sheets should be plain and of the same quality and colour as the headed paper. Approximately one inch of space should be left at the foot of the first and each subsequent page before beginning a continuation sheet. See also **Paper economy**.

Each continuation sheet should be headed giving the page number, the date, and the addressee. The setting out of this heading will vary according to the style of layout being used. With the indented method, the required information is usually given on a single line—the addressee beginning at the left-hand margin, the page number in the centre and the date finishing flush with the right-hand margin, as in this example:

Mr. E. James   – 2 –   2nd May, 1976

However, if this would result in a crowded line, the page number should be centred on a separate line above the other information.

With the fully-blocked (and sometimes the semi-blocked) method, the information is typed so that each item begins at the left-hand margin point. It can be in single, one-and-a-half or double spacing.

```
–2–
14 June 1976
Mr J Thomas
```

Often, however, the semi-blocked style is typed as follows, with the date finishing flush with the right-hand margin.

```
– 2 –
Mrs G Harris                          2 July 1975
```

Circular letters. When a firm wants to send out large numbers of a letter with the same wording, reproductions are used, known as circular letters. Sometimes this is done by typing a master for a spirit duplicator, an offset litho duplicator or a stencil for an ink duplicator, and running off the required number of copies. However, general modern practice is to make circular letters look like individually typed letters by using a typewriter that will automatically type as many copies as necessary (see **Special purposes typewriters**). Alternatively, the required number of copies may be printed.

Except when small numbers are needed it is usual to omit the inside name and address: where this information is typed in, care should be taken to see that the type matches that of the copies as closely as possible.

Frequently, circular letters begin with the salutation Dear Sir or Dear Madam or Dear Sir/Madam. If the circulated letters are sent over a period of several days, or even weeks, a specific date is not included on the circular: sometimes just the month and year are given (as December 1976) or the date is represented by the words Date as Postmark.

On circular letters there is usually no reference. If the method of reproduction allows, a signature is included—otherwise the name of the signatory is represented in typed or printed form.

Civil Service letters. To help obtain a more efficient typing service, the Civil Service now uses a basic simplified method of letter display on A4 or A5 paper and usually uses window envelopes. However, the different Departments are given a limited autonomy in being able to decide whether to use a modified fully-blocked or semi-blocked style: but consistency within a Department is mandatory.

Letter headings are designed so that the inside name and address, the reference(s) and date are typed within two parallel lines that extend the full width of the typing line. The design also requires the telephone number (extension), reference(s) and date to begin at the same point of the scale—approximately two-thirds of the way across the typing line. A tab stop is set at this point, which can also be used for the signature block if the Department elects to use this style as opposed to beginning all parts of the signature block at the left-hand margin.

The following main points should be noted. Typed examples are given on pages 143 and 144.

1. *Inside name and address.* Full stops and commas are omitted completely. The inside name and address is blocked in single spacing within the two parallel lines already mentioned, each line of type beginning 20 mm (or $\frac{3}{4}$ in.) from the left-hand edge of the paper, for use with window envelopes (see **Envelopes**). One space separates initials before a name and groups of letters after a name, as in Mr B S Small OBE JP. Abbreviations for Departments are used instead of the full names (this applies also in the body of the letter): for example, HMSO (Her Majesty's Stationery Office) and DHSS (Department of Health and Social Security). The town is always typed in capital letters and the postcode typed last, usually on a separate line with one space between the two parts of the code. If an envelope is used, the name and address is typed in the manner described in this paragraph.

2. *References.* The common business method of using the initials of the dictator and typist is not used. Instead, the reference consists of initials denoting the section, etc., and file number; and references are typed in the positions provided on the right-hand side within the parallel lines.

3. *Date.* No punctuation is used and it is simplified as in 19 July 1976. Dates in the body of a letter are typed in a similar way. The date is typed in the position provided at the right-hand side of the paper, below the reference.

4. *Margins.* These should be 9 elite (7 pica) character spaces on the left and 6 elite (5 pica) character spaces on the right of both A4 and A5 paper. On the headed paper used with window envelopes, the horizontal lines bounding the address area indicate the margins. Typing should begin at the first space inside the edge of the lines on the left and should not extend beyond the edge of the lines on the right.

The margins are reversed when typing on the back of paper so that the typing is superimposed.

5. *Salutation.* This is typed leaving at least two line spaces below the bottom line of the address panel. The name is often given, for example, Dear Mrs Kennedy or Dear Mr Fox; otherwise Dear Sir,

Dear Sirs, or Dear Madam. The salutation is never followed by a comma.

6. *Subject headings.* These start at the left-hand margin and are typed in closed capitals (without underscoring) with no final full stop.

7. *Body of letter.* Blocked paragraphs and single spacing are used; a line space is left between paragraphs. Spacing after punctuation marks is always one space after a comma, semi-colon and colon; two spaces after a full stop, question mark and exclamation mark. All numbers are typed as figures, except the number one or when a number is the first word in a sentence. However, when numbers are used in phrases as figures of speech, they should always be typed as words, e.g., one in a million, in two or three cases, threefold. Fractions, except when used as figures of speech, should be typed in figures. Recognized abbreviations are typed without stops, for example, UNESCO, ie, etc, BEA. Numbered paragraphs begin at the left-hand margin and are followed by a full stop and three spaces. They are blocked, including the numbers. Sub-paragraphs are indented five spaces and blocked, including the letters a, b, c, etc.—which are always followed by a full stop and three spaces. Roman numerals are not used. The numbers and letters preceding paragraphs and sub-paragraphs are never enclosed in brackets (this would be more time consuming since the shift key would have to be used for both brackets). When referring to the time of day, the 24-hour system is used (see **Time**).

8. *Continuation sheets.* Both sides of the letter paper (which has different 'faces') are used and the typing lines are backed up one with another and the margins reversed so that the typing is superimposed. However, if starting higher on the back of a sheet would avoid the need for a continuation sheet, this is done: this practice obviously results in a saving of time, paper, and filing space. Where continuation sheets are needed, the second and subsequent pages are numbered and headed with the addressee's name, the reference number, and the date. When typing overleaf or on a continuation sheet, one line of a paragraph should not be separated from the main part of the paragraph. Catchwords should not be used.

9. *Complimentary close.* This begins either at the left-hand margin or at the standard right-hand tab stop, according to the style being used by the Department: it should not be followed by a comma.

10. *Name of writer.* This is typed below the signature space and is not enclosed in brackets. It begins at the same point as the complimentary close. 'Mr' should not be typed, but when the writer is a woman, the style of address used by her should be typed before the name.

11. *Designation.* This is typed on the line following the name of the writer, beginning at the same point of the scale. Branch/division details, etc., are typed on the next line, beginning at the same point.

12. *Enclosures.* These should be indicated at the end of the letter by typing ENC or ENCS at the left-hand margin, followed by a figure denoting the number of enclosures. Dashes or dots against the reference to enclosures in the text should not be used.

13. *Ampersand.* This is normally used instead of 'and' in the names of firms (Messrs Smith & Jones) and in branch titles such as O & M. However, on legal documents the names of firms must be typed *exactly as printed on their letter headings,* which may have 'and' or 'Company' or 'Limited' in full.

14. *Security classifications.* If a rubber stamp or pre-printed paper is not available, the security classification (SECRET, CONFIDENTIAL, etc.) should be typed in spaced capital letters in the centre of the top and bottom margins of each page, and added attention may be drawn to the caution by underscoring it or by enclosing it in a box. Classified matter must never be despatched in window envelopes.

Form letters. Many firms send out form letters or cards (sometimes known as skeletons) for routine correspondence. These contain a basic wording so that only certain specific particulars have to be typed in before despatch. Such a practice, where applicable, is efficient and, of course, a great time-saver for the typist.

The form letters or cards are usually printed or duplicated, and either a blank space or a space with a line or dots beneath it is left in the places where information has to be inserted.

If the original of the form letter is typed, it is desirable that the typist uses a typewriter with the same pitch for completion of the particulars. Also, she should try to match the colour and density of the type. If this is not possible, many firms prefer the details to be completed in a contrasting colour.

The details that have to be typed in will, of course, depend upon the nature of the document. The margin stops should be adjusted to match those of the form letter and the line spacing should be similar to the original, if typed. Once the correct positions of the paper guide, margin stops, etc., have been set, a large number of a similar form letter may be rapidly typed with little or no additional adjustment of the typewriter mechanisms being necessary.

Where particulars have to be typed in over ruled or dotted lines, it is essential that the base of the type appears *slightly above* the line or dots. Use of the interliner or variable line spacer will be necessary for this purpose. Where information has to be inserted in the body of a sentence,

Ministry of Documents
National Museum of Documents and Research
Document House 42 Sovereign Street London W1X 2AA
Telex 38678   Telephone 01-222 2870 ext 427

A B Smith Esq ARIBA
192 High Street
NOTOWN
Newshire
AMN 23D

Your reference
ABS/MNO
Our reference
LA 14/102/01
Date
1 October 1968

Dear Mr Smith

NEW LETTERHEADINGS

We were very interested in the comments made in your letter to us dated
20 September. This subject is one that has been given detailed attention by
us over the last year or so, and it is now culminating in the adoption by
Government Departments of a drastically revised style of letterheading. This
letter is typed on an example of this new style.

The changes have come about for 2 reasons. The first was a general desire
by those responsible for our design work to bring Civil Service practice more
into line with the better styles now used commercially. This meant looking
not only at the general appearance of the letterheads but also at the
typefaces used and at the content of the printed material. The inclusion of
telegraphic detail, for instance, was considered to be no longer necessary.

The second reason was a need to introduce a design which would assist the
typist to place the addressee details in the correct position to match the
aperture in standard window envelopes that were being introduced for general
use. The Civil Service has not hitherto used window envelopes for its formal
correspondence, but it is intended to adopt this practice as widely as
possible as a means of obtaining greater typing productivity. This latter
purpose will also be served by the fact that the typist will be able to work
to a single tabulation stop for the insertion of the telephone extension
number, the 2 references and the date. The same tabulation stop will also
be used where the final salutation is placed to the right - although many
departments are likely to place this against the left margin.

The new style chosen is intended to serve both aesthetic and practical ends.
It will also create a distinctive 'house style' for the Civil Service. We
have therefore achieved a number of the objectives you proposed in your
letter; and we think that you will not find the results displeasing.

Yours sincerely

N.O.Price

N O Price
Design Division

Specimen typed letter (A4)

Reproduced with the permission of the Controller of Her Majesty's
Stationery Office

at least one character space should be left before starting to type the
fill in. (See also **Lines, typing on.**)

Some firms that consider form letters too impersonal, keep a number of specimen letters from which the typist copies routine wording according to need. These are typed as individual letters and specific details are included in the body of the letter in the normal way; such letters are often used to remind customers of overdue accounts.

MINISTRY OF DOCUMENTS
Document House 42 Sovereign Street London W1X 2AA

Telex 38678   Telephone 01-222 2870 ext 427

A B Smith Esq ARIBA	Your reference
192 High Street	ABS/MNO
NOTOWN	Our reference
Newshire	LA 14/102/01
AMN 23D	Date
	1 October 1968

Dear Mr Smith

NEW LETTERHEADINGS

This subject is now culminating in the adoption by Government Departments of a drastically revised style of letterheading. This letter is typed on an example of this new style.

The changes have come about for 2 reasons. First was a general desire by those responsible for our design work to bring Civil Service practice more into line with the better commercial styles. Next was a need to introduce a design that would assist the typist to place the addressee details in the correct position to correspond to the aperture in standard window envelopes which are now to be used as widely as possible for correspondence. The new design has several features to assist the typist.

Yours sincerely

N.O.Price

N O Price
Design Division

Heading in Univers type

Specimen typed letter (A5)

Reproduced with the permission of the Controller of Her Majesty's Stationery Office

Form letter layout. Sometimes a secretary or senior typist may be called upon to plan or modify a form letter, so she should understand the basic principles to be borne in mind.

Forms that are badly designed and worded are inefficient in that much time can be wasted sorting out queries: in addition, they encourage rather than prevent inaccuracies.

It should be remembered that forms are a means of conveying routine information from one person to another. They often also serve as records, storing facts until they are required—when quick reference to the relevant information should be available. Thus the layout of the forms is very important.

The content of the forms should be arranged in logical sequence and sufficient room should be left for completion of the necessary points. Crowded and cramped design leads to confusion and inefficiency.

The layout should be arranged so that good use can be made of the tabulator: and if the original is typed, the line spacing and margins should be consistent so these can be permanently set by the typist when completing the forms.

In advanced typewriting examinations, candidates are sometimes asked to draw up a simple form from unarranged data.

Personal letters. Sometimes a typist/secretary may be asked to type personal letters for her employer or she may wish to type her own personal letters at home. In the former case the employer might wish to use his home address: often, however, the letter will be typed on business headed paper.

With personal letters it is common practice for the dictator to handwrite the name of the addressee in the salutation after the typed word Dear. At the same time he will sign his name after the complimentary close (usually the informal Yours sincerely), sometimes using only his first name. The typist should not, as a general rule, type his name below the signature space nor include his designation. If the letter is being sent to a business address the envelope will be headed Personal (see **Envelopes**).

Many typists type their own personal letters at home. If they do not use headed paper with their address printed at the top, the address has to be typed. A good method here is to set a tab stop approximately two-thirds across the typing line and begin all lines of the address (using double or one-and-a-half spacing) at this point. The date would also begin here. The same tab stop can be used for the complimentary close which, if writing to a friend, will be informal, i.e., Yours sincerely, Sincerely, Yours, etc. If the letter is of a business nature, however, the more formal Yours faithfully or Yours truly will be used.

If the typist is writing to a personal friend she will not normally type an inside name and address: but this will be necessary if the letter is of a business nature.

Continuation sheets should be numbered (and headed in the usual manner if the letter is a business one).

```
                                          Laburnum Cottage
                                          29 Park Grove
                                          EXETER
                                          EX3 25P

                                          26 May 1976

        Dr J Standing
        50 Thornton Road
        South Park
        LIVERPOOL   L16 4WN


        Dear John

        Thank you very much for entertaining me to dinner during
        my recent visit to Liverpool.  It was really very kind of
        you to do so and the evening highlighted an otherwise
        tedious business trip.

        Do let us know when you are coming to Exeter so that my
        wife and I may repay your kind hospitality.

                                          Yours sincerely
```

An example of a personal letter

A suggested example of a personal letter (with inside name and address, the letter having been dictated to the typist) in a semi-blocked style is given above—although personal letters may, of course, be set out in any of the forms.

Letters out of alignment. See **Errors, their cause and remedy.**

Line indicators. See **Parts of a typewriter.**

Line space selector. See **Parts of a typewriter.**

Line space selector drills. See **Drills.**

Lines, typing on. A typist often has to insert information into a form letter, etc., so that she types above lines or lines of dots. This should be done so that the base of the typed characters appears *slightly above* the line. Care should be taken to ensure that the typist does not type through the line, nor should the typewritten insertions appear too high in relation to the rest of the typed or printed matter.

If the original is printed, the typist will have to use the variable line spacer for finding the correct typing position for each line. On the other hand, if the original is typewritten, it will only be necessary to find the correct position for the first line and to ensure that the line spacing is set as on the original (see also *Form letters* under **Letters**).

If the insertion runs to several lines they should all begin at the same left-hand margin point, and the right-hand margin should be kept as even as possible.

Literary work. A person who acts as secretary to an author will be required to type a large quantity of literary matter. This could take many forms—novels, short stories, articles, essays, etc.,—and a skilled typist should know how to tackle such work. As in all typewritten matter, consistency within a single piece of work is essential: headings and sub-headings should be uniform in style; likewise margins, position and style of numbering pages, method of typing sub-paragraphs, and so on.

Since typists of literary work will often have to type corrected matter, a knowledge of correction signs is necessary (see **Typewriter and manuscript correction signs**).

The following alphabetical list gives definitions of some of the specific terms used in literary work. It also gives details of general points to observe when typing literary work: however, it is important that the typist follows the wishes of her employer since there is seldom *one* method that is rigidly correct.

Addendum. (plural addenda). Thing(s) added. Lists notes of an explanatory or additional nature added at the end of a work; also describes notes added to the front of a book showing matter that has been accidentally omitted.

Bibliography. A list of books, magazine or newspaper articles, etc., which indicates the sources from which information has been taken by the author. A bibliography is usually included either at the end of a chapter or at the end of the work, depending on its nature and extent. It includes the author, the title of the work, place and date of publication, and sometimes the pages to which reference is made. A bibliography lists the authors alphabetically according to surname, with the first name(s) or initial(s) following. The name of the author is followed by the other relevant information.

Contents page(s). This is a survey of the contents of a book, and its value to the reader (particularly if the book is of a technical nature) is similar to that of an index in that it can help him to pick out the section or chapter to which he wants to refer. It can assist a prospective buyer in deciding whether the book covers all aspects of the subject necessary to him: therefore it is important that the contents page is comprehensive and clear enough to give a 'bird's eye view' of the whole book.

Draft. A preliminary copy of a work. Usually typed in treble spacing on inferior quality A4 paper with a wide left-hand margin for amendments and additions. As with most literary work, only one side of the paper is used. Abbreviations may be used in a draft. (see also **Drafts**).

Dropped head. Each chapter or section of a book, etc., usually begins lower on the page than the following pages: the term 'dropped head' is used to indicate this arrangement. The dropped head should be uniform in depth for each chapter or section.

Fair copy. This is the corrected draft typed in its final form. All alterations and additions should be incorporated in it and no abbreviations except the generally accepted ones should be used. The fair copy should be typed in double spacing on one side only of good-quality A4 paper and should be consistent in layout, capitalization, margins, etc.

Fit. When a lengthy piece of typing is divided among several typists, various points must be observed to ensure that the different parts dovetail or 'fit' unobtrusively.

1. The same size and kind of typeface should be used (pica, elite, etc.).
2. The density of the ribbon ink should be approximately the same.
3. The paper should be of the same size and quality and only one side should be used.
4. Consistency should be observed in matters of layout and style. For instance, margins should be the same, both horizontally and vertically; the page numbers should appear in the same position and be typed in the same way; the method of typing headings and sub-headings and numbering paragraphs and sub-paragraphs should be similar; the type of paragraphs used should be consistent for the main paragraphs and for sub-paragraphs; the depth of the line spacing should be the same, and the system of spacing after punctuation marks and the method of typing numbers should be similar.
5. If possible, each typist should be given complete chapters or sections.

Footnotes. These are typed in various ways, the purpose of the typescript determining the method used.

1. When an article, etc., is not being prepared for a printer, the footnote(s) should be typed at the foot of the page where the reference(s) occurs. If more than one footnote is to appear on a page, care should be taken to ensure that enough space is left at the foot of the page to take them and still leave 25 mm (1 in.) after the last footnote. The footnotes should be separated from the text by a line of underscore running the full width of the typing line or from edge to edge of the paper: one line of space should be left on either side of this line. The footnotes should be typed in single spacing in blocked form with a line of space between each footnote. The footnotes may begin at the left-hand margin or be inset five or six spaces from each margin. If there are not more than three footnotes on a single page, the footnote signs (asterisk, dagger, double dagger (see **Combination characters and special signs**)) are sometimes used. However, because of their limited use and the extra time needed to type them, many people prefer the numbering or lettering method instead. If a page contains more than three footnotes, arabic numbers or lower case letters (usually enclosed in brackets) should be used. The footnote sign, number or letter in the text should always be raised half a space above the normal typing line and there should be no space between the word in the text and the footnote sign, number or letter. In the actual footnote, however, the footnote sign, number or letter is not usually raised and is often separated from the text of the footnote by one space.

2. If the typed work is to be printed according to methods (1) and (2) given below, each footnote should be separated from the text by a line of underscore running the full width of the typing line, both above and below the footnote. One line of space should be left between the text and the line of underscore both at the beginning and end of the footnote; likewise, one line of space should be left between the line and the text of the footnote at both ends. The footnote itself should be typed in double spacing.

When footnotes are *printed* there are four main ways of dealing with them: (1) they appear at the foot of the same page as the reference; (2) they appear as side or 'shoulder' notes; (3) they are listed at the end of individual chapters; (4) they appear all together as an appendix to the book. For methods (3) and (4) printers often prefer the footnotes all to be typed on a separate sheet(s), so they do not have to refer back in the copy of the text for them.

Frontispiece. This is an illustration which faces the title page. It may be printed on the back of the half-title page or may be inset (stuck in).

Half-title. This is the page that comes before the title page and it usually contains only the name of the book.

Back (verso) of half-title. This is often blank but it may contain details of other books by the same author or other books on similar or allied subjects. In fiction, a synopsis of the story is sometimes set here. In addition, a frontispiece (see above) may be positioned here.

Headings (see also **Headings**). Prominence should be given to the important aspects in the headings by skilful use of the various heading devices—spaced capitals, closed capitals, initial capitals, underscoring, etc. Consistency should be observed within a single work.

Headlines. The line at the top of a page containing running title, page number, etc. When they are continued from page to page they are known as 'running headlines' (see below).

Hook in. Where there are too many words for one line of poetry, or of an index or some similar setting, those at the end can be 'hooked in', i.e., carried to the end of the preceding or succeeding line and separated from it by a bracket sign.

Inset matter. Any matter that is inset is usually typed in single spacing and inset equally from both margins, unless blocked layout is being used. See also **Inset matter.**

Italics. If a word or group of words is underlined, this indicates to the printer that italics should be used.

Margins.
1. The left-hand margin of a draft is usually 50 mm (2 in.) wide to accommodate corrections and additions, and the right-hand margin 25 mm (1 in.).
2. The margins of a fair copy for a printer are usually 25 mm (1 in.) on the left and 10 mm (or $\frac{1}{2}$ in.) on the right.
3. If the fair copy is not to be printed but is to be bound in some way, a margin of 40 mm (or $1\frac{1}{2}$ in.) should be left on the left-hand side as a 'stitching margin', with a right-hand margin of 10 mm (or $\frac{1}{2}$ in.). If both sides of the paper are used, the wider margin appears on the left-hand side of the odd numbered pages and on the right-hand side of even numbered pages.
4. Top and bottom margins, six line spaces except on the first page of a chapter or section where a dropped head is used (see above).

Pagination.
1. Preliminary pages are normally numbered separately from the main text, using small roman numerals. The text pages are numbered in arabic figures.
2. The half-title, title and acknowledgments pages (and their versos) are numbered as preliminary pages, but the number does not appear in print.

3. All pages of a text (except the first) should be numbered in type-writing, using arabic figures. The figure should appear in the same position on each page (either in the centre or at the right-hand side) on the third line down from the top of the page, with the text beginning on the seventh line down, so that six line spaces are left above the beginning of the text. The figure may be followed by a stop, be enclosed in brackets, have a hyphen or dash on either side of it, or stand alone. Consistency of style should be observed.

Paper. For economy, inferior quality paper can be used for drafts. However, good-quality paper should be used for typing the fair copy. Flimsy paper should be used for carbon copies. One side only of the paper should be used, except for some documents that are to be bound in some way. In general, A4 paper is used for typing literary work.

Plays. See separate entry.

Poetry. See separate entry.

Proof reading. A typist should, of course, always carefully check her work. When fair typing from a draft, however, she may make errors which are not easily detectable. If the matter is to be printed and such errors are not detected until after the typesetting, they will prove costly to rectify and cause delay in the timing schedule. Therefore it is desirable that one person should read aloud the copy and a second person check the fair-typed version. See also **Proof reading.**

Quotations. Lengthy quotations are usually inset using single spacing. If a quotation consists of more than one paragraph, double quotation marks should be typed at the beginning of each paragraph and at the end only of the last paragraph. Quotations, or direct speech, within quotations are indicated by single quotation marks.

Running headlines. Running headlines assist the reader to find his place in a book. The style adopted varies but a commonly used method is for the book title to be on the left-hand pages on the same line as the the page number, and the chapter or section title to be on the right-hand pages on the same line as the page number.

Short page. The term used to indicate a page that contains less than the usual amount of matter—e.g. the last page of a chapter or section.

Stitching margin. See under **Margins.**

Tailpiece. This is a decorative ending to an article, programme, book chapter, or section, etc. (See **Tailpieces.**)

Title page. This contains some or all of the following:

1. Title of book.
2. Sub-title.
3. Author's name.
4. Editor's name.
5. Illustrator's name.
6. Edition number and/or number of the volume and number of volumes in the set.
7. Publisher's monogram or symbol.
8. Publisher's name and address.
9. Date of publication—but this is usually put on the back of the title page.

Back (verso) of title page. This page is often used for notes about the book, the publisher, and the printer that would be out of place on the title page but are nevertheless either useful or necessary.

Location drills. See **Drills.**

Lock, carriage. Some typewriters, particularly portables, are fitted with a special locking mechanism for the carriage. The lock securely fastens the carriage when it is in its central position and prevents any sideways movement, and should always be used when the typewriter is being moved.

When typewriters are not fitted with a carriage-locking device, the carriage should be secured by moving the two margin stops to the centre of the carriage.

At the end of the working day, and when the typewriter is being left unattended for any considerable period of time, the typist should always 'lock' the machine—in case it should be moved for any reason during her absence (see also **Care of the typewriter**).

Mainspring and escapement. See **Parts of a typewriter.**

Maintenance of typewriter. See **Care of the typewriter** and **Overhauling typewriter.**

Maltron keyboard. See **Arrangement of keyboard.**

Manuscript abbreviations. See **Abbreviations.**

Manuscript correction signs. See **Typewriter and manuscript correction signs.**

Manuscript, typing from. All professional typists require the ability to type from manuscript. In addition, most typewriting examinations include at least one manuscript typewriting task.

Before beginning to type from manuscript, the typist should read through the whole passage—or part of it, depending on the legibility of the writing—to make sure that it is clear and makes sense. Often, a word that is not immediately legible, makes sense as one proceeds with reading the whole: the same word may be repeated in a more legible form or in a different context that suggests its meaning. Also, as the typist becomes more familiar with the subject matter and the particular characteristics of the handwriting, words that at first were unreadable become clear. If there is any doubt at all about spelling, a dictionary should be consulted.

The typing of a sentence should not be started until everything in it is perfectly understandable. Otherwise errors and even gibberish may occur—with the result that the work will have to be retyped and time lost.

All manuscript abbreviations should be typed in full, except the generally accepted ones such as i.e., e.g., etc. If the manuscript has been revised and corrected by the writer, care should be taken to see that 'ballooned' portions, etc., are inserted in the correct place. Also, all marginal corrections (see **Typewriting and manuscript correction signs**) should be observed. Sometimes a manuscript that has been corrected ready for typing may still contain errors: if these are obvious ones, they should be corrected, but if there is any doubt, the writer should be consulted if possible.

Sometimes a manuscript will include a 'Note to Typist' that contains various instructions. Remember to follow the instructions—but do not type the words 'Note to Typist' as unthinking typists often do.

Sometimes a typist may be confronted with rough manuscript notes which she must expand into well-produced typewritten copy. If little alteration or expansion is necessary, the typist can mark up the manuscript original: otherwise it will pay her to type a rough draft (for possible further refinement) in double or treble spacing, before attempting to produce the finished version.

If a typist is given an *uncorrected* manuscript for typing, she should carefully mark up on the manuscript copy all her corrections (preferably in another colour) before beginning to type the final copy.

Margin release key drills. See **Drills.**

Marginal headings. See **Headings.**

Margins (see also **Literary work**). The following points should be noted.

1. In typewritten work, left- and right-hand margins may be equal, or the left-hand margin may be wider than the right-hand one: it is

generally considered bad practice for the right-hand margin to be wider than the left one.

2. Margins that are equal give a pleasing appearance and are advisable in work that contains a considerable amount of centring since headings should always be centred to the typing line. If margins are equal, it is a simple matter to move the carriage to the centre point of the paper and backspace once for every two characters or spaces in the heading. Centring headings over matter where the margins are unequal is a more complicated procedure (see **Headings**).

3. In work that contains little or no centring, a left-hand margin of 25 mm (or 1 in.) and a right-hand margin of 10 mm (or $\frac{1}{2}$ in.) are commonly used.

4. In display and tabular work, left- and right-hand margins should be equal, and there should be equal space at the top and bottom of the paper.

5. In work of a continuous nature, the top and bottom margins of the paper should both be six line spaces (unless a 'dropped head' is used (see **Literary work**)). To secure a uniform top margin, the paper should be inserted into the typewriter until it is just visible along the alignment scale. The line-space lever should be set for single spacing and turned up seven times. Typing should begin on this line—thus leaving six clear line spaces above the typing. See the entry **End of paper** for suggested methods of obtaining a uniform space at the foot of typewritten pages.

6. The margins and layout of some documents such as Specifications and Minutes of Meetings vary and are complicated, particularly if the blocked method of layout is not being used. The appropriate section of the book should be consulted.

7. The left-hand margin of a *draft* is often 50 mm (or 2 in.) wide (and the line spacing treble) to take any necessary corrections and additions; the right-hand margin should be 25 mm (or 1 in.).

8. If a fair typed copy of a document is to be bound in some way, a margin of 40 mm (or $1\frac{1}{2}$ in.) should be left on the left-hand side as a 'stitching margin'; with a right-hand margin of 10 mm (or $\frac{1}{2}$ in.). If both sides of the paper are used, the wider margin appears on the left-hand side of the odd numbered pages and on the right-hand side of even numbered pages.

9. The margins for A5 paper used portrait-style (narrower side at the top) are usually 10 mm (or $\frac{1}{2}$ in.). When A5 paper is used landscape-style (wider side at the top) the margins can be 10–25 mm (or $\frac{1}{2}$–1 in.) according to the length and nature of the copy.

Irregular margins. If the typewriter is in good working order, the left-hand margin set at the required position, and the typist returns the carriage correctly (see *Carriage return lever* under **Parts of a typewriter and their uses**), there should be no problem about securing an exactly even left-hand margin. A mechanic should be called in if a regular left-hand margin is not obtainable with proper use of the machine, since the left-hand margin stop may need attention.

A regular right-hand margin is more difficult to obtain. Consult the entry **Division of words at line ends.**

Margin setting drills. See **Drills.**

Margin stops. See **Parts of a typewriter.**

Matching in and matching up. 'Matching in' describes the process of completing form letters so that the added particulars match, as closely as possible, the colour and density (also pitch) of the form (see also *Form letters* under **Letters**).

'Matching up' means adjusting the paper correctly so that the characters appear in correct alignment, both vertically and horizontally, when a completed piece of typescript has to be reinserted into the typewriter for a correction to be made (see also **Correcting errors**).

Mathematical typing (see also *Dual unit typewriter* under **Special purpose typewriters** and **Combination characters and special signs**). In this technological age there are many specialized fields that employ highly technical terms and signs—for example, mathematics, science and medicine.

It is possible to obtain typewriters with special keyboards for such specialized work where the amount of work justifies the expenditure. In addition, a 'typit' attachment enables a typist to type symbols and characters that are not included on her keyboard. Typits are separate typebars, of which there are more than 1,000 symbols available, ranging from scientific and mathematical letters and symbols to symbols used in pharmaceutics, linguistics, astronomy and meteorology. The typist inserts the typits into a modified typebar guide fitted onto her machine.

However, typists are often required to do mathematical or simple scientific typing using a standard keyboard with perhaps only one or two special characters fitted. Such a situation requires a high degree of typing skill and the ability to display the required matter in a clear, attractive and consistent manner. Some symbols will probably have to be carefully written in by hand, using a black biro.

Mathematical and scientific language and signs are very exact and the typist should follow the copy very carefully. Some general typing suggestions for mathematical work follow.

1. If there is continuous prose before and after a mathematical expression, the typist should ensure that she leaves a clear and equal

space above and below the mathematical typing, making due allowance, of course, for superior and inferior characters.

2. (a) A space should be left on either side of the plus, minus, equals, multiplication, and division signs in simple expressions (provided the author has not given specific instructions to the contrary), as in the following example.

$$x + y - z = a \times b$$

(b) No space should be left either side of these signs if they connect simple expressions within brackets or form part of a superior or inferior expression.

$$(x=ab) \qquad (a^2 - 4c) \qquad z^{n+2}$$

(c) A space should be left either side of these signs before and after brackets or braces.

$$b + (c^2 x d^3) - x$$

3. When vertical fractions and expressions are used, the whole numbers, addition, subtraction, multiplication, equals, and division signs should be centrally positioned, as in the following examples. (See also **Fractions.**)

(a) $\qquad 4\dfrac{15}{16}$

(b) $\qquad \dfrac{3a^2 + b^3}{2abc} + \dfrac{6b^2 - c^3}{3ac} = 4xz$

4. If a long equation can all be typed on one line by omitting a few spaces, it is better to do this rather than split the equation and use a second line. However, this expedient should be resorted to only if absolutely necessary, and after consultation with the author, if possible.

Mats, typewriter. When in use, a manual typewriter should always be placed on a pad of felt or rubber, approximately 10 mm (or $\frac{1}{2}$ in.) thick. If the four feet of a typewriter stand on such a mat while the machine is in use it will be less noisy in operation, and vibration of the typewriter parts will be lessened as the mat will, to some extent, act as a shock absorber.

Such mats, however, should *not* be placed under electric typewriters or the airways on the underside of the machine will become blocked, resulting in overheating of the motor and consequent failure. Also, the fan of an electric typewriter may draw in felt fluff or dust and thus cause other maintenance problems. Only typewriter mats recommended by the electric machine manufacturers should be used: alternatively, a small pad can be placed under each foot of the typewriter.

Meetings. A good typist/secretary will sometimes be called upon to produce typewritten work in connection with meetings. To do this successfully, she should be conversant with basic meeting procedure and terminology, and the main documents concerned with meetings.

Main documents

1. *Notice of meeting.* This is sent by the Secretary to every person entitled to attend the meeting. It states the day, time, place and purpose of the meeting and should be sent out well before the meeting so that necessary arrangements for attendance can be made.

2. *Agenda.* This is a list of the items to be discussed at a meeting. Usually they are numbered and given in the order in which they will be dealt with. An agenda is drawn up by the Secretary in consultation with the Chairman, and the business of the previous meeting and the requests of members are taken into consideration.

Business is normally dealt with in the following order.

(a) Minutes of the last meeting read (or taken as read if they are circulated with the agenda), confirmed, and signed by the Chairman after any necessary alterations have been made.

(b) Business arising from the minutes not covered elsewhere in the agenda.

(c) Apologies for absence.

(d) Correspondence.

(e) Other items as appropriate—such as the election of officers, reports, and other special points on the agenda.

(f) Any other business.

(g) Date of next meeting.

If the election of a Chairman were necessary, this would be the first item of business and the election would be carried out under the supervision of the retiring, or a temporary, Chairman.

An agenda is often sent out with the Notice of the Meeting. Increasingly, the fully-blocked style is being used for meeting documents although some traditional bodies prefer to retain the fully-displayed method with centring and indented paragraphs—despite the extra time and effort involved.

An example of a combined notice and agenda, in the fully-blocked style follows.

Meetings

THE CENTRAL LAWN TENNIS CLUB

The Annual General Meeting of the Central Lawn Tennis Club will be held in the
Committee Room at 27 Green Street, Northampton, on Friday, 17 February 19--
at 1950 hrs.

A G E N D A

1   Minutes of last meeting
2   Matters arising therefrom
3   Apologies for absence
4   Correspondence
5   Chairman's Annual Report
6   Treasurer's Annual Report and Balance Sheet
7   Election of: Honorary Secretary
                 Honorary Treasurer
8   Consideration of plans for extending the Club's facilities
9   Any other business
10 Date of next meeting

B SANDERS
Hon Secretary

10 February 19--

The notice and agenda for a less formal meeting would obviously
differ in some respects from the foregoing example and would vary
according to the purpose of the meeting. An example follows.

JOHNSON ELECTRICAL COMPANY LIMITED

NOTICE OF MEETING

To all Sales Representatives

A meeting of all sales representatives will be held in the Sales Manager's
office at Head Office on Tuesday, 14 November 19--. The meeting will begin
promptly at 1600 hrs and it is expected that all sales representatives will
attend. Anyone unable to attend should contact the Sales Manager immediately,
stating the reasons for his proposed absence.

The agenda is set out below.

A G E N D A

1   Apologies for absence
2   To discuss reasons for recent poor sales figures and measures to improve them
3   To receive and discuss revised price lists
4   Any other business

D SMITH
Sales Manager

7 November 19--

Agendas are frequently typed with a wide right-hand margin to
enable members to make notes at the meeting. Sometimes a special
Chairman's Agenda is prepared which includes, for the Chairman's
benefit, special notes under each item: the right-hand side of the paper
is left free for his notes.

3. *Minutes.* The Secretary will be required to take notes at meetings. These notes will form the basis of the Minutes—which should be a brief, accurate and clear record of the business transacted. He/she must make a note of the precise wording of every motion and resolution passed, together with the names of the proposers and seconders. If a member requests that a particular point be minuted, it should, at the Chairman's discretion, be included.

The Secretary must ensure that all the main arguments for and against a motion are recorded. The ability to do this well is a difficult task that requires both skill and experience. Some discussions may be lengthy and notes should be made only on the points that have a real bearing on the matter under discussion.

It is a good practice for the Secretary to keep a special shorthand notebook for meetings, to number them consecutively as they become full, and to write on the front of each the starting and finishing dates.

As soon as possible after the meeting, the Secretary should type the Minutes in draft form on A4 paper in double or treble spacing. They should be written in the third person and in the past tense and should be checked against the agenda and notes to ensure that nothing has been omitted. The approval of the Chairman should be obtained before the Minutes are typed in their final form.

Sometimes Minutes are written in a bound Minute Book with a wide left-hand margin ruled down each page for the insertion of headings. However, it is now common practice for Minutes to be typed and inserted in a loose-leaf Minute Book. Some organizations number each Minute. Often the numbers are consecutive for a series of meetings, i.e., they do not start at **one** for each meeting. A common method here is to indicate the year of the meeting; for example, Minute 279.76 refers to minute no. 279 at a meeting held in 1976. By this method the first minute of the first meeting of the year is numbered **one** (e.g. 1.76) and by December of that year the Minutes might have reached, say, 350 (350.76). Often the subjects discussed are indexed at the back of the Minute Book, listed alphabetically under their subject headings.

Since the Minutes are the official record of meetings, their safe keeping is very important, and since leaves can be lost or removed they are usually kept locked up when not in use.

Minutes are usually recorded in the following order:

1. Description of meeting, place, date, and time.

2. List of those present with the Chairman's name first. If the meeting is a general one with a large number of members present, the number only is usually recorded.

3. Reading (if necessary) and confirmation of the Minutes of the last meeting.

4. Matters arising from the Minutes.
5. Apologies for absence.
6. Correspondence.
7. Other business, in the order listed on the agenda.
8. Any other business.
9. Date of next meeting.

At the foot of the Minutes a space should be left for the signature (at the next meeting) of the Chairman, and his name typed below the signature space. This should be followed by the designation 'Chairman'. The date of signing will be typed last; this is sometimes handwritten at the time of signing.

The following is a simple example of typed Minutes of a meeting in the fully-blocked style.

M I N U T E S   O F   M E E T I N G

A meeting of the Entertainments Committee of the Whitstable Traders Association was held in the committee room of the Council Offices on Tuesday 12 January 19— at 1800 hrs.

PRESENT

Mr James Brown (Chairman)
Miss Ann Buxton
Mr C Creed
Mr R Watson (Secretary)

MINUTES

The minutes of the last meeting, held on 10 October 19— were read, approved and signed by the Chairman.

MATTERS ARISING

There was only one matter arising from the minutes. The Secretary reported that the recent application for a bar licence at this year's Annual Dinner and Dance had been approved.

APOLOGIES

The Secretary said that Mr Matthews was unable to attend as he was out of the country on important business but hoped to be present at the next meeting.

ARRANGEMENTS FOR THE ANNUAL DINNER AND DANCE

Miss Buxton announced that she had made arrangements for the Paul Smithson Group to play at a fee of £100 (one hundred pounds). She also stated that the printing of tickets was in hand.

Mr Creed reported that catering arrangements would be in the hands of the same firm as last year but that there would be an increase of 15% in the charges.

He also stated that there would be an increased charge for the use of the hall. After a lengthy discussion it was agreed to increase the price of a double ticket to £6.50.

The Secretary pointed out that it would be necessary for at least 150 double tickets to be sold for all expenses to be covered. It was agreed that this year a maximum of 200 double tickets (ie 400 present) should be sold in view of the complaints of overcrowding last year.

ANY OTHER BUSINESS

There was no other business and the Chairman declared the meeting closed at 1950 hrs.

DATE OF NEXT MEETING

The date of the next meeting was fixed for 15 March 19—

J BROWN
Chairman

An alternative method of setting out Minutes is illustrated below:

SPORTS COMMITTEE MINUTES

A Meeting of the Sports Committee of The Benning Welfare Association was held in the Sports Pavilion on Monday, 30 June 19— at 1930 hrs.

<u>Present</u>

Mr J H Thomas (in the chair)
Miss D Ashton
Mrs I Gardner
Mr A Evans
Mr J Ripley
Mr H Spence
Mr R T Bird (Secretary)

Minutes

The minutes of the last meeting were read, adopted and signed by the Chairman.

Matters Arising

Mr Evans reported that a reunion of the members of the Football Club proved very successful.

Financial Statement

A statement of the current financial position of the Committee was read and adopted. In addition, the statement for presentation to the Annual Meeting to be held on 14 July 19— was approved.

Tennis

Miss Ashton pointed out that there was a lack of facilities for members wishing to play tennis. She stated that the one grass court belonging to the Committee was proving inadequate owing to the constant demand caused by the Club members' enthusiasm, and asked whether the Committee could see its way to secure a second court. Mr Ripley mentioned that members of the tennis section had contributed a large proportion of the funds at present in hand, and that he considered Miss Ashton's recommendation justifiable. The Chairman pointed out that the application would have to be submitted in the first place to the Board of Directors for their approval.

```
          RESOLVED: That the Secretary be
          R41       instructed to make
                    application to the Board
                    of Directors for the
                    provision of a second
                    grass court adjoining
                    the existing grass
                    court.

Date of Next  It was decided to hold the next
Meeting       meeting of the Committee on
              Tuesday, 23 July 19—.


              Chairman
              23 July 19—
```

Extract from the Minutes of a Sports Committee Meeting. By permission of Mr John Harrison, author of *Secretarial Duties* (Pitman).

Some meetings terms

Addressing the Chair. All remarks should be addressed to the Chairman, and members should not discuss matters amongst themselves or the meeting would soon get out of hand. If the Chairman is a man, the speaker should begin 'Mr Chairman'. A woman Chairman is usually addressed as 'Madam Chairman'. The Chairman controls the meeting and ensures that only one person speaks at a time.

Ad hoc. Of Latin origin, meaning 'for this purpose'. Therefore an ad hoc committee is one appointed to carry out a particular task. Such committees are also called special or special purpose committees.

Amendment. A proposal to alter the wording of a motion: it must be proposed, seconded, and put to the meeting in the usual way.

Any other business. Frequently abbreviated to A.O.B. Usually included on an agenda so that, if there is time, items other than those stated on the agenda may be discussed at the Chairman's discretion.

Attendance record. Unless the meeting is a very large one, the names of members present are included in the Minutes. Frequently, a sheet of paper is passed round for members to sign. Alternatively, an attendance register is sited at the entrance to the room or hall, which members sign as they enter.

Casting vote. A casting vote is used only when there is an equal number of votes for and against a motion. A casting vote is made by the Chairman.

Closure. A motion 'that the question be now put'—submitted with the intention of ending a lengthy discussion on a matter before the meeting. If the motion is seconded and carried, the motion under discussion must be put to the vote immediately, without further discussion. If the motion to close the discussion is defeated, deliberations may continue.

Co-opted member. A person appointed to serve on a committee as an additional member, usually because he/she possesses specialized knowledge for a particular purpose. A co-option can only be made by a majority vote of existing members of the organization.

Ex officio. From the Latin, meaning 'by virtue of office'. An ex officio member of a committee is entitled to sit on it because of some other position he/she holds.

Honorary member or officer. An honorary member of an organization is not required to pay the normal membership subscription. An honorary officer undertakes a particular duty for the organization *without payment*, e.g., Honorary Secretary, Honorary Treasurer.

Lie on the table. A motion that a particular matter should 'lie on the table' means that no action should be taken on it until an agreed future date.

Memorandum and Articles of Association. The Memorandum sets out the objects for which an organization is formed. The Articles of Association are the regulations governing the internal management of the organization—the rules governing membership, activities, etc.

Motion. A motion is a proposal put forward at a meeting. The mover of a motion is called the proposer and the required supporter is known as the seconder. The proposer speaks on the motion and also has the right of reply at the *end* of the discussion. The seconder may speak on the motion only once. When a motion is put to the meeting it becomes the question, and if passed by a majority vote it becomes a resolution. A resolution cannot be rescinded at the meeting at which it is adopted.

Nem con. From the Latin *nemine contradicente* meaning 'no-one dissenting', i.e., no votes have been cast against a motion although some members may have abstained from voting.

Next business. A motion 'that the meeting proceed with the next business' is a means of delaying a decision on a matter under discussion.

Out of order. A remark by a member may be called out of order if it involves a breach of the governing rules.

Point of order. This is a question raised regarding meeting procedure or a query concerning the standing orders or constitution. An immediate decision should be made by the Chairman.

Proxy. A person may be appointed by proxy to represent someone else—and vote on his behalf—at the meeting, subject to this being permissible in the regulations of the organization.

Putting the question. At the end of discussion on a motion, the Chairman 'puts the question' by announcing 'The question before the meeting is . . .'. Voting then takes place.

Quorum. The minimum number of members who must be present at a meeting to make it valid. The quorum is laid down in the regulations of the organization.

Resolution. See *Motion.*

Rider. An addition to a resolution *after* it has been passed. A rider differs from an amendment in that it adds to, rather than alters, the sense of the resolution. A rider must be proposed, seconded and put to the meeting in the usual way.

Right of reply. The proposer of a motion has the right of reply after it has been fully discussed. This is followed immediately by the voting. (See also *Motion.*)

Standing orders. These are the rules governing the conduct of meetings of a particular organization. They are also referred to as the Constitution. In general, the standing orders may not be altered in any way except at an annual or special meeting.

Sub-committee. A sub-committee is appointed by the committee of an organization to carry out a specific task.

Teller. A person appointed to count the votes at a meeting.

Unanimous. When *all* members of a meeting have voted in favour of a motion, it is said to have been carried unanimously (see also *Nem con*).

Memos. Memos (or memorandums/memoranda, as they are now less frequently called) are written communications between individuals within an organization. Frequently they are sent from one person to another within the same building but sometimes they are sent to another person working for the same organization in an external section or department. In the former case they would be delivered by hand and in the latter, usually sent by post, especially if the distance was considerable.

Some firms use printed memo forms which are headed by the word Memorandum or Memo and the firm's name, etc: also printed are a combination of the words To, From, Our ref, Your ref, Date, and Subject—with appropriate spaces for the typist to type in the required information, sometimes with the guidance of dots. Under the printed heading there is often a line ruled across the form from margin to margin.

Many organizations, however, do not use printed forms and often plain paper suffices with the typist typing in the necessary headings and information as she proceeds with the memo. Layout of memos varies very considerably from firm to firm. Many organizations now use the fully-blocked form of layout since this is the quickest and therefore the cheapest method.

Memos do not require an inside address, salutation or complimentary close. If the memo has a subject heading this is often typed in closed capitals but it is sometimes typed with initial capitals and underscored—although the latter method is obviously slower. The body of the memo is typed in single spacing with a line space left between paragraphs, which may be blocked or indented. Below the message there is usually a space left for the initials or signature of the sender, and the name and/or the designation of the sender may or may not be typed, according to preference and circumstances. The style of English used in memo writing is usually concise and colloquial unless the memo is to be used for an official purpose. Enclosures are normally indicated as for letters (see **Letters**).

Some firms now use a blocked style of memo and omit the words To and From. The name of the addressee and his designation appear at the top with the name and designation of the sender at the bottom beneath the initials or signature: the date and reference (if there is one) usually appear last.

A5 paper (with the longest dimension at the top) or A4 paper is used, according to the length of the memo, and the margins likewise are dependent on the length—although if a printed heading followed by a line is used, it is to set the margins to coincide with the line.

Although a variety of layouts are in common use, there is usually consistency within a single organization (particularly with regard to position of date and reference) to facilitate filing, etc. Three styles of memo, not using printed headings, follow.

```
MEMO

To    Sales Manager
From  Accounts Manager

W SIMPSON & SONS LTD

The above firm is now considerably above its
credit limit and no further orders should be
accepted from them until a considerable part of
their balance is cleared.

Since you have good personal contacts with this
```

firm I should be grateful if you would send them a tactful letter.

B Milner
Ref BM/AS/1286

Date

MEMORANDUM

Mr A Turner
Educational Section

Date

COPY FOR NEW CATALOGUE

This is to remind you that you promised to let us have the copy for your new catalogues by today at the latest. The stock of catalogues for your Section is nearly out so this matter is urgent.

Please let me know the situation.

G S Kennedy
Publicity Manager

GSK/ML/Sec 6

M E M O R A N D U M

To: Company Secretary   From: Managing Director

Date: Ref: AL/bc

Annual Booksellers' Exhibition and Dinner

Further to our telephone conversation earlier today, I am attaching two tickets for tonight's Annual Booksellers' Exhibition and Dinner.

Please note that the Exhibition will begin

Menus

at 1730 hrs and <u>not</u> at 1830 hrs as stated on the
tickets. I have been unable to cancel my other
engagement for this evening so should be most
grateful if you and a guest would attend on my
behalf.

Encs. 2

Menus. Menus may be elaborately displayed and centred or typed

T H E   W H I T E   H A R T   H O T E L

BRIGHTON

<u>Luncheon Menu</u>

Tomato Soup
or
Grapefruit

* * *

Fried Fillet of Plaice - Sauce Tartare
Roast Chicken, Stuffing and Bread Sauce

* * *

French Fried Potatoes
Roast and Creamed Potatoes
Fresh Garden Peas
Spring Cabbage

* * *

Peach Melba
Fruit Tart
or
Cheese and Biscuits

* * *

Coffee

--ooOoo--

Example of a displayed menu

168

```
THE   WHITE   HART   HOTEL

BRIGHTON

Luncheon Menu


Tomato Soup
or
Grapefruit

----------

Fried Fillet of Plaice - Sauce Tartare
Roast Chicken, Stuffing and Bread Sauce

------------------------------------------

French Fried Potatoes
Roast and Creamed Potatoes
Fresh Garden Peas
Spring Cabbage

----------------------------

Peach Melba
Fruit Tart
or
Cheese and Biscuits

----------------------

Coffee


------
```

Example of a blocked menu

simply using the blocked method with every item beginning at the left-hand margin point. Whichever method is used, the different courses are usually separated from each other by several line spaces with a series of asterisks, dots, hyphens, etc., typed along the centre of the space. Also, the typing should be centred on the page (see **Centring—horizontal and vertical**). If a menu is for an important occasion the displayed method is often preferred with, possibly, an ornamental border and tailpiece (see **Ornamental typing** and **Tailpieces**).

MESSAGE FOR

Mrs Taylor

WHILE YOU WERE OUT
Mr Anderson

OF **Southern Typewriters Ltd**

TELEPHONE NO **Hampton 50936**

Telephoned	✓	Please ring	✓
Called to see you		Will call again	
Wants to see you		Urgent	

MESSAGE **Mr Anderson will be in this area tomorrow and would like to see you to discuss the typewriters you wish to part exchange for new ones. Please ring him back today before 1600 hrs.**

Date **10 July 1976**   Time **1045 hrs**

Received by **Mary Bowen**

Example of a typed message

Messages, typing of. Most secretaries and personal assistants will have to take and pass on messages for their employers. Whether the message is taken from a telephone call or a personal visit, certain essential facts will have to be recorded. These are: name of person for whom the message is intended; name and telephone number of the caller (sometimes also the name of his firm and/or his address); message; date and time of the message; signature of the person taking the message.

Therefore, in the interests of speed and overall efficiency, most firms use printed message pads so the person recording the message merely has to fill in the appropriate spaces.

In the first instance the message will obviously be handwritten and in many cases, particularly if the message is a simple one, the first effort will suffice. Often, however, if the message is long and complicated—and not well or logically presented by the caller—it will be considered necessary to rearrange and rewrite the original notes: in this case a new message sheet should be made out and, if possible, typed.

Messrs. See **Titles, decorations, qualifications, forms of address, etc.**

Metrication. The metric system is based on new pence for money, the metre for length, the kilogram for weight, and the litre for liquid—to mention but the most common everyday measurements. The system is more logical than the old one of pounds, shillings and pence; yards, feet and inches; gallons, quarts, pints and gills; and tons, hundred-weights, pounds and ounces. This is because throughout the entire metric system TEN is the number on which everything is based—and we all know how easy it is to add, multiply and divide by ten, compared with the odd assortment of numbers we had to work in under the traditional system.

The metric system is convenient for all purposes in industry, commerce, education, and everyday life. Teaching, learning, and working in metric reduces errors and saves time—as research has proved.

The British decision to change over to the metric system was made in 1965, and although the changes created problems, these were soon overcome and everyone agrees the new system is an improvement—although some people feel that the old units of measurement were part of our cultural heritage. However, with the vast increase in international trade, a world-wide system was obviously desirable and necessary.

A list of some of the metric units and symbols in most common use is given below.

Unit	Unit Symbol
kilometre	km
metre	m

Unit	Unit Symbol
centimetre	cm
millimetre	mm
litre	l*
millilitre	ml
tonne	t*
kilogramme	kg
gramme	g
newton	N
newton per metre	N/m
kilonewton	kN
second	s
degree Celsius	°C
joule	J
kilojoule	kJ
watt	W
kilowatt	kW
candela	cd
lumen	lm
ampere	A
volt	V

*The unit should be written in full if there is any doubt as to the use of the symbol, e.g., the unit symbols 'l' for litre and 't' for tonne can be confused with the number one and the imperial ton.

Typing of unit symbols, units of measurement and numerical values

1. The same symbol should be used for the singular and plural, e.g., 1 m, 2 m.

2. No full stops or other punctuation marks should be used, e.g., 3 mm, 4 kg.

3. A single space should separate figures from their symbols as in the examples given above.

4. The correct case of type should be used for symbols. Where a unit is named after a person, i.e., W after Watt, A after Ampere and C after Celsius, an upper case character is used. It is also used where the lower case character has a different meaning, such as M for Mega- and m for milli-.

5. Where it is necessary to use a thousand marker, it can be provided by means of a space—as the comma is in general use in metric countries for the decimal marker—e.g., 1 000 000. See also **Money, typing of** on this point.

6. Figures and symbols should not be divided at line ends.

7. Quantities should be used in the terms of one unit only, e.g., 10.100 m (not 10 m 100 mm).

Degrees centigrade. Celsius is the new name for centigrade. There are *two* symbols for degrees Celsius. °C is used for temperature *readings* (e.g. from a thermometer); degC is used for temperature *differences*. The diagram shows that the temperature has fallen from 20°C to 15°C; this is a fall of 5 degC.

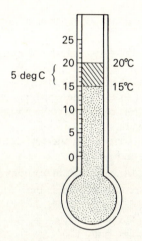

Mille. See **Combination characters and special signs.**

Minus sign. See **Combination characters and special signs** and **Mathematical typing.**

Minutes of meeting. See **Meetings.**

Minutes sign. See **Combination characters and special signs.**

Money, typing of. (The rules for sterling used in this section apply to other currencies.) The £ symbol, and p when typed after a figure to represent pence, should never be followed by a full stop—except when the latter occurs at the end of a sentence. The £ symbol and pence abbreviation should never both be included in a single money expression.

An amount of money, represented as figure, should not be divided at the end of a line.

When the decimal point is used in money items it is typed using the full stop, in its normal position on the line. In some countries, type-writers have a decimal point key which types the point above the line.

A halfpenny is represented in fraction form, e.g., 58½p, £188.26½.

Typing money in continuous prose

(a) Any sum over £1 that includes pence is usually shown as a decimal, e.g., £6.55, £100.06.

(b) Any sum amounting to £1 or over, but not including pence, can be shown with or without the decimal point, e.g., £10, £500 (or £10.00 and £500.00). Such amounts can also be represented in words only, e.g., ten pounds, five hundred pounds.

(c) Amounts under £1 can be typed with or without the £ symbol and decimal point.

    i. When not using the £ symbol, the pence can be shown either with just the abbreviation for pence (p)—or the word 'pence' typed in full as in the following: 75p, 10p, 75 pence, 10 pence. The number, when using the word 'pence' can be typed as a figure or word, but consistency should be observed within a single piece of work.

    ii. If the £ symbol were used, the two examples in (**i**) would appear as £0.75 and £0.10.

(d) Millions of pounds can be shown in a variety of ways:

    i. 'It amounts to six million pounds but . . .'
    ii. 'It amounts to £6,000,000 but . . .'
    iii. 'It amounts to £6m but . . .'
    iv. 'It amounts to £6m. but . . .'
    v. 'It amounts to £6 million but . . .'

Typing money in column form

(a) Care should be taken to ensure that the units always line up.

(b) If the column consists of pence items only, the column should be headed with the abbreviation p so that figures only appear below it. It is cumbersome and a waste of time to repeat the p for every item. The total will, of course, need to include the £ symbol if the items add up to more than £1: the decimal point should be used in the total with the pence correctly aligned with the column.

(a) p	(b) p
5	17
10	45
7	6
16	81
38p	£1.49

(c) If the column consists of pounds only, it should be headed with the £ symbol centred over the longest item (unless the blocked method of display is being used, in which case it will appear over the first digit).

(d) If the column consists of amounts in pounds and pence, the decimal point should be used (see also (e)) and the column headed with the £ symbol typed over either the units of the pounds or over the decimal point (the latter is generally considered the most logical position). However, if the blocked method of display is being used, the £ symbol can appear over the first digit.

Note: In the first amount of money .05 = 5p and in the last amount .50 = 50p. There should always be two digits following the decimal point to avoid confusion on this point.

Note also that the £2 in the third sum is followed by two noughts but the last item (50p) need not be preceded by a nought.

(e) Some invoices, etc., include a vertical line to separate the pounds from the pence: in this case the decimal point is *not* used. It is usual to head the pounds column with the £ symbol and the pence column with the pence abbreviation.

Examples of (c), (d) and (e) follow.

(c) £	(d) £	(e) £	p
200	10.05	5	10
5,350	169.75	18	55
12,160	2.00	4	$15\frac{1}{2}$
	$45.10\frac{1}{2}$		65
	.50		
£17,710	£227.40$\frac{1}{2}$	£28	$45\frac{1}{2}$

(f) Where invoices, etc., do not include a vertical line to divide the pounds from the pence, the items should be typed as in (c) or (d)—whichever is applicable.

(g) Money totals should be typed in one of the ways illustrated in (c) and (d).

    i. If the items are typed in double spacing, *one line of space* should be left either side of the top line as in (c); likewise, there should be one line of space between the total figure and the first of the double lines. The variable line spacer or interliner should then be used before the second line is typed. Note that the £ symbol should appear before the pounds figure in the total and the lines should not extend above or below the £ symbol.

   ii. If the amounts in a money column are typed in 1½ spacing or in single spacing, a more balanced appearance is obtained if *half a space* is left either side of the top line of the total; likewise, half a space should be left between the total figure and the first of the double lines.

In some offices the practice of using a space instead of a comma is adopted for sums of one thousand pounds, or higher. For instance £6 000 is typed instead of £6,000; likewise one million pounds would be shown as £1 000 000. However, in Britain the Decimal Currency Board has made no recommendation about the use of the space to mark off the digits in groups of three as, in money sums, the use of the comma is widespread as a thousand marker and is in fact used in other EEC countries. In their official booklet, *More Points for Businessmen* it is stated: 'There is therefore no need to disturb the widespread current use of the comma until there is general and universal acceptance of some different system.' (see also **Metrication** on this point.)

Moving a typewriter. See **Care of the typewriter** (No. 13).

Multi-Number system of enumeration. See **Enumerating sections, paragraphs and pages** and **Blocked layout.**

Multiplication sign. See **Combination characters and special signs** and **Mathematical typing.**

NCR (No carbon required) paper. This kind of paper is being increasingly used for the production of copies and it has several advantages over conventional carbon paper. It is frequently used for forms where a number of copies are required, and is made up in sets of the required number and colour(s), lightly attached at the top. Its use saves the typist a considerable amount of time in the handling of paper and carbons—an important factor when one considers that it has been estimated that the cost of *using* forms with carbons is approximately fifteen times the cost of the actual forms!

The popularity of NCR paper is thus growing. Obviously the main reason is that as paper work expands, the trend is to cut costs and simplify procedures rather than increase staff.

Certainly carbonless stationery allows more copies to be made if only because there is less bulk in the typewriter. To make four carbon copies the typist needs to insert the original, four sheets of carbon paper and four copy papers. However, using NCR paper, it is necessary to insert only five sheets to get an original and four copies—so obviously the copies will be clearer and the typewriter can produce more copies than by the carbon copy method.

An important advantage of NCR paper is that it is cleaner to work with than carbon paper since the copies do not smudge. Thus work is made more congenial, hands do not continually get dirty from the carbons, and time is saved in hand-washing, etc.

As office space becomes increasingly expensive, storage space becomes an important factor and any measure that cuts down the amount of cupboard space required for stationery supplies is welcome. In addition, when staff are under pressure, the use of NCR paper for telex and computer installations means that machines can be left unattended for longer periods as there is more paper in the same size cartons because no bulk is taken up by carbons.

There are now many types of NCR paper on the market and it is possible to describe here only a few of them. Although there are a number of different products, most of them are the type that have three different sorts of coating, known as CB, CF and CBF. If you wish to take only one copy, place a CB sheet (meaning the coating is on the back) on top of a CF sheet (meaning the coating is on the front) and when the two matching sides are thus brought together, a copy is produced on the bottom sheet by applying pressure, either by handwriting or typing. The coating on the back may be obvious but that on the front has to be invisible or it would, of course, affect the appearance of the finished copy.

The third type of coating (CFB) is required only if you are taking *more than one copy*. An intermediate sheet of CFB is placed in the 'sandwich' between the CB sheet on top and the CF sheet on the bottom. This has a coating on the front *and* the back so that it receives the copy from the CB sheet above it, and passes it on to the CF sheet underneath. For each additional copy you require, place another CFB sheet in the 'sandwich'.

Because it is important that sets are assembled correctly, and also to save handling time, most firms have their printers make up sets of the required number of sheets ready for the clerical staff to write or type on.

There is also usually some form of colour coding to enable departments to pick out their own copies quickly and to aid distribution.

IDEM carbonless paper is produced by Wiggins Teape. The first Wiggins Teape NCR paper was produced in 1956 and continuing research and development have resulted in IDEM which gives more and clearer copies and is easier to photocopy. The firm claims the copies *cannot* smudge for the image is *in* the paper, not on it. The top sheet has an emulsion coating on the back, composed of millions of tiny capsules containing two colourless dyes. The front of the bottom sheet that receives the copy is coated with a clay material. When pressure is applied by typing or writing, this causes the capsules to burst, the dyes penetrate the clay surface and the chemical reaction produced forms the blue copy that cannot smudge. Again, CB, CF and CFB sheets are supplied and used as already described. One useful point is that IDEM paper can be printed on the back without affecting the copying process. This can be most useful when information must appear on a form but not necessarily on the portion available for taking copies (for example, Conditions of Sale).

Another type of NCR paper—Action paper—is produced by 3M. Action Paper 200 is the conventional chemical transfer paper with the three basic sheets, CB, CF and CFB. Action Paper 100, however, is 'self-contained', which means that it works on its own to make a copy and can, therefore, be used *behind* any type of paper, not needing a paper with CB coating on top of it. Once the top sheet of ordinary paper (such as a letter-head) has been placed in position, there is no need to bother about the correct order of the other sheets as they each act on their own. Again, a chemical reaction takes place *within* the paper as a result of minute plastic capsules holding a colourless chemical dye breaking on pressure.

'Kores direct copy paper' is available in white, pink, blue, yellow, green, or gold. This product has only one coating, enabling it to be used as the top *or* middle sheet in a set while the bottom sheet can be your own paper (as opposed to the 3M Action Paper 100 where the top copy is your own paper). Because the coating makes the back of the paper blue, it is strictly of one-sided use only, unlike IDEM paper which can be printed on the back.

NCR paper undoubtedly has an important future in office use for both typewriting and handwriting.

Notice of meeting. See **Meetings.**

Numbering sections, paragraphs and pages. See **Enumerating sections, paragraphs and pages.**

Numbers (see also **Cardinal numbers** and **Roman numerals**). The student of Typewriting is often perplexed to read the complicated 'rules' propounded in some textbooks about when figures or words should be typed. These rules are lengthy, complex and listed under various headings: General and Literary Work; Correspondence; Commercial Work; Legal Work, and so on. Needless to say, even teachers and examiners in Typewriting are confused by them and often at variance. To many typewriting students they remain an unsolved mystery!

A swing of the pendulum has taken place and many authorities now state that all numbers can be typed as figures except the figure **one** (unless used in conjunction with other numbers, as in Catalogue No. 1342) and when a number starts a sentence. Such a straightforward method is certainly an improvement on the former maze of 'rules' with all their 'ifs' and 'buts'.

Commonsense and our general education tell us that such items as the following should be typed as figures.

1. Expressions of weight, quantity, and measurement, e.g., 3 kg, 10 reams of A5 paper, 10 m, 20°C.

2. Numbers in invoices and all forms of financial statement.

3. Numbers in statistical tables and reports.

4. House numbers, postcodes, references (where applicable), policy and certificate numbers, and after the abbreviation No. (for number). In addition, it is common knowledge that a figure is always used in conjunction with the % symbol and before the abbreviations a.m. and p.m. and in the 24-hour clock (0640 hrs, etc.).

There are, of course, certain documents where both figures and words are used—for instance, cheques and legal documents. Also, to avoid confusion, a number is often first typed as a figure and repeated in words in brackets, e.g., 'We are prepared to offer a fee of £80 (eighty pounds)'.

Again, it is largely commonsense that tells us that words and figures should not be mixed in certain cases. For example, we should type 10,000 or ten thousand, *not* 10 thousand. A notable exception here is when typing millions, e.g., we can type £6,000,000 or £6m or £6m. or £6 million.

An easy, generally-accepted method. A good general rule to follow is the now widely-accepted one that in connected matter, numbers from 1 to 9 may be typed as words or figures and numbers from 10 upwards always as figures. In addition, a word, not a figure, should begin a sentence. However, the latter, although widely accepted and practised, is not really logical and leads to inconsistencies. For example, why should one have to type 'Two out of every 10 votes were cast for Mr Longman' rather than '2 out of every 10 votes were cast for Mr Longman'? To many people the latter example is clearer and more consistent.

Although one is always taught to be consistent in the typing of words and figures, there are occasions when the author may quite reasonably wish to mix them for emphasis purposes—in company reports for instance.

It should be noted that a space may be used instead of a comma as a thousand marker (except in currency) when there are five or more figures standing on their own. Examples are 873 480 and 3 563 219. With four-digit numbers standing on their own it is not necessary to use a space or a comma, e.g., 3000. However, when figures are set out in column form the units, etc., should line up, as in the following example.

$$820 \ 439$$
$$3 \ 000$$
$$24 \ 063$$
$$23$$
$$1 \ 724 \ 878$$

The typist should note that if her keyboard does not have a special key for the figure **one,** she should use lower case **l** *not* upper case **I**.

Numerous pages, handling of. A good method for keeping pages in order if a piece of work is lengthy is as follows:

The first page, when completed, should be laid on the desk or table face upwards while the typist proceeds with the second page. On completion of page number two, the first page should be turned face downwards and number two laid on it, face upwards. This operation should be repeated throughout the whole of the work—so that only the last top copy page is facing the typist for her to refer to if necessary.

If carbon copies are being taken, care should be observed to ensure that they are kept in their correct order—all the first carbon copies together, and so on. This will help ensure that the density of impression of each set is similar. Each carbon copy, as it is completed, should immediately be placed face downwards.

Office composing machines. See **Special purpose typewriters.**

Offset lithography duplicating (see also **Reprography processes**). Offset lithography is based upon the principle of the mutually repellent properties of oil and water. Masters are prepared on special metal or paper plates which are coated with a greasy substance.

Masters for this method of reproduction can be prepared by a typewriter using a special litho ribbon and special offset litho paper plates. Alternatively, a master can be made by putting a typewritten original through an electrostatic copier. The quality of reproduction is very high: an effect similar to printing can be obtained and for this reason the masters are often prepared on a high-quality typewriter that provides a variety of type-faces and type sizes, and a justified right-hand margin.

Quite understandably, offset lithography is considered the aristocratic method of duplicating. The main disadvantages of the system are the high cost of the machines and master plates, and the comparatively difficult machine operation and costly machine maintenance.

When preparing offset master plates, the typist should take care, with a manual typewriter, to maintain a firm, even touch—just sufficiently heavy to give a clear impression. With an electric typewriter, the typing pressure control should be at a low setting. *Heavy* typing produces *light* copies. The specially coated plates used for masters are available in a variety of colours, and two or more colours can be combined—but a separate master has to be produced for each colour and each colour requires a separate run through the duplicating machine.

It is important to use the correct type of master for the number of copies needed: the masters have different serial numbers.

Making corrections when typing a master. When making corrections on a master, care must be taken to avoid smudging and damaging the special coating. Ordinary typewriter erasers are not suitable but it is possible to obtain a special 'offset' eraser which is non-abrasive. It is necessary to remove only the surface ink and a light 'lifting' stroke should be used to do this.

As when typing spirit masters or stencils, each master should be very carefully checked. Proof reading at all times is most effective when it is done by two persons—one reading to the other: alternatively, a person other than the typist is often more likely to spot errors.

Special ballpoint pens, pencils, and crayons are obtainable for the production of signatures and lines, but on some masters an ordinary pencil is suitable. Lines are best made with a ruler rather than use of the underscore key.

Omission of words (**ellipsis**). Sometimes words are deliberately omitted in sentences (usually in quotations). If the omission occurs at the beginning or in the middle of a sentence, three spaced full stops are used to indicate this: if at the end of a sentence, four spaced full stops are used, the fourth one indicating the end of the sentence. This is illustrated in the following example.

```
". . . the field of human conflict . . . by so
many . . . ."
```

If the omission occurred *between* sentences, it would be indicated as follows:

```
"After all, what is money? . . . I shall define
money . . . ."
```

Omitting letters, line or phrase. See **Errors, their cause and remedy.**

One finger word drills. See **Drills.**

One hand drills. See **Drills.**

Opaquing liquid. See **Correcting errors.**

Open puctuation. This is the name given to the method of typewriting using a minimum of punctuation. In the case of letters, for instance, employing the open punctuation method means omitting all punctuation marks except in continuous prose—e.g., the body of the letter and a postscript. An examination of the first three letter examples under **Letters,** *Business letters* will clarify this. It will be seen that the only punctuation mark, apart from those in the body of the letter, is a comma between PAISLEY and Scotland. Even this comma could have been omitted, either by typing PAISLEY and Scotland on separate lines or dividing them by two or three character spaces: some form of division here is obviously necessary.

When typing abbreviations, full stops are omitted in open punctuation. This point is fully dealt with and examples of both 'traditional' and 'open punctuation' given under the entry **Abbreviations.**

Punctuation can also be omitted after letters or figures when enumerating sections, sub-paragraphs, and pages. See **Enumerating sections, paragraphs and pages** for a full explanation and examples.

Open punctuation is frequently used in conjunction with the blocked methods of layout and is an extension of the attempt to rationalize and speed up the work of the typist.

Ordinal numbers. See **Cardinal numbers.**

Ornamental typing (see also **Tailpieces**). Except with certain types of work, such as menus, programmes and some notices, elaborate ornamentation should be avoided. However, it is possible to produce both simple and elaborate ornamental borders with a typewriter (see opposite). Some people have an inclination for this type of work, and produce impressive pictures using solely the keys of a typewriter.

Overhauling typewriter. If a typewriter is in frequent use it should be professionally serviced at least two or three times a year. In addition, a typewriter needs to be overhauled periodically: the frequency

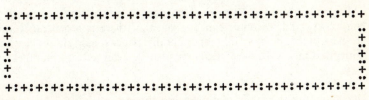

Some suggestions for ornamental borders

will depend upon the amount of use and the care with which the machine is maintained (see **Care of typewriter**). Overhauling is a costly process and the typist should take every step to ensure that it needs to be undertaken as seldom as possible. When the typebars begin 'sticking' at the printing point, i.e., they do not spring back sharply after being struck, this is a sure sign that the typewriter needs overhauling.

Overhauling consists of stripping the machine down and cleaning every part; also oiling all necessary parts. All the mechanisms should be checked and adjusted where necessary and worn parts of the typewriter should be replaced with new ones. With frequent use, the type faces become worn and the impressions made are blurred—not clear and sharp as with a new machine. This can be overcome by having new type faces fitted to the typebars. If the frame of the typewriter has become very scratched, chipped, and worn, it can be treated and resprayed.

If all the above operations are carried out the typewriter, once over-hauled, should be nearly as good as new. The work should, of course, be carried out in the workshop of a professional and reputable typewriter engineer.

Because of the high cost of new typewriters, many people are instead purchasing good, reconditioned machines which have been treated as described above. A competent and reputable firm will guarantee the machine for at least six months.

Overtyping. Typing the correct letter over a faulty one is rightly considered one of the worst errors a typist can make.

In the early stages of learning typing (before an eraser is allowed) a typist often resorts to this method of correcting a mistake. This should be *strictly forbidden* by the teacher and any offender severely chastised: otherwise it may become a habit, proving difficult to eliminate.

In production work of any kind nothing looks more unsightly than overtyping mistakes. The fact that the correct letter is typed over the error is proof that the typist was fully aware of her mistake, but was too lazy to correct it.

In most typewriting examinations, overtyping and -xing out mistakes are penalized more harshly than other kinds of error.

Pagination. See **Literary work.**

Paper bail. See **Parts of a typewriter.**

Paper economy. Paper has become an increasingly expensive commodity and, because of heavy demand, there is a general world shortage of it. Therefore it is important that paper should always be used with the utmost economy. Economy can be achieved in a number of ways.

1. Attention should be paid to the size of paper used in relation to the amount of typescript that must be contained on it.

2. Low-grade paper should be used for drafts and unimportant work.

3. The typist should work with particular care and accuracy when using high quality, expensive paper (such as business letterheadings), stencils, etc., to avoid extravagant 'restarts'.

4. Carbon copies should always be made on the cheaper flimsy paper. When continuation sheets are required, *both sides* of the carbon copy paper should be used: in this case it will be necessary to use a flimsy capable of being read on both sides and yet consistent with the number of carbon copies being taken. Such a practice economizes not only on expense but also on storage space for filing.

If the above points are observed, the annual saving to firms, both large and small, can be considerable.

Paper for typewriting. British stationers carry stocks of many sizes and shapes of paper, although on the Continent a standard and rational system of paper sizes, originally drawn up by the Deutsche Industrie Normen (DIN) has been established for many years. The International Paper Sizes system is based on three standard sheet sizes— designated A, B, and C and these can be subdivided to provide sheets of commonly-required dimensions: printings and writings from size A, posters and some envelopes from size B and envelopes from size C.

The British Standards Institution (BSI), in co-operation with the International Standards Organization (ISO), has recommended introduction of the A, B, and C sizes in this country and the transition is virtually complete. Most firms, large and small, have adopted International Paper Sizes (IPS) for the whole of their stationery requirements. In addition, most typewriting examining bodies now require candidates to use A sizes of paper.

International Paper Sizes are based on a perfectly proportioned rectangle of which the longer side is the diagonal of a square. Following this formula, one can continue to halve the longer side or double the shorter one and still retain the same proportions—a clear aid to economy in design costs. The basic sheet of the A series also has the advantage that it has an area of one square metre, thus facilitating calculations of the weight of the paper in grammes per square metre.

Thus the basis of the A sizes is a rectangle which retains the proportions of the original each time it is halved. AO, which is the largest size, has an area of one square metre; A1 is half this size; A2 half the size of A1, and so on. The higher the figure which follows the A, therefore, the smaller the paper. A4, which measures 210 mm × 297 mm, is becoming the most widely used paper size for it is replacing both quarto (10 × 8 in.) and foolscap (13 × 8 in.). A5, which is 148 × 210 mm (i.e., half the size of A4), is the smallest paper size in general use and is replacing octavo (8 × 5 in.) and sixmo (8 × 6½ in.). Some firms, however, which find A4 too large for many of their requirements, and A5 too small, are using in addition a size of paper which is two-thirds the size of A4: folded singly, this fits exactly into a DL envelope. In the interests of economy, many of these firms have their compliments slips, etc., printed on the remaining one-third of the A4 paper. This is illustrated on p. 189.

Thus, an easily-understood numerical code is replacing mysterious terms such as quarto, foolscap, octavo, and sixmo.

The IPS details for the B and C series are given below.

B & C SERIES
trimmed sizes

		millimetres	equivalent to nearest $\frac{1}{8}$ inch
BO	....	1000 × 1414	$39\frac{3}{8} × 55\frac{5}{8}$
B1	....	707 × 1000	$27\frac{7}{8} × 39\frac{3}{8}$
B2	....	500 × 707	$19\frac{5}{8} × 27\frac{7}{8}$
B3	....	353 × 500	$12\frac{7}{8} × 19\frac{5}{8}$
B4	....	250 × 353	$9\frac{7}{8} × 12\frac{7}{8}$
B5	....	176 × 250	$7 × 9\frac{7}{8}$
CO	....	917 × 1297	$36\frac{1}{8} × 51$
C1	....	648 × 917	$25\frac{1}{2} × 36\frac{1}{8}$
C2	....	458 × 648	$18 × 25\frac{1}{2}$
C3	....	324 × 458	$12\frac{3}{4} × 18$
C4	....	229 × 324	$9 × 12\frac{3}{4}$
C5	....	162 × 229	$6\frac{3}{8} × 9$
C6	....	114 × 162	$4\frac{1}{2} × 6\frac{3}{8}$
C7	....	81 × 114	$3\frac{1}{4} × 4\frac{1}{2}$
C8	....	57 × 81	$2\frac{1}{4} × 3\frac{1}{4}$

As already mentioned, A4 and A5 are the two sizes of paper now in most common use. The following table gives the number of spaces across a page of A4 and A5 in both elite and pica pitch; also the number of lines to the page.

	A4	A5 (shorter dimension at top)	A5 (longer dimension at top)
Spaces across the page			
Elite (12 to the inch)	100	70	100
Pica (10 to the inch)	82	59	82
Lines down the page			
Elite and Pica (both 6 to the inch)	70	50	35

841 mm	
	Sizes
	A1 594 × 841 mm
	A2 420 × 594 mm
	A3 297 × 420 mm
A1	A4 210 × 297 mm
	A5 148 × 210 mm
	or
	210 × 148 mm
	A6 105 × 148 mm
	A7 74 × 105 mm

594 mm

420 mm   420 mm

A3

297 mm

210 mm   210 mm

148 mm   A5

297 mm   A4

594 mm

A2

105 mm   105 mm

74 mm   A7

148 mm   A6

Diagram showing the symmetrical division of AO paper

Paper for typewriting

Some uses of the main sizes of paper

Brief (13 × 16 in.)	Barristers' briefs and other legal documents; certain financial statements and other documents requiring a large size of paper.
Draft (10 × 16 in.)	Certain legal documents and legal accounts; other documents requiring a large size of paper.
A4	Business letters, long memos, agendas, minutes of meetings, tabulated statements, literary work, reports, specifications, bills of quantities, tenders, long invoices, etc.
A5	Memos, debit and credit notes, short invoices (all used with the longer dimension at the top), short letters, single actors' parts for small parts in plays, short notices, etc.
A6	Postcards, index cards, receipts.
A7	Compliment slips, business cards, index cards, labels, and dockets.

Paper quantities

1 quire = 25 sheets (formerly 24)
1 ream = 20 quires (i.e. 480 or 500 sheets)

Qualities of typewriting paper. Typewriting paper is available in a variety of qualities and weights, the two most commonly used being known as bond and bank. Bond papers are of better quality and greater weight than bank papers, although each type is available in various qualities and weights.

Bond papers (which are bright white in colour) are used, in the main, for original documents and high-quality work. The quality of bond is such that erasures can be made without obvious damage to the paper. The expert typist will know that there is a 'right' side (for typing on) and a 'wrong' side to the paper. A close scrutiny of bond paper will reveal a difference in the surfaces of the two sides, the side for typing on being smoother than the reverse side. Most bond papers are watermarked and this can be seen by holding the paper up to the light. The paper should be inserted into the typewriter so that the watermark can be 'read', in the same way as a letterheading.

Bank papers are cheaper and lighter in substance and should be used for unimportant work, drafts, and carbon copies. It is difficult to make good erasures on bank papers since the surface of the paper rubs away as soon as an eraser is applied.

The lighter-weight bank papers are known as 'flimsies' and should be used for taking carbon copies: the weight of the flimsy used will depend on the number of carbon copies required (see **Carbon copying**).

GOODFIRM LIMITED
104 London Road,
WINCHESTER, Hants.

Telephone	Telegrams	Telex
01-834-0272	FIRLIM	8340272

GOODFIRM LIMITED
104 London Road,
WINCHESTER, Hants.

Telephone	Telegrams	Telex
01-834-0272	FIRLIM	8340272

With compliments

Example of an A4 sheet being used for both correspondence purposes
(the top two-thirds) and compliments slip

Bank paper is available in a variety of tints, a different tint often being used for each different department in a large organization.

Paper grips. See **Parts of a typewriter.**

Paper guide. See **Parts of a typewriter.**

Paper handling drills. See **Drills.**

Paper injector/ejector. See **Parts of a typewriter.**

Paper rest. See **Parts of a typewriter.**

Paragraph headings. See **Headings.**

Paragraphs. There are three types of paragraph: blocked, indented, and hanging. An example of each one follows.

Blocked paragraphs
This is the simplest form of paragraph since each new line, including the first, begins at the left-hand margin. It is necessary to turn up twice between blocked paragraphs when double spacing is used, or it will not always be possible to see where a new paragraph begins. This paragraph is typed in the blocked style and is preceded by a shoulder heading.

Indented paragraphs
The first word of each indented paragraph begins five or six spaces from the left-hand margin. A tab stop should be set for this purpose to save time and avoid unnecessary tapping of the space bar. This paragraph is shown in the indented style and is preceded by a shoulder heading.

Hanging paragraphs
In hanging paragraphs the first line 'overhangs' to the left the second and following lines of the paragraph by two or three spaces (consistency is essential). Since most of the lines will be typed beginning two or three spaces to the right of the first line, the left-hand margin should be set at this point to save time. The margin release key and backspacer should be used for typing the first line of each new paragraph. This type of paragraph is less frequently used than the first two, described above, and is used mainly for sub-paragraphs. It has the effect of throwing into prominence the first word and this point can be used to good effect in the composition of sub-paragraphs. This paragraph is typed in the hanging style and is preceded by a shoulder heading.

Parts of a typewriter and their uses. (See also **Electric typewriters** for the main differences between electric and manual machines, both in construction and required operation techniques). The different parts of a typewriter vary to some extent between different manufacturers: also, some of the parts are known by different names. The instruction booklet supplied with the typewriter should be consulted on doubtful points.

An alphabetical list and description of the main parts (and their uses) of a typewriter follow.

Alignment scale. (see *Line indicators.*)

Backspace key. Each time this key is fully depressed, it moves the carriage back one character space. Used mainly for:

(a) underscoring single words
(b) typing certain combination characters
(c) retyping a lightly-struck key
(d) in conjunction with the tabulator bar/key in column work
(e) half-space correcting.

Bell, warning. (See separate entry **Bell, warning.**)

Card guide. The metal attachment situated above the printing point close to the front of the platen. Together with the paper grips, it helps to hold firm cards, labels, thick envelopes, etc., for typing.

Carriage. The whole of the top part of a typewriter which moves from right to left the width of a character each time a key or the space bar is struck. Carriages are available in different lengths and on most office models are easily interchangeable.

Carriage release levers. These two levers (one situated at each end of the carriage) are operated by the appropriate thumb while the rest of the hand clutches the platen knob to secure good control of the movement of the carriage. They enable the carriage to be moved quickly from one position to another independent of the escapement (the mechanism which allows the carriage to move one space from right to left each time a key or the space bar is struck).

Carriage return lever. This lever is situated on the left-hand side of the carriage and should be used to move the carriage when a new line is required. The depth the carriage moves will depend upon the setting of the line-space selector.

The carriage return lever should be struck firmly and sharply with the index finger of the left hand. The hand should be kept flat, palm down. The carriage should be 'thrown' back with just enough force to ensure that it reaches the left-hand margin stop. If this throw is skilful, the typist will be able to return her left hand to the keyboard during the latter part of the movement of the carriage and will be able to perform the movement without the aid of sight. In no circumstances should the carriage return lever be grasped by the thumb and fingers, thus causing the carriage to be drawn back instead of 'thrown' back.

Cylinder. (See *Platen*).

Drawband. This band, which draws the carriage along, is attached at one end to the mainspring (an adjustable coiled spring which provides the motive power to move the carriage) and at the other end to the carriage.

Escapement. See *Mainspring and escapement*.

Feed rollers. These are small rubber rollers that are situated beneath the platen. When the platen release lever is in its normal position for typing, they grip the paper and hold it firm. Moving the paper release lever forward releases the pressure on the feed rollers so the paper can be freely moved.

Interliner. This lever is usually situated on the left-hand side of the carriage. When pulled forward, it temporarily releases the platen from the line-space ratchet so that the platen may be moved smoothly to any required point: when the lever is re-engaged, the platen returns to the original typing line position. The interliner is sometimes used when typing superior and inferior characters and certain combination characters; also when typing on lines.

Keyboard. This consists of four rows of keys with the space bar at the bottom. The bottom three rows contain all the alphabetical letters (with some other characters) and the top row (lower case) contains all the figures. Most typewriters have a special key on the top row for the figure **one**, but if this is not provided, lower case **l** must be used instead, also, if there is no special key for zero, capital **O** must be used.

Last line indicator. See **End of paper.**

Line indicators. These are located at the right and left of the ribbon at the printing point. The top edge of the ribbon approximately lines up with the top edges of the line indicators which are a series of vertical marks. As one types, it will be seen that the upper tips of the vertical lines correspond to the base of the typewritten characters. With the assistance of the paper release lever and the variable line spacer, these lines are used to position the paper correctly after erasing so that the correct letters will line up with the typing line. It will usually be found that each vertical mark on the line indicators is positioned in the middle of each letter (**O** is a useful one to take as a guide). However, typewriters vary slightly and the typist should become familiar with her machine before making corrections after erasing.

The line indicators are often known as the alignment scale.

Line space selector. This mechanism controls the depth of spacing between the typewritten lines. It may be set for single, double, or treble spacing and most modern typewriters provide for half spacing ($1\frac{1}{2}$, $2\frac{1}{2}$) as well. It should be noted that when the line space selector is set at single spacing (1) there is no space between the lines of typewritten work: when it is set at double spacing (2), one line of space is left between the typing, and so on. There are six line spaces to the inch for both pica and elite type.

Mainspring and escapement. An adjustable coiled spring (the mainspring) provides the power that moves the carriage. The movement of the carriage is governed by the escapement so that the carriage moves forward one space each time a key is struck. The escapement consists of a toothed wheel which is engaged by two 'spacing dogs'. When a key is struck, one of these dogs releases the escapement wheel and the other is engaged in the escapement wheel to stop it after the key has been struck.

Margin stops. These are used to fix the points where the typewriting begins and ends on each line. A warning bell rings (see **Bell, warning**) a few spaces before the carriage reaches the point where the right-hand margin stop is set, where the carriage locks. To type beyond this point, the typist should use the margin release key. Also, if she wishes to type in the left-hand margin (to type numbers, etc.) she will need to press the margin release key at the same time as moving the carriage to the right by use of the carriage release lever.

Paper bail. This is the movable, swivelled metal bar that extends across the front of the platen. The paper bail is marked with a paper scale: each short vertical mark represents one movement of the carriage. There are longer vertical marks at every fifth position and numbers are shown for **0, 10, 20, 30, 40,** etc. It will be seen that the horizontal scale at the back of the carriage (where the margin stops are situated on some machines), is identical to the paper bail scale and any other paper scales on the typewriter.

The paper bail is fitted with paper grips (the number depending on the length of the carriage) which help hold the paper firm against the platen.

Paper grips. These are movable rubber rollers fitted to the paper bail. They hold the paper firmly against the platen and should be adjusted to the required position before typing.

Paper guide. The adjustable, right-angled metal plate situated on the left-hand side of the paper shelf, against which the left-hand edge of the paper should be positioned as it is inserted into the typewriter. This guide should normally be set at zero on the scale. It enables successive sheets of paper to be fed into the typewriter at exactly the same point so that the margin and tab stops, once set for a piece of work, do not need to be re-adjusted with the insertion of each sheet of paper.

Paper injector/ejector. Where provided, this is a lever situated on the right-hand side of the carriage for the rapid insertion and removal of paper from the typewriter.

Paper release lever. When moved forwards, this lever moves the feed rollers away from the platen so the paper in the typewriter can be freely moved if inserted crookedly, etc. The paper release lever should be used when removing paper from the typewriter (if there is no paper ejector) or if the paper is re-inserted into the machine for the correction of errors.

Paper rest. The support behind the platen, on which the paper rests as it is fed into the typewriter. Sometimes called the paper table.

Platen. This is the roller that runs almost the entire length of the carriage and around which the paper is curved and held in position by the feed rollers for typing. When the platen becomes worn and pitted, it should be replaced if the typewriter is to continue producing good-quality work. During typing, the type bars rise and strike against the platen. If typing on a single sheet of paper or using very thin paper taking only one carbon copy, a backing sheet should be used to help protect the platen and prolong its life.

Platens are available either hard or medium. A hard platen should be used if a large number of carbon copies is being taken. A medium platen is best for stencil cutting and general typewriting work.

Platen turning knobs. These two knobs (situated at each end of the platen) are turned to move the paper into the required position. With most typewriters, it will be noticed that when either of these knobs is turned slowly, there is a regular clicking sound: each 'click' indicates a *half-space* movement of the platen. This device is often used when typing superior or inferior characters, some combination characters, etc.

Printing point. The point to which all the type bars rise so that the appropriate typeface strikes the paper and prints the required character.

Ribbon and ribbon guide. (See also **Ribbons for typewriters.**) The inking medium which often consists of a length of ribbon about half an inch wide, wound on two spools. The ribbon travels from one spool to the other, reversing (usually automatically) when the end is reached. It is held in position for typing by the ribbon guide, round which it is threaded: this is situated just in front of the platen.

Ribbon position indicator. This usually has a colour code. When set at blue, the top half of the ribbon is used and when set at red, the bottom half of the ribbon comes into operation. If set at the white marker, the ribbon is disengaged so that the type comes into direct contact with the paper. The ribbon should be disengaged for stencil cutting.

Scales. The various scales that run nearly the full length of the platen (see *Paper bail*) are provided to assist the typist with typewriting display work.

Shift keys and shift lock. These are two keys, one situated at the lower right-hand side of the keyboard, the other opposite on the left-hand side.

Each type bar has two faces. When typing without using a shift key or the shift lock, the lower case face is printed, but use of the shift mechanism brings the upper case character into operation. In the case of letter keys, for example, the shift key enables a capital letter to be typed. With keys other than letters, the upper case character is shown above the lower case one on the key face.

The shift key should be depressed by the little finger of the hand not required for typing the letter, etc. The shift key should be held down firmly with the full weight of the hand supporting the little finger. Care must be taken to synchronize depression of the shift key and the required character, otherwise the upper case character will not appear in alignment with the typing line. A skilled operator can type upper case characters with scarcely any loss of time due to shift-key operation.

If a whole word, heading, sentence, etc., is required in capital letters, the typist should depress the shift lock, which 'locks' the typewriter mechanism permanently in the upper case position until released by pressing either of the shift keys.

Space bar. This is the long bar at the front of a typewriter that extends nearly the full length of the keyboard. The carriage moves forward one blank space each time it is depressed—which should always be with the right-hand thumb, except for some left-handed people who find use of the left-hand thumb easier.

Tabulator. Most typewriters have the following.

(a) A tab-set key for fixing the required tab stops (usually indicated by a plus sign on the key).

(b) A tab-clear key to clear a previously-set tab position (usually indicated by a minus sign on the key). The carriage must be moved to the tab position before it can be cleared.

(c) A lever which will clear all set tab stops by a single depression.

(d) A tab bar or key which, while depressed, moves the carriage quickly, independently of the escapement, to each tab position in the order set.

The tabulator should always be used at the beginning of the first line of each indented paragraph, to prevent unnecessary tapping of the space bar. In addition, of course, it should be used in all column work. When starting a new piece of work, the typist should remember to clear all tab stops before setting the required ones.

Some typewriters have decimal tabulators: they work on the same principle but there are five or six tab keys instead of the usual one (for units, tens, hundreds, etc.).

Touch control adjuster. This is provided on many typewriters so that the typist can adjust her machine to her personal touch pressure.

Type basket. This is situated below the printing point and contains all the type bars, at the end of which the metal typefaces are fixed. Each typeface contains two different characters, one for lower case typing, the other for use in conjunction with the shift key or shift lock. When a key is struck, the appropriate type bar rises to the printing point and prints the required character on the paper through the typewriter ribbon.

Transparent paper holders. These are two pieces of transparent plastic (which can usually be pulled forward for cleaning) and are situated to the right and left of the printing point. They have a number of uses:

(a) At their base are situated the line indicators (see *Line indicators*).

(b) They help hold secure small paper, cards, or envelopes, for typing.

(c) Ruling with a ball-point pen or stylus (for stencils) can be carried out speedily and efficiently by using the small hole(s) provided. Vertical lines can be ruled by inserting the point of the pen, etc., into the hole, pulling the interliner forward and then rotating the platen the required distance. For horizontal ruling, use the carriage release lever to move the carriage for obtaining the required line(s).

Variable line spacer. This is situated at the end of the left platen turning knob and often takes the form of a convex knob. When depressed (or in some cases pulled out), the line-space ratchet is released so the platen may be smoothly moved to any required position. Unlike the interliner, the paper does *not* return to its original typing line position when the variable line spacer is released.

The variable line spacer is used for the following purposes.

(a) When typing on ruled or dotted lines.

(b) When filling in form letters.

(c) When typing the second of double lines under a figure total.

(d) When typing superior or inferior characters—although the half spacer or interliner is preferable here because of the ease with which the original typing line can be re-established.

(e) To help find the original typing line when making a correction after erasing.

Per cent sign. See **Combination characters and special signs.**

Personal letters. See **Letters.**

Photocopying (See also **Reprography processes**). The term 'photocopier' is often applied to all copying machines whether or not the principle involved is based on a negative and positive process. Many different types of copying machines are on the market (some needing special fluid and many requiring special paper) and with all of them it is possible to make copies from a typewritten original.

The now widespread commercial use of copying machines has led to the virtual disappearance in most offices of the pure copy typist. A copier produces an *identical* copy or copies of an original whereas a copy typist is likely to make mistakes—which may not be detected even by expensive proof reading methods. In addition, a copier can produce better copies much more quickly and cheaply than a copy typist.

Copying machines will generally produce from three to ten copies more economically and quickly than any of the duplicating methods. For one or two copies only, carbon or NCR paper is widely used. When deciding on the method to be used when more than about ten copies are required, one should consider, in addition to cost, various other factors involved—such as the purpose for which the copies are required and the speed with which they are needed.

The quality of the copies produced on a copying machine from a typewritten original will depend mainly on the quality of the original. The type impressions should be even and dense in appearance, on good quality paper.

Phototypesetting. See **Special purpose typewriters.**

Phrase drills. See **Drills.**

Pica. See **Pitch.**

Pin point type. See **Cheques.**

Pitch. This term refers to the spacing on the typewriter, i.e., the space occupied by each individual letter or character. The two most common pitches are pica (10 characters to each inch) and elite (12 characters to each inch). See also **Proportional spacing** and **Typeface styles.**

Platen. See **Parts of a typewriter.**

Platen restorer. Unless precautions are taken, the platen of a typewriter will soon become badly pitted—which will lead to poor-quality, uneven typing (see **Backing sheets**). It is possible to purchase a 'platen restorer', which can also be used on other machines that use a platen—such as teleprinters and accounting machines.

The platen restorer is supplied in a bottle with a sponge attached to the top. Using the sponge and a sparing amount of restorer, the typist should rub across the worn part of the platen, turning it until the whole surface has been treated. Badly-worn platens may need several applications—unless their condition is such that replacement of the platen is necessary.

Although the use of such a platen restorer can help, the old adage 'prevention is better than cure' is very appropriate in this situation.

Platen turning knobs. See **Parts of a typewriter.**

Plays. Much has been written about how plays should be typed. A close look at the instructions in various typewriting textbooks, however, will show considerable differences and contradictions. It is important to realize that the circulation and use of a play in typescript applies only to plays *before* they have been published.

Once a play is in print, a theatrical company wishing to stage that play will purchase (or borrow from a public lending library, in which case no pen or pencil marks are permitted) as many copies as there are characters in the play. The only occasional exception here is with a *very short part*, in which case the appropriate portions will be photo-copied (with the publisher's permission). In these days of high labour costs, the typing of individual actor's parts is usually uneconomic.

It is more satisfactory for a theatrical company, whether professional or amateur, to purchase the required number of copies of the play for the cast. It is important that each actor gets the feeling of the play *as a whole*—and he can only do this by having the complete play and becoming familiar with it. Each actor can mark up his own part according to his particular preferences and in a way that will be most meaningful and useful to him as an individual. Moreover, it will probably be necessary for the producer to make some alterations to the stage directions, etc. These can easily be marked in when the copies are owned.

Stage producers, for the reasons given, rarely borrow sets of plays from public libraries but they are widely used for play reading in education.

If a play is being typed, prior to publication, the main criterion is that it should be *clearly and pleasingly set out in a consistent style*. If the play is subsequently published it will be printed in the house style of the publisher and the copy will be marked up by the editor accordingly.

Should a typist be asked to type a play, she should follow the instructions of the author with regard to layout and styling. If these are not given she should, in consultation with the author, decide upon her own method after looking at published plays. She will probably be surprised to see the considerable variations in styling from one publisher to another!

Pocket envelopes. See **Envelopes**

Poetry. (See also **Literary work**.) If a single poem is to be typed on a sheet of paper (A5 for short poems, A4 for longer ones) it should be positioned so that it appears centrally on the paper. Single spacing should be used and one or two line spaces left between verses. The title of the poem should be centred over the typing: it can be typed in closed capitals or with initial capitals and underscored. One or two line spaces should be left between the title and the first line of the poem. The poet's name is usually typed at the end of the poem with one or two lines of space between the last line of the poem and the poet's name: it may be (a) preceded by a dash; (b) enclosed in brackets; (c) typed in closed capitals; (d) typed in lower case and underscored. The poet's name is usually typed so that it lines up with the longest line of the poem.

If a poem has a chorus, this begins further to the right than the rest of the poem. A chorus is printed in italics and in typewriting it should be underscored.

When a poem is being quoted, quotation marks should appear only at the beginning and end of the poem.

Poetry is not intended to be read at eye speed but at speech speed. Therefore, whereas prose is presented in lines of a uniform length to assist speed of reading, the condensed language of poetry is presented in shorter lines of irregular length which reduce the speed of reading to the advantage of understanding.

A glance through an anthology of poetry will show that there are no hard and fast rules about capitalization and indentation. However, the way a poem is typed or printed often helps to identify the metre, to relate rhyming lines and to distinguish between verse and chorus. For instance, many poems are typed or printed so that rhyming lines begin at the same point of the scale. Thus when alternate lines rhyme, the second, fourth, sixth lines, etc, are indented two or three spaces from the point at which the first, third, fifth lines, etc. begin. This is illustrated in the following first verse from 'The Soldier' by Rupert Brooke.

If I should die, think only this of me:
    That there's some corner of a foreign field
That is for ever England. There shall be
    In that rich earth a richer dust concealed;
A dust whom England bore, shaped, made aware,
    Gave, once, her flowers to love, her ways to roam,
A body of England's, breathing English air,
    Washed by the rivers, blest by the suns of home.

Where there is no rhyming (as in blank verse) or where successive lines rhyme—as in the following poem 'Silver' by Walter de la Mare—there is no indentation.

SILVER

Slowly, silently, now the moon
Walks the night in her silver shoon;
This way, and that, she peers, and sees
Silver fruit upon silver trees;
One by one the casements catch
Her beams beneath the silvery thatch;
Couched in his kennel, like a log,
With paws of silver sleeps the dog;
From their shadowy cote the white breasts peep
Of doves in a silver-feathered sleep;
A harvest mouse goes scampering by,
With silver claws, and silver eye,
And moveless fish in the water gleam,
By silver reeds in a silver stream.

Walter de la Mare

In the following poem 'The Owl', the relationship between indentation and rhyming will be readily apparent.

THE OWL

When cats run home and light is come,
    And dew is cold upon the ground,
And the far-off stream is dumb,
    And the whirring sail goes round,
    And the whirring sail goes round;
      Alone and warming his five wits,
      The white owl in the belfry sits.

In all the above examples it will be seen that each new line begins with a capital letter. However, in much modern poetry this convention does not apply and a capital letter is often used only where normal punctuation would demand it. Also, many modern poets prefer no indentation even where there is rhyming, and all lines begin at the same point of the scale.

If a line of a poem is considerably longer than the normal line, in order to maintain balance it is often 'hooked in', i.e., some of the words are carried to the succeeding or preceding line after a bracket sign. Also, in order to maintain a symmetrical appearance, discretion should be used if some lines are very uneven in length: in addition to 'hooking in' long lines, very short lines should start further to the right than the other lines or be centred to the width of the poem.

When typing poetry, the typist should follow the preferences of the author or the copy from which she is typing.

Portable typewriters. It is estimated that the sale of portable typewriters is greater than that of standard office machines. Therefore it is hardly surprising that typewriter manufacturers offer a wide range of attractive portable models ranging from a small, lightweight model to machines (both manual and electric) that are solidly constructed and incorporate many features of the standard office typewriter (13 in. carriage, choice of typestyles, full tabulation facilities, etc.).

All portable typewriters are designed to fit into a carrying case with a handle and most have a carriage locking device, so there is no movement of the carriage when being carried around.

Portable typewriters are a boon to professional people who need both to travel and type. In addition, they are used extensively in the home, because their storage and portability raise no problems.

The British Standards Institution, in its investigations on an international basis for typewriter keyboards, recommended a 32-key triple-shift keyboard for a portable typewriter.

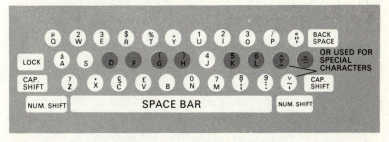

The British Standards Institution suggested keyboard arrangement

It will be seen that this keyboard has three banks of keys instead of the standard four: such an arrangement would obviously assist in making the typewriter lighter without any loss of general quality and sturdiness. Use of the Roman alphabet would suit many languages of world importance without favouring one language more than another.

Postcards. Postcards are used for business and personal correspondence when the communication is short and not private in content. IPS (International Paper Size) postcards are A6 (148 × 105 mm). Two other sizes still used are 157 × 99 mm (5½ × 3½ in.) and 128 × 99 mm (4½ × 3½ in.): the latter, however, are usually thick and more suitable for handwriting invitations, etc., rather than for typewriting.

Business firms usually have their address, etc., printed at the top of postcards, but if this information has to be typed, the following is a good practice. Begin typing the address on the fourth line from the top of the card, starting at the left-hand margin and using one or two lines only (single spacing if two lines are used): then turn up half a space and type a line right across the card from margin to margin.

Postcards do not require an inside address, salutation or complimentary close. The date and reference (if there is one) are best typed immediately under the sender's address (leaving one line space after the sender's address or the line referred to above), both beginning at the left-hand margin in single spacing. One line space should then be left before beginning the message which should be typed in single spacing with a line space between paragraphs, which may be blocked or indented. The margins used will vary according to the length of the message but are seldom more than 25 mm (1 in.).

On some modern typewriters there are card clips near the ribbon vibrator to help keep cards firm for typing. Nevertheless, a medium weight of card is recommended because it is difficult to ensure a straight line of typing or uniform space between lines if thick cards are used, since thick cards do not easily curve round the platen. If you have to type near the bottom of the card, use a backing sheet, as this will help ensure that the typewriter grips the card and prevents the bottom line(s) from 'running off' crookedly.

The same rules as for envelope typing apply when typing the name and address on the reverse side of the communication—which *must* be reserved exclusively for the address and postage stamps (see **Envelopes**).

For rapid typing of large quantities of postcards or other cards see under **Envelopes** (*Rapid envelope and card typing*).

Posture and position at typewriter. It is important that the typist should always sit in a comfortable position at her typewriter, completely relaxed with no trace of stiffness or tension. Such a position will help avoid fatigue—often the cause of errors and low-speed production of work.

In addition, during the early learning stages, unless the posture and position of the typist remain fairly constant, the task of mastering the keyboard is made more difficult because the spatial effect of the key reaches will vary.

The following points should be observed.

1. The front of the typewriter should be parallel to the front edge of the desk, not protruding beyond it, nor pushed back so that there is a space between the front of the typewriter and the edge of the desk.

2. The height of the typist's chair should be such that when she is seated with her back well supported by the curved back of the chair, both feet can rest comfortably on the floor—preferably with one foot slightly in front of the other, to help give balance. The legs should never be crossed or 'wound' round the chair. Purpose-designed, height-adjustable typewriter chairs are therefore necessary: the seats should be upholstered with softly-rounded fronts. (See **Chair, Typewriting.**)

3. The relative height of the typewriter and chair should enable the forearms to be at the same slope as the keyboard.

4. The typist's chair should be at a distance from her typewriter so that she can adopt the correct slope of the forearms without having either to stretch the upper arms forward or to crouch. Unless the correct relative position and height of the chair and typewriter are maintained, the typist will experience fatigue and develop various aches and pains. Many typists tend to sit too low at their machines so that they have to lift the upper arms as well as the forearms when typing. This causes unnecessary strain on the muscles.

5. The wrists should not be 'humped' but should be kept down—yet not so low that they rest on the typewriter frame. When typing, there should be a minimum of wrist and arm movement: the movement should be restricted as much as possible to the *fingers*.

6. The trunk should be relaxed with a very slight forward lean. The arms should hang in a relaxed manner with the elbows *slightly* out from the sides: this enables the fingers to assume (without any straining of muscles) the same lateral position as the keys when the finger tips are positioned above the home keys.

7. When copy-typing, the copy (see also **Copyholders**) is usually to the *right* of the typewriter, well lit and in a sloping position—to help avoid eye strain and consequent headaches with possible damage to the health. When the copy is on the right-hand side, it is on the opposite side (with manual typewriters) to the carriage-return lever: this prevents the hand sweeping between the eyes and the copy each time

the carriage is returned—which tends to make the typist lose her place in the copy.

If the habit of *always* positioning the copy on the right is developed and maintained the typist can, when necessary, more easily adjust from a manual to an electric typewriter and vice versa. The typist who habitually uses an electric model *may*, occasionally, have to use a manual machine.

Although the foregoing points should, in general, be observed, slight shifts of position are, of course, necessary if one types for prolonged periods.

Prefix and suffix drills. See **Drills.**

Pressure-sensitive letters. See **Correcting errors.**

Printing point. See **Parts of a typewriter.**

Production typing. This is the term used to distinguish realistic 'business' typewriting tasks that involve display, intelligence, and decision making on the part of the typist, from straightforward copying/speed typewriting (see **Speed/accuracy tests**).

Many typists are obsessed with their 'speed' but since this is invariably based on straightforward copying work it bears little relation to the speed of work in an office where varied business typewriting tasks are required of the typist. Such tasks, of course, include the typing of letters (often complicated ones with subject headings and inset tabular matter), financial statements and reports, etc., from manuscript —often with necessary rearrangement of the material.

An employer is naturally concerned with the *production speed* of his typists and secretaries but this is difficult to measure because of the variety and differing degrees of complexity of the work involved.

Typing 'production' tasks at maximum speed with quality production requires the following:

1. Orderly habits of work with the different sizes and types of paper and other working requirements efficiently arranged so they are immediately accessible. Materials should be laid out so they can be used with a minimum of arm and body movement. The working area should be kept clear of personal belongings and everything except materials pertaining to the job in hand.

2. Using correct typewriting techniques—'touch' typing, good posture and position at the typewriter, correct and rapid return of the carriage (with manual machines), and so on. All such points are important to the expert typist if she is to work at maximum speed and efficiency with a minimum of fatigue. Well-taught students will have developed these good habits from early on in their training.

3. A feeling for the artistic and pleasing display of work and the ability to make rapid decisions about margins, division of words, line spacing, and the best size of paper for a particular task. If the task involves complicated display of tabular matter, the typist should be completely familiar with a reliable system of calculation which she can put into effect quickly. (See **Display.**)

4. The typist should *understand* what she is typing. Therefore the work should be quickly read through before typing starts to ensure that everything is clear and makes sense. Corrections, position of 'ballooned' portions, and specific instructions should be clearly marked on the copy so they will not be overlooked during the typing.

5. A sound knowledge of typewriting 'theory' and good, highly-regarded typewriting usage.

Many typewriting students display a sense of urgency about speed/ accuracy tests but lapse into desultory habits when on production work. To help overcome this tendency the teacher should set a target production time for each piece of work: if the class is divided into groups this time should, as a rule, vary according to the ability of the group.

Candidates cannot pass worthwhile public examinations in typewriting unless they can tackle production work with speed and accuracy. Therefore attention to all the points mentioned is important, particularly for advanced level examinations.

Programmes. The successful typing of programmes of any kind demands skilful application of the rules for display work (see **Display**). Programmes may be of a varied nature—for conferences, musical events, athletics and sports meetings, social events, etc.—and because their nature *is* so varied, the typing of any one programme will call for a keen sense of artistic display on the part of the typist. Programmes are usually typed for mass reproduction so it is worth while ensuring that the finer points of typewriting detail are observed. Some general points to bear in mind follow.

1. If one sheet of unfolded paper is used, margins at the right and left should be equal, and there should be equal space at the top and bottom of the paper. See **Centring—horizontal and vertical**.

2. A4 paper is usually used but if the programme is a very short one, A5 size can be used.

3. Unless the blocked method is being used, a heading should be centred and if it consists of more than one line, each line should be carefully centred with the others. See **Headings.**

4. Long lines in a heading can be divided but care should be taken to ensure that division occurs in suitable places. For example, WELCOME YOU TO A CHEESE AND WINE PARTY could be divided as WELCOME YOU / TO A / CHEESE AND WINE PARTY, but

WELCOME YOU / TO A CHEESE / AND WINE PARTY would
be poor division.

5. Prominence should be given to the important aspects in the heading
by skilful use of the various heading devices—spaced capitals, closed
capitals, initial capitals, underscoring, etc.

6. If the programme is of a suitable type (e.g., a musical programme
or listing the characters and cast of a play), a neat appearance is obtained
if the right-hand margin is kept exactly even. This will involve backspacing from the right-hand margin position for the last item on each
line.

7. Leader dots should be used if there is a wide gap between columns,
to help direct the eye from one item to the next one on the same line
(see **Leader dots**).

8. In typing programmes there are no hard and fast rules about layout, capitalization, underlining, etc., but consistency is essential in any
one programme. For example, the items in a musical concert may or
may not be numbered according to preference: the type of work (violin
solo, song, duet, etc.) could be typed in closed capitals or in lower case
with initial capitals, beginning at the left-hand margin: the name of the
piece and the artist could be typed in the centre of the page (each on a
separate line) and the name of the composer typed last, finishing flush
with the right-hand margin. Alternatively, the composer could be typed
in the centre beneath the title of the piece and the name of the performer
typed last, finishing flush with the right-hand margin. Capitalization
and underlining can be used to advantage—and their use varied from
one programme to another—but consistency must be observed within
a single programme.

9. Programmes lend themselves to the successful use of ornamentation
—ornamental borders, tailpieces, etc. (see **Ornamental typing** and
Tailpieces).

10. A typed programme often has a more professional appearance if
the paper is folded and the matter presented on the four resulting 'pages'.
If this method is used, extra care will have to be used in displaying the
matter so that it fits tastefully on to the different pages. The margins
on the two pages in the middle (pages 2 and 3) should be arranged so
that there is equal space on the extreme left and right and equal space
either side of the central crease: a pleasing appearance is obtained if
these four margins are equal. The following diagrams will help make
clear the arrangement of the programme if the paper is to be folded.

FRONT SIDE OF PAPER

Fold

Back page Left hand	Front page Right hand

REVERSE SIDE OF PAPER

Page 2 Left hand	Page 3 Right hand

It will assist the typist if she makes a light pencil mark in the centre of the page where the fold is to be.

11. Sometimes a typist will be called upon to display a programme for printing. However, if a programme is typed for duplication by the spirit or ink method, great care should be taken to ensure that the master is correctly positioned on the drum: otherwise the careful efforts made to place the matter artistically on the master will be largely wasted.

Proof reading (see also **Correcting errors**). Proof reading or checking for errors is an essential part of every typist's job and in typewriting instruction students should be compelled *from the very first lesson* to proof read their own work. They will be developing a good habit and will become error conscious (although the teacher should take care that they do not produce 'correct' work at the expense of sacrificing correct *techniques* of work).

In all production work, careful proof reading is necessary to ensure that the work is accurate and mailable. The proof reader should develop the habit of reading *word for word* as opposed to 'skimming'—since our eyes have a way of passing over the lines of typescript and seeing what we *think* should be there and not what we have actually typed. Particular attention should be paid to points that will not be readily apparent in the typescript alone, such as dates, figures, addresses, and proper nouns: also complete sentences can be omitted (particularly if there are two sentences in juxtaposition, each beginning with the same word). Finished work should, of course, always be checked against the original or shorthand notes.

A completed sheet of typescript should always be proof read before it is removed from the typewriter since corrections are so much easier to make when the paper is still in the machine.

Many typists find proof reading an irksome chore because they look upon it as a non-productive operation: they are often anxious just to 'get on with the next job'. Unmailable work, however, is of no value.

When checking important work (such as printers' proofs) extra care must be taken since undetected errors can prove particularly costly and time-wasting. A fast and reliable method here is for one person to read the proof copy aloud whilst a second person checks this against the original. See also **Literary work** (*Proof reading*).

Proportional spacing. On most typewriters the space occupied by each letter or character is the same, the two most common 'pitches' being pica (**10** characters to the inch) and elite (**12** characters to the inch). However some modern typewriters have proportional spacing which means that the space occupied by the letter, symbol or figure varies to suit its size and shape.

Proportional spacing is achieved by a special escapement which provides a certain number of units to the inch. Every character occupies the number of basic units (each unit being $\frac{1}{32}$ in. or 0.8 mm) appropriate to its width and shape. For instance, the letter **i**, being a narrow character, needs less than half the space required by the letter **m**. All characters have varying unit values according to their size and shape, and the movement of the carriage is proportional to the needs of the letter or character typed. The various typewriter manufacturers use different unit systems. The IBM Executive and the Singer-Friden Justowriter work on a 5-unit system (the narrowist character, **i**, having 2 units; the widest, **m**, having 5 units). The VariTyper and the Hermes Ambassador work on a 4-unit system. However, the IBM Selectric Composer (see **Special purpose typewriters**) uses a 9-unit system: the type fonts (golf balls) each carry 88 characters which vary in width from 3–9 units.

Some typewriters with proportional spacing have two space bars— one giving a movement of two units and the other three units. The backspace key moves the carriage back one unit at a time. Proportional spacing typewriters can be used to produce a justified right-hand margin (every line ending at the same point on the scale) to give a neat finish to the work (see **Justified right-hand margin**). These typewriters produce typewritten work with a pleasing appearance since proportional spacing follows a basic principle of letterpress printing. However, they can present problems to the typist.

The setting out of tabular matter on a typewriter with proportional spacing needs special care since an ordinary letter and space count for display purposes is obviously not sufficient since each character has its own space value. Corrections can likewise cause difficulty unless the error is detected and corrected immediately it is made. For instance, if the typist wanted to correct a letter with a 5-unit value to one of a 2-unit value, an ugly gap would be visible after the correction was made: a converse correction would give a crowded appearance.

Punctuation marks. A competent typist/secretary should have a sound knowledge of punctuation. She should be familiar with all the punctuation marks and their good usage (see also **Combination characters and special signs**; also **Abbreviations** and **Open punctuation**). If she takes dictation in shorthand her employer will normally expect to be able to leave all punctuation to her. However, he may dictate certain stylistic marks which express fine shades of meaning (such as the semi-colon and colon) if he is fastidious about such matters.

Except in advanced audio work, it is customary for more punctuation marks to be dictated to the audio-typist than to the shorthand-typist. If the dictation is to be transcribed by an unknown typist in a centralized or departmental pool, the dictator will usually include most punctuation marks in his dictation, although commas are seldom given. Most dictators find such a practice irksome and distracting to the flow of their thoughts. When the transcriber is *known* to the dictator he will give punctuation marks according to his knowledge of her English ability and familiarity with his preferences. A first-class audio-typist should always *listen for meaning* and have a sufficiently good command of sentence construction and English in general to be able to punctuate competently. In the ideal audio situation the dictator should need to dictate only punctuation marks that are stylistic (exclamation mark, colon, semi-colon, etc.) or those that cannot be anticipated by the transcriber (such as the start of a new paragraph).

It does not come within the scope of this typewriting work to give full instructions about the good usage of punctuation marks: this is the concern of instruction in the use of the English language. Points mentioned here will be confined mainly to *the way punctuation marks should be typed*, although the hyphen, which many typists find particularly difficult, is given special attention.

Spacing after main punctuation marks. There are a number of methods in common use: the generally acceptable ones follow.

Character spaces after:	(a)	(b)	(c)	(d)	(e)
comma	1	1	1	1	1
semi-colon	1	2	2	1	1
colon	1	2	2	2	2
full stop/question mark/ exclamation mark	2	3	2	2	3

Method (a) is the most widely used, probably because it is the easiest to learn and teach and is the quickest to carry out since it requires the least finger action. Whichever method is adopted, it is important that the typist uses it consistently to give a pleasing and professional appearance to her work. One space after a full stop, or any other punctuation mark having the same force as a full stop (e.g., question mark, exclamation mark), is not considered good practice and is usually penalized in typewriting examinations.

1. *Apostrophe.* This is used to indicate the omission of a letter or to denote possession, and is typed as in the following examples.

209

The girl just couldn't make up her mind about the choice of a career. Eventually the boy's lost hat was discovered in a ditch.

2. *Brackets.* If only one set of brackets is required, the upper case characters are typed, as in the following example.

Section 3 of the Conditions of Sale (see page 10) states that . . . .

Where matter is to be enclosed in brackets within brackets, this should be done by using square brackets for the outer set (see **Combination characters and special signs**).

I feel I should draw your attention to the fact that major legislation [The Employment Protection Act, The Trades Union and Labour Relations Act (TULRA—which replaced the Industrial Relations Act), also the Sex Discrimination Act] is not mentioned although it is important in this particular context.

3. *Colon.* There should be no space between the word and colon that follows it, as in the following example.

This action appears desirable: its implementation, however, will depend upon the decision of the Managing Director.

4. *Dash and hyphen.* Typists often confuse the hyphen and the dash. A *dash* uses the hyphen sign and has a space before and after it: if a dash begins a line it should be typed at the left-hand margin point and followed by one space. An alternative, but less frequently used, method of typing the dash is to use two unspaced hyphens with no space before or after them. Examples of the two methods follow.

My opinion - which has remained consistent - is that . . . .
My opinion--which has remained consistent--is that . . . .

A *hyphen* has no space before or after it and in continuous prose is used as follows.

(a) In some compound nouns, e.g., hot-house, humming-bird. When compound nouns are first used in the language they generally include a hyphen but in time the hyphen is often dropped. A study of good English usage will show that some writers include hyphens in certain compound nouns whereas others do not—and write the word as one without a hyphen or space between the two parts. Therefore, the use of the hyphen in many compound nouns is arbitrary—but the typist should follow the expressed wishes of her employer on this point and make sure she is consistent in the way she types each compound noun, especially within a single piece of work.

(b) In compound adjectives such as: the bright-eyed child, the fully-blocked letter. A typist should understand the difference between the adjectival use of such words and their adverbial use, where no hyphen should be used, e.g., the child was bright eyed; the letter was fully blocked. This is a frequent source of confusion.

(c) When dividing a word at the end of a line of typing (see **Division of words at line ends**).

(d) After certain prefixes (e.g., pre-Victorian, ex-chairman) and particularly where the same letter that ends the prefix begins the following word—as in pre-eminent, co-ordination, co-operative. Note also the difference in meaning between re-lease and release; re-mark and remark; re-press and repress.

5. *Exclamation mark.* This is typed by using the single quotation mark, backspacing once and typing a full stop. An example follows.

Mary won the beauty competition—although she thought she would come last!

6. *Hyphen.* See under *Dash* and *Hyphen.*

7. *Question mark.* This is typed with no space between the question mark and the preceding word, as in the following example.

Why have you locked the garage door?

8. *Quotation marks.*
(a) When only a single word or phrase requires quotation marks either single or double quotation marks may be used, but consistency of style is important. Both the following can be considered 'correct':

By popular request she sang 'The White Cliffs of Dover'.
By popular request she sang "The White Cliffs of Dover".

(b) Single or double quotation marks may be used to enclose a simple quotation within a sentence. Examples follow.

On the staff notice board there appeared the following last Monday morning: 'Flexi-time, which was discussed at the last staff meeting, will be introduced at the beginning of next month'.
On the staff notice board there appeared the following last Monday morning: "Flexi-time, which was discussed at the last staff meeting, will be introduced at the beginning of next month".

(c) Direct speech is indicated by double quotation marks:

Mr Brown asked, "How long will it take to build the bridge?"

(d) When a word or phrase requiring quotation marks occurs within direct speech it is typed as follows.

"What are we going to do about these 'drop-outs' to ensure they become responsible members of our society?" he asked.

(e) When a quotation consists of several paragraphs, double quotation marks are placed at the beginning of each paragraph but at the end only of the final paragraph.

9. *Semi-colon*. No space is left after the word immediately preceding the semi-colon, as in the following example.
"You may believe what you are saying; many, however, would disagree with your opinion."

Qualifications. See **Titles, decorations, qualifications, forms of address, etc.**

Qualities of typewriting paper. See **Paper for typewriting.**

Question mark. See **Punctuation marks.**

Quotation. See **Inset matter** and **Literary work.**

Quotation marks. See **Punctuation marks.**

Radio scripts. Radio scripts are a specialized form of typing and relatively few typists will ever be required to type them. As with most typewriting documents there are some variations in styling and layout.

When the final draft has been approved by the script editor and his colleagues, it is typed on A4 paper or on a duplicating master and the required number of copies are duplicated or copied for the cast and technicians. The pages are normally attached at the top left-hand corner. Soft paper is used for the copies—in order to minimize the rustling of paper as the pages are turned over near sensitive microphones.

A page of a typical radio script follows, and a list of points to note is given at the end.

–1–

```
                THE GOLDEN CHAIN by Gale Pedrick

 1. ANNOUNCER:  In Paris – the Paris of 1884 – it
                has been a day of misty sunshine.
                The very pavements seem to give
                forth a pale and pearly radiance.
                The famous Parisian motor-horn
                has yet to sound its contemptuous
                farewell to the old era, its
                impudent welcome to the new. That
                day is coming very soon. The
                Paris of our story is removed
                merely by a decade and a half
```

from the follies and conceits of
the Second Empire. Leisure and
grace still pervade the streets;
and are to be observed in the
elegant carriage of the lady in
blue velvet, whose enormous hat
hides her face, but cannot
obscure completely the golden-red
curls. One would say at once, a
lady of fashion — but that the
blue of her dress is faded, and
that the dress itself is in the
mode of yesterday.

(BRING UP STREET NOISES)

2. COCHER: Where to, Madame?

(HORSE WHINNIES)

3. CORA: To the publishing house of
Monsieur Levy.

4. COCHER: Surely. Gee-up there.

(CLATTER OF HOOVES ON COBBLE
STONES)

(FADE THEN HOOVES UP AGAIN)

5. COCHER: Whoa! Whoa . . . there!

(HOOVES STOP. IN THE
BACKGROUND VOICES ARE
RAISED IN STREET ARGUMENT)

6. COCHER: We have arrived, Madame. This is
the house of Monsieur Levy, the
publisher.

7. CORA: Thank you, driver. Please wait
for me.

8. COCHER: Certainly, Madame.

(THE VOICES STOP ABRUPTLY,
THEIR OWNERS TOO INTERESTED
IN WATCHING CORA ALIGHT)

9. MAN: Forgive me, Madame. You've
dropped something — a piece of
paper.

```
10. CORA:        Thank you. How careless of me.
                      (DOOR SLAMS SMARTLY. THE
                      BABBLE OF VOICES BREAKS OUT
                      AGAIN)

11. WOMAN 1:     Who was it, Pierre?

12. WOMAN 2:     A hoity-toity piece, that's
                 plain.

13. MAN 1:       (With the air of one imparting a
                 great secret) It was the top . . .
                             -1-
```

Points to Note.

1. Speeches in single spacing (to minimize the turning over of pages) with a line of space between each speech and effect. No line-end division.

2. Speeches should be numbered consecutively on *each* page, i.e., the speeches on the second page would begin again at one.

3. Each page is numbered both at the top and bottom in the centre of the sheet. Only one side of the paper is used for typing.

4. Directions for effects are typed in capital letters and enclosed in brackets—beginning five or six spaces to the right of the speeches.

5. Directions for interpretation by speakers are typed in lower case and underscored, enclosed in brackets: they begin at the same point as the speeches.

Rapid envelope and card typing. See **Envelopes.**

Receipts and payments account. See **Income and expenditure account.**

Reference, sources of. An efficient typist/secretary carries in her head only information that is frequently required. An important part of her efficiency lies in knowing where she can speedily obtain information that she will need from time to time; and having to hand a selection of reference books that will be of most value to her in her particular job. She should visit the Reference Department of the local library and become familiar with all the reference books that are available for other information she may at some time need. If she is unable to find what she needs no doubt the reference librarian will be able to assist.

Some information about the type sources of reference follows.

1. *Abbreviations and initials.* Abbreviations in common use and their meanings are given in *The Complete Dictionary of Abbreviations*

compiled by R. Schwartz (Harrap), *Everyman's Dictionary of Abbreviations* by J. Paxton (Dent) and *Cyclopaedia of Initials and Abbreviations*.

2. *Clergymen.* Information about the clergymen of the Church of England is given in *Crockford's Clerical Directory*. Clerical directories are available for other religious denominations.

3. *Directors of companies.* A detailed record of all directors is given in *The Directory of Directors*, published yearly.

4. *English language.* A typist/secretary should always include the following in her collection of reference books.

(a) A good dictionary.

(b) *Roget's Thesaurus of English Words and Phrases.* In this work words are arranged according to their meaning compared with a dictionary where they are arranged alphabetically. A full list of synonyms and closely-related words and phrases is given which often helps one find the best word for a particular context—le mot juste! An index of all words dealt with is listed (with page references) in alphabetical order, at the end of the book.

(c) Fowler's *Modern English Usage.*

5. *Government reports.* These are published by Her Majesty's Stationery Office: there is a branch in most large towns. *Hansard* is the official report of proceedings in Parliament. Reports are verbatim (i.e., given word for word as spoken in Parliament) and cover both the House of Commons and the House of Lords.

6. *Hotels.* Motoring and other travel organizations publish handbooks which list and classify hotels, using symbols for grading, such as the star system used by the AA and RAC to cover the UK and Europe. *The Hotel Guide* is prepared by The British Hotels and Restaurants Association.

7. *Law.* Details of judges, magistrates, county court registrars, solicitors, barristers, etc., are given in The *Law List*.

8. *Local authority matters.* A variety of information (area, rates, population, names of officers, etc.) about local authorities in England and Wales is provided in *The Municipal Year Book* and *Public Utilities Directory*.

9. *Manufacturers and merchants.* Suppliers and manufacturers are listed alphabetically, according to the goods and services provided, in *Kelly's Directory of Manufacturers*.

10. *Medicine.* Information about qualified medical practitioners is

given in *The Medical Directory*. There is also a *Register of Nurses* and a *Dentist's Register*.

11. *Office stationery, machines, etc.* A wealth of information about all types of office stationery, machines and sundry items is given in *The Manual of Stationery, Office Machines and Equipment*, published by The British Stationery and Office Equipment Association.

12. *Place names and details.* A good gazetteer is very useful for checking the spelling and details concerning places in the British Isles. A world atlas is likewise desirable for verifying the spelling and situation of towns and cities abroad.

13. *Post Office publications.* The Post Office publishes many leaflets and books. Some of the more important ones follow.

(a) *The Post Office Guide* is published annually and is kept up to date by supplements. It gives details of postal, telephone, and telegraphic facilities; savings, remittances, and other services.

(b) *London Post Offices and Streets* lists all post offices in London and gives the postal district of all London roads.

(c) *Post Offices in the United Kingdom.*

(d) *Postal Addresses* lists all towns and villages and states which county they are in.

(e) *Postcode Directories.* A separate directory is published for each major town and its surrounding districts which are included in the same postcode area. These directories can be consulted at all main post offices.

14. *Ready reckoner.* A ready reckoner is a useful aid in most offices, providing a speedy means of arriving at answers to calculations involving multiplication, discounts, percentages (very useful for VAT), etc.

15. *Street directories. The Post Office Directory* is published for London, with a separate edition for each county. These directories give the names of all roads (arranged alphabetically) and the responsible occupiers of each house, office, shop, and flat: the private residents' section gives the names of the residents, arranged in alphabetical order. Trades and professions are also listed. In addition, *Kelly's Street Directories* are available.

16. *Technical terms.* If a typist/secretary works for a firm engaged in a particular technical trade or profession, she should have among her reference books the technical dictionary appropriate to her work. Such technical dictionaries include *Short Dictionary of Architecture, Authors' and Printers' Dictionary, Chambers' Technical Dictionary, Black's Medical Dictionary* and *Dictionary of Legal Terms*.

17. *Telephone directories.* The appropriate telephone directory (or set of directories for London) should be readily to hand in any office. Names (arranged alphabetically), addresses and telephone numbers of subscribers (apart from ex-directory subscribers) can be obtained from them. The classsified section (or yellow pages) is useful for finding the names, addresses and telephone numbers of particular trades or professions, listed alphabetically.

18. *Telex information.* Companies in the UK, together with their addresses and telex number, that are linked to the telex circuit are listed alphabetically in *The United Kingdom Telex Directory.* It also gives full details of the telex service. Directory information about subscribers in other countries can be obtained from the official directories published by their Administrations. In addition, a number of private companies produce national or international telex directories but none of them is approved or sponsored by the Post Office.

19. *Titles and forms of address.* The books listed below provide a variety of information about eminent people. In addition, the correct form of address is given; also the correct sequence for typing decorations, honours, qualifications, professional titles, etc. (see also **Titles, decorations, qualifications, forms of address, etc., typing of**).

(a) Black's *Titles and Forms of Address.*
(b) *Burke's Genealogical and Heraldic History of the Landed Gentry.*
(c) *Debrett's Peerage and Titles of Courtesy.*
(d) *Kelly's Handbook to the Titled Landed and Official Classes.*

(See separate heading for *Who's Who.*)

20. *Trade journals.* A trade journal is a magazine relating to a particular trade and it is published at regular intervals (weekly, monthly, or quarterly). Trade journals specialize in information relating to the trade in question and keep the readers informed of latest developments: they also provide a plentiful supply of useful advertisements. For details about publications relating to any particular trade or profession, reference should be made to the Newspaper Press Directory or Willing's Press.

21. *Travel information.* (Road, Rail, Sea, and Air.)

(a) *Road. ABC Coach and Bus Guide*, the *AA Members' Handbook*, the *RAC Club Guide and Handbook*, and local bus and coach company brochures and leaflets.
(b) *Rail.* In Britain, British Rail publish timetables which give detailed routes of trains and the stations at which they stop. These time-tables are invaluable when planning itineraries. Boat services connected

with British Rail are also covered and a continental edition is available.

The *ABC Railway Guide* gives only the times of departure and arrival of trains between London (or the town of issue in a local *ABC*) and the stations of destination.

(c) *Sea. ABC Shipping Guide;* also company brochures.

(d) *Air. ABC World Airways Guide;* also booklets published by individual airlines.

22. *Who's Who.* Short biographies of living eminent people can be found in *Who's Who*; *Who Was Who* covers eminent people who have died. There are several other forms of *Who's Who* such as *Who's Who in Art, Who's Who in the Motor Industry, Authors' and Writers' Who's Who, International Who's Who,* etc.

23. *Year books.* Various organizations publish year books. These give details of meetings, standing orders, members and officers, statistics, and other information useful to members.

24. *The Statesman's Year-Book* (Macmillan). Published annually, this book provides detailed statistics on political, economical and social topics for all countries of the world.

25. *Pear's Cyclopaedia.* This reference book, which is published annually, has sections dealing with a wide variety of subjects including an English dictionary, gazetteer, legal data, office compendium, details about prominent people, synonyms and antonyms and a ready reckoner.

26. *The Typist's Desk Book* (Pitman). This useful book is divided into four sections and includes information on centring, forms of address, styles of typewriting layout, punctuation, reference books, specimens of letters and documents, spelling check list, pronunciation of proper nouns and abbreviations.

27. *Whitaker's Almanack.* This comprehensive reference book, which is published annually, contains useful current information on a wide variety of topics, including the following: the calendar year, astronomy, tides, information about world affairs, detailed information of a varied nature about the UK, statistics, local government, national parks, and miscellaneous information about literature, music, drama and films, broadcasting, art, sport, trade unions, banking and finance.

Other sources of information

The typist/secretary may require certain current information that is not available from a reference book. The following is a brief guide to some of the sources available.

Information	*Source*
Banking and foreign currency	Bank
Books, newspapers, magazines, etc.	Reference section of local library
Court procedure	Local Justices' Clerk
Employment	Local office of the Department of Employment and Productivity Local Youth Employment Office
Income tax, etc.	Local office of the Inland Revenue
Interpreters, translations, etc.	Local Chamber of Commerce Language Department in local college; local travel agents; embassy of country concerned
Local government matters	Local office of the District or County Council
Motor taxation, etc.	Local Motor Taxation Office
National Insurance	Local office of the Department of Health and Social Security
Overseas trade, home market, etc.	Local Chamber of Commerce
Postal, telephone matters, etc.	Local main post office
Stocks and shares	Stockbroker—who is issued with the official Stock Exchange List daily
Travel	AA or RAC office; airport; British Rail; travel agency; appropriate bus company or steamship company

Remedial drills. See **Errors, their cause and remedy.**

Removing paper from typewriter. When the typing is complete on a sheet of paper it should be removed in one of the following ways. On no account should the paper be grabbed and merely 'yanked' out of the typewriter, as this can cause damage to the machine.

1. If the typewriter is fitted with a paper injector/ejector lever (situated on the right-hand side of the carriage) this should be used since it is provided to assist with the rapid insertion and removal of paper from the machine.

2. If there is no paper injector/ejector lever, the paper release lever should be used. This lever is situated on the right-hand side of the carriage and when moved forwards, it moves the feed rollers away from the platen so the paper can be speedily and silently removed from the typewriter without damage.

3. If the typist is very near the bottom of the paper when she wishes

to remove it from the typewriter, she can turn one of the platen knobs to move the paper on the required short space.

When carbon copies have been taken, the typist should carefully grip all the papers between her left first finger and thumb when removing them from the typewriter to ensure that the papers remain intact and in their correct order during the process of removal.

Reprography processes. A variety of methods is used in offices to produce one or more copies of a document. The different methods are dealt with under the following headings: **Carbon copying; Ink duplicating; Offset lithography duplicating; Photocopying; Spirit duplicating.** (See also *Office composing machine* under **Special-purpose typewriters.**)

Instructions on the manipulation of the different machines are not included, since such information comes within the sphere of Office Practice.

Automatic typewriters are also used to produce large numbers of a letter or other document—each copy giving the appearance of being individually typed. See **Special-purpose typewriters.**

The method selected from the above list will depend upon a number of factors including: resources available; number of copies wanted; purpose for which the copies are required; and the cost.

In typewriting, the reprographic methods given above can be classified into two main branches: *duplicating*, which means the production of copies from a specially prepared master; and *copying*, which means the production (by carbon paper or copying machines) of copies from an original. In general, duplicators are used to produce numerous copies, and carbon paper and copying machines are utilized for a few copies only.

In all duplicating and copying work that requires a typed original, the typist largely controls the quality of the copies. Clean fingers help ensure clean masters, and clean type assists in the production of clear, sharp copies. Masters for duplicating should always be carefully handled by the edges and they should never be bent or folded.

Rhythm. Most skills have their own distinct rhythm or pattern of movement and it is widely recognized by industrial and educational psychologists that the human body is highly susceptible to rhythm. It is a vital part of our psycho-physical makeup and is made use of wherever possible in learning processes. Much has been written about rhythm in typewriting but here it is important to distinguish between a tick-tock metronomic rhythm and the uneven yet definite rhythm pattern of the expert typist.

It is now generally agreed that typists should type to a regular beat only when learning new reaches and typing unmeaningful matter; and in certain remedial drills in order to rectify a ragged uneven touch (with manuals) and incorrect manipulation of the shift key.

The learner has to train the stimulus-response bonds to act in a certain way. Much practice is needed before the response (the typing of a letter or word) becomes automatic to the stimulus (in the case of copy typing, the sight of a letter or word). Each of the eight fingers used for typing controls a number of different keys and for each key the mind has to master not only which finger must be used but also the direction in which it should move. Typewriting is thus a complex perceptual-motor skill.

All skills are actions that have to be *learnt*, as opposed to certain reflex actions which are fully developed when we are born—such as blinking in the glare of a bright light and moving the hand quickly away from a hot object that would cause harm. Skills are basically of two types: sensory-motor and perceptual-motor.

With sensory-motor skills, conscious mental effort is required in the early learning stages (e.g., tying up shoe laces and skipping) but after many repetitions the actions become completely automatic and are performed without conscious thinking. Sensory-motor skills are therefore sometimes known as conditioned reflexes.

Perceptual-motor skills, on the other hand, have an intellectual content to a greater or lesser degree. Perceptual-motor skills follow a definite but varying pattern in which conscious thinking is always necessary to some extent: performance of these skills can thus never be completely automatic. They require constant co-ordination of the mind and body, and the mind must be constantly working and selecting. Short-hand and Typewriting are good examples of perceptual motor skills.

In learning Typewriting, control of the speed of movement is necessary in the very early learning stages, and the learners are usually required to type in unison to a regular beat. However, if an expert were asked to type each letter as a uniformly-timed movement, her speed and skill would suffer.

As stated earlier, the learner should, as a general rule, type to a regular, metronomic rhythm only when typing on a letter response basis. The learner also has to develop independent finger action (each finger moving individually with as little movement as possible of the rest of the hand): and metronomic rhythm can assist here.

At as early a stage as possible, the learner typist should begin to develop an 'automatic' vocabulary. For instance, when she first types the word 'and', it is three quite separate letter responses. With practice, however, the typist soon acquires the ability to type this and other high-frequency words and letter combinations as *single responses* and is hardly aware of the fact that she is typing several letters. The words and letter combinations have become part of her automatic vocabulary and the earlier laborious conscious thought required when typing them is largely eliminated.

It follows from this that the learner typists should be expected to type meaningful matter as early as possible. Not only does this speed up development of the skill but it also motivates the learners. Typing lines of mumbo-jumbo, although perhaps necessary at first, does tend to dampen enthusiasm.

For this reason, typewriting teaching machines which flash up the work to be typed, one letter at a time at regular intervals, are of educational value only in keyboard mastery. Although the programmes for such machines include words, phrases, and sentences, the students can see *only one letter at a time*. Thus skill is actually retarded, since all typing must be on a letter-response basis: it is not possible to type words or letter combinations rapidly as single responses. To develop an automatic vocabulary the student must be able to see or hear (in the case of audio-typing) the word *as a whole*. In addition, constant typing on a single-letter basis is tiring.

It is only natural that, once basic skill has been mastered, the typist should want to develop her own speed and rhythm—and, to a considerable extent, the position of the keys on the keyboard in relation to the matter being typed affects the rhythm and speed that can be achieved. Therefore, any teaching method that required the typist to type easy words and connected prose, letter by letter at a uniform speed, should be discarded as early as possible.

Many teachers, however, feel that regular-beat typing to specially-prepared musical records or tapes helps relieve the intense concentration required in the early learning stages of typing: in addition, it introduces a different and pleasant activity into lessons, helping to keep boredom and fatigue at bay. The point is also made that having to type to a regular beat helps carry the learners forward. Not many people would argue against this and a few minutes' typing to music in a lesson can do no harm—particularly if the students are typing material which requires a letter-response approach. However, typing to regular-beat music should always be tackled intelligently and both the teacher and students should always be fully aware of the particular reasons for its use.

Regular-beat typing is in fact difficult, particularly at high speeds. This is largely because of the unscientific arrangement of the letters on the keyboard (see **Arrangement of the keyboard**). If a typist were to type every letter at uniform speed she would obviously have to slow down her typing to the speed at which she could type the most difficult reaches and letter combinations.

If a class were expected to type in this way at high speed, the skill of many members of the class would suffer. No matter how homogeneous a class may appear, speed in operation of the typewriter will vary considerably with different members of the class. Therefore, to expect a class to perform regular-beat typing to music at high speeds will actually impede the development of skill for many of its members. The faster typists will have to slow down, while the slower ones will be forced to type spasmodically and without control because the speed expected is too high.

The learner typist should constantly be aware of, and strive to emulate, the action pattern of the expert. In this connection, skilful demonstration accompanied by competent analysis and verbalization are important in skill development (see **Demonstration**).

The rhythmic pattern of an expert typist is not metronomic: it is an alternation of rapid and less rapid groups of key striking. For instance, when typing high-frequency words and letter combinations that form part of the typist's automatic vocabulary, the typing will be rapid. On the other hand, low-frequency words and words that are difficult to type because of the letter combinations will be slow. Example of the latter are 'address' (typed entirely with the left hand), 'zoology', 'zest', 'minimum', and 'poll'. Therefore some words and phrases will be typed rapidly whilst others will be typed slowly. However, the two responses (letter and word) will be blended by the expert into a variable and flowing rhythm—a rhythm in which spasmodic key striking is eliminated and all actions are performed with complete economy of movement. Such a rhythm will have nothing to do with metronomic beat: nevertheless, it will have its own distinctive features and pattern.

Ribbon and ribbon guide. See **Parts of a typewriter.**

Ribbon position indicator. See **Parts of a typewriter.**

Ribbons for typewriters. These are mostly made of inked fabrics which may be cotton, silk, or nylon. The degree of inking varies from light to medium and heavy. For some electric typewriters a plastic carbon-coated ribbon (which should be used only once) is also available and is used where the appearance of the typewritten work is of maximum importance and for typing masters for reproduction processes. By use of a special attachment, carbon ribbons can be used on manual typewriters as well.

Irrespective of the fabric used, ribbons may be single or two coloured (bichrome) with black or black and red record being the most popular. Other colours are obtainable so that the user can match the typewriting with the colour used in the letterheading, or for any other special requirements.

Record ribbons are inked with a fast dye which makes the typewritten impressions permanent. This is the most commonly-used type of

223

ribbon and easy, neat corrections are obtainable with it. A black record ribbon is always used for typing legal documents. Bichrome ribbons are uneconomical unless a second colour is in frequent demand. If a second colour is required only occasionally, this can be effected by placing a piece of carbon paper of the necessary colour between the ribbon and the paper.

Typewriter ribbons, which can be of different widths and lengths, are carried on two spools, the size and type of which vary with the make of machine. So that the correct ribbon for any particular make of typewriter can be easily determined, suppliers have now grouped machines taking the same ribbon spools, coding each group with a letter or number. In this way, the number of different spools has been reduced to manageable proportions. Charts listing the various groups are available from the manufacturers. When ordering ribbons, it is very important to furnish the supplier with all the necessary details; these are normally printed on the ribbon container.

To help prevent the ink on typewriter ribbons from drying out, each ribbon is usually wrapped in silver paper or other non-porous material, and put in a closely-fitting container before being sent out by the manufacturer.

Sometimes ribbons are supplied on a right-hand spool only (although most are interchangeable): therefore, when fitting a new ribbon, it is advisable to wind the old ribbon on to the right-hand spool in the typewriter so that the new ribbon will be fitted on the right-hand side.

Instructions for fitting a new ribbon are given in the Instructions Booklet supplied with the typewriter, but if this is not available one should note very carefully how the ribbon is fitted and wound before removing the old one for replacement. This varies considerably from one make of machine to another: to give but one example—on some machines the ribbon approaches the spool from the back and on others from the front.

It is usually easier to thread a new ribbon at the printing point if the shift lock is engaged, as this gives easier access to the ribbon vibrator.

The ribbon mechanism is fitted with a device so that when one spool becomes full and the other empty, the direction of the ribbon is automatically reversed: if the automatic reverse mechanism does not work, there is usually a ribbon reversing switch so that the direction can be changed manually.

Typewriters have a ribbon switch which enables the typist to select the part of the ribbon (top or bottom) she wishes to use. The ribbon switch has a colour code—blue (or black) indicating the top of the ribbon and red indicating the bottom. In addition, there is usually a white mark which, when enagaged, switches the ribbon completely out of action for the purpose of stencil cutting. This ribbon switch is, of course, essential when using bichrome ribbons—so that the second colour can be easily brought into action. If a plain black or other single-colour ribbon is being used, the ribbon switch will enable the bottom half of the ribbon to be fully used once the top half becomes worn. If the ribbon spools are interchangeable, many typists prefer to change the side of the ribbon so that the top of the ribbon is in constant use: this produces speedier typing as the ribbon does not have to rise to its highest extent when each key is struck, as when the ribbon switch is moved to the red position.

Cartridge ribbons are fixed into a case which is slotted into the typewriter, thus facilitating the loading of a machine with the maximum of speed. Different types of ribbon can be used for specific purposes by this method, but so far there are only a few typewriters fitted with this device. See also **Correcting errors** (*Correction ribbons*).

Roman numerals. The figures that we use in everyday life are known as arabic numbers (1, 2, 3, etc.) because they derive from the Arabic system of numbering which, because of its efficient groupings into tens, is widely used throughout the world. 1, 2, 3, etc., are known as cardinal numbers; 1st, 2nd, 3rd, etc., are known as ordinal numbers. The latter should not be followed by a full stop.

The Romans used a quite different system of numbering, based on letters of the alphabet. It is a very cumbersome method and any kind of calculations using it are extremely difficult. Today, roman numerals are less and less frequently used but they have certain uses in typewriting and typists should therefore understand the system.

Roman numerals consist of seven symbols known as Units and Fives as follows:

Units	Fives
I (1)	V (5)
X (10)	L (50)
C (100)	D (500)
M (1,000)	

If difficulty is experienced in memorizing the symbols above X (10)—remember that CD and LM both occur together in the alphabet. M is the 'highest' letter used and represents the highest figure employed (1,000): its 'partner', L, represents the lowest of the figures above X. Split L and M and insert the C and D, thus putting the letters in ascending order. Thus:

$$L = 50$$
$$C = 100$$
$$D = 500$$
$$M = 1,000$$

Roman numerals

(a) The four unit symbols can be repeated two or three times:

I (1)	X (10)	C (100)	M (1,000)
II (2)	XX (20)	CC (200)	MM (2,000)
III (3)	XXX (30)	CCC (300)	MMM (3,000)

(b) A unit or repeated unit may be used after another symbol of higher value to indicate addition:

VII (7)	LXX (70)	DCCC (800)
XII (12)	CIII (103)	MXXX (1,030)

(c) Each unit symbol I, X, and C may be placed before its immediately following 'five' or 'ten' symbol to indicate subtraction of that single unit from the 'five' or 'ten' unit:

IV = 4	XL = 40	CD = 400
IX = 9	XC = 90	CM = 900

N.B. These figures—4, 9, 40, 90, 400 and 900—are the only numbers where a higher number is taken and the corresponding difference placed in front as a subtraction.

(d) When changing arabic numbers to roman ones, each figure has to be taken separately, in turn:

$$868 = 800 + 60 + 8$$
$$800 = 500 + 300 = DCCC$$
$$60 = 50 + 10 = LX$$
$$8 = 5 + 3 = VIII$$

Therefore 868 is represented in roman numerals as DCCCLXVIII.

(e) A horizontal stroke placed over a roman numeral multiplies it by 1,000:

$\overline{VII} = 7,000$ $\qquad$ $\overline{IX} = 9,000$ $\qquad$ $\overline{M} = 1,000,000$ (one million)

The following table illustrates some of the above points.

arabic	large roman	small roman	arabic	large roman	small roman
1	I	i	20	XX	xx
2	II	ii	30	XXX	xxx
3	III	iii	40	XL	xl
4	IV	iv	50	L	l
5	V	v	60	LX	lx
6	VI	vi	70	LXX	lxx
7	VII	vii	80	LXXX	lxxx
8	VIII	viii	90	XC	xc
9	IX	ix	100	C	c
10	X	x	1,000	M	m

Note that capital **I** is used for large roman numeral 'one'. Capital **I** should never be used for arabic 'one': if the typewriter does not have a special key for the arabic figure 'one', lower case **1** should be used. Roman numerals are traditionally typed so that the last symbol lines up, as shown in the table, although increasingly they are being aligned to the *left*, partly because of the problems caused when using them for enumeration in 'inset' matter with the blocked style. They are only followed by a stop when used for numbering paragraphs (as an alternative to being enclosed in brackets or standing alone: in the latter case three character spaces should be left after the last symbol in the roman numeral before the typewritten matter).

Some uses of roman numerals
Large roman numerals are used:

(a) For monarchs, e.g., Queen Elizabeth II, King Henry VIII.
(b) On old-fashioned cloack dials—where 4 often appears as IIII.
(c) For Books of the Bible.
(d) Usually to number Acts in a play, the Scenes being denoted by arabic figures, or small roman numerals.
(e) Sometimes on foundation stones.
(f) Sometimes to number chapters of books.
(g) In Acts of Parliament—small roman numerals being used for sub-sections.
(h) In some schools to denote form or class numbers, e.g., Form VI.
(i) For numbering paragraphs and sections (see **Enumerating sections, paragraphs and pages**).

Small roman numerals are used:

(a) For numbering preliminary pages in books and typescripts.
(b) Sometimes to number Scenes in plays, although arabic figures are usually preferred (see (d) above).
(c) For Chapters of the Bible, the number of the Book being denoted by a large roman numeral, the verse by small roman numerals and the lines by arabic figures, e.g., II Romans iii, 26.
(d) For numbering paragraphs and sections (see **Enumerating sections, paragraphs and pages**).

Ruling (see also **Display**). A study of typewriting textbooks will reveal a variety of instructions for ruling tabulated work—some simple and straightforward, but others complicated and difficult to master.

Many typewriting students find typing tabulations difficult, and unnecessarily complex instructions about ruling merely add to their fear of this kind of work—about which they often develop a phobia.

For instance, what does the average student make of the following quotation (but *one* of a list of ruling instructions)?

> To find the point at which to mark the vertical line, proceed as follows: (a) Move to tab stop following vertical line. (b) Divide number of spaces between columns by 2 and take next highest figure, e.g., 3 spaces between columns—divide by 2 = $1\frac{1}{2}$, call it 2; 5 spaces between columns = $2\frac{1}{2}$, call it 3. (c) From tab stop back space 2 (or whatever the figure is), and put a pencil mark.

(a) *Ruling with ballpoint pen and ruler.* If a tabulation has been well typed and an equal space left between each column (see **Column work with column headings**), ruling up is a simple matter if the following procedure is adopted.

1. Remove the paper(s) from the typewriter and start by ruling in the outer frame of the table. There should be an equal space between the body of the typing and this line all round the table. Since vertical lines between columns should be centralized, measure the space allowed between columns, halve it, and work so that this same space will appear around the perimeter of the tabulation.

2. Insert a series of light pencil dots (two for each of the four outside lines is sufficient) equidistant from the typing, at the appropriate position. Rule through these dots lightly with a soft pencil. Since pencil marks can be easily erased later, extend the lines a little further than necessary *to ensure that they meet and form neat right angles.*

3. Neatly ink over the outer frame with a good-quality biro (black or red is recommended) and ruler.

4. Next rule in all lines that run the full length and width of the table. The space between columns should be measured and halved and two or three pencil dots per line inserted (one near the top, one near the bottom and possibly a third one roughly in the centre) to help get the line absolutely straight. The lines can be lightly pencilled in first and then inked over. The same basic principle and practice should be applied for horizontal ruling. With practice, the typist will find that she can dispense with the pre-ruling in pencil.

5. Other lines should then be ruled in, using the same method.

6. Any pencil marks that are visible should be carefully erased with a soft rubber.

7. If any of the headings need to be underlined, this should be carefully done with ruler and the same ballpoint pen. Use of a good-quality ballpoint pen obviates the problems caused by ordinary pen and ink, i.e., risk of smudging, uneven lines, frequent wiping of the ruler, and constant use of blotting paper.

The ruling should *help make the work appear pleasing to the eye*

Therefore it should not be too obtrusive and thick. A good-quality ballpoint pen or fine felt tip pen produces attractive work—but a *broad* felt-tip should not be used. Pencil ruling is not generally acceptable.

8. If carbon copies have been taken, the four corners of the work should be carefully secured with small paper clips. This will prevent the carbons moving during ruling and throwing the ruling out of alignment. Any marks that may be made on the carbon copies by the paper clips can later be erased with a soft rubber.

(b) *Ruling with the typewriter.* This is a slow process which many students find difficult and few manage to master. The underscore key is used for the ruling, the horizontal lines being typed in first. The paper(s) must then be removed from the typewriter and reinserted sideways for ruling the vertical lines. The vertical lines should be typed mid-way between the columns and guide marks are therefore necessary. These can be inserted lightly by pencil or by typing dots (with the ribbon position indicator in the stencil position, and using a *very light* touch) in the appropriate places.

Apart from the fact that this is a slow method of ruling, many typists experience difficulty in obtaining neat right angles to the outer frame and in getting the lines exactly in the right place. Moreover, the 'stencil' dots are difficult to erase satisfactorily and when carbon copies are taken, there is a tendency for the papers to move slightly when reinserting them into the typewriter for the vertical ruling—with disastrous consequences.

(c) *Mixed ruling with the typewriter underscore and ballpoint pen.* To help avoid the difficulties described in the last paragraph, some typists type in the horizontal lines with the underscore key, remove the work from the typewriter and then rule in the vertical lines with ink. Guide marks (using one of the methods already described) are usually inserted for the vertical ruling.

It is obviously desirable that the ruling should be all in the same colour: therefore, if a black typewriter ribbon is used for the horizontal ruling, a black ballpoint pen should be used for the vertical ruling. However, it is usually apparent that the mixed ruling method has been used, and this detracts from the appearance of the work.

This method is obviously slower than that described in (a), as well as having other disadvantages.

(d) *Ruling by use of the notches on the alignment scale.* It will be seen that most typewriters have four small notches (round holes) on the transparent plastic alignment scale, just below the paper bail. These notches can be used for drawing lines with a pencil or biro.

For horizontal ruling, insert the pencil or biro in one of the notches and move the carriage along the appropriate distance by means of the carriage release lever. To make a vertical line, release the platen ratchet and move the paper up or down by turning one of the platen knobs.

If this method is used, great care must be taken to ensure that the lines end at exactly the right point—particularly if a ballpoint pen is used and carbon copies are being taken. If the lines are drawn in by pencil, they should be inked over later, since pencil ruling is not generally acceptable.

This method of ruling is also slower and less reliable than that described in (a).

Running headlines. See **Literary work.**

Scales. See **Parts of a typewriter.**

Seconds sign. See **Combination characters and special signs.**

Section mark. See **Combination characters and special signs.**

Semi-colon. See **Combination characters and special signs.** Also, **Punctuation marks.**

Serial number of typewriter. Every typewriter manufactured is given a serial number which is placed on the typewriter (in a non-eradicable form) on a non-removable part: usually this number is found on the carriage for ease of checking but, since the carriage can be removed and changed, it is duplicated on the typewriter frame beneath the carriage.

When an organization purchases a typewriter, the date of purchase and other details are recorded in a stock book, together with the serial number of the machine.

Should a typewriter become lost or stolen it can be traced by means of the serial number. Also, if a typewriter is being sold or part exchanged for a new one, its serial number can give the intending purchaser a useful guide to its age.

Servicing typewriter. See **Overhauling typewriter** and **Care of the typewriter.**

Seven hundred common words. See **Word frequency, its signficance in typewriting.**

Shift key drills. See **Drills.**

Shift keys and shift lock. See **Parts of a typewriter.**

Shift keys, demonstration of use. See **Demonstration.**

Short page. See **Literary work.**

Shoulder headings. See **Headings.**

Side headings. See **Headings.**

Sloping fractions. See **Fractions.**

Solidus. See **Extra typewriter characters.**

Space bar. See **Parts of a typewriter.**

Space bar drills. See **Drills.**

Spacing after punctuation marks. See **Punctuation marks.**

Special-purpose typewriters. Most visitors to the Business Efficiency Exhibitions are bewildered by the wide range of special-purpose typewriters and the variety of features each incorporates. This section deals with but a few of these machines and their uses: a whole book could be written on this subject alone.

Automatic typewriters. Automatic typewriters are electrically operated, and once masters have been prepared they can automatically reproduce the material so that each copy gives the impression of being an original.

The first automatic typewriter, the Auto-Typist, was manufactured in America in 1932, its master consisting of a roll of perforated paper similar in appearance to that used on the once popular but now obsolete pianola. The success of the Auto-Typist led other manufacturers of typewriters to develop their own automatic machines, and a wide range is now available, each incorporating its own sophisticated features. The Flexowriter range of automatics (the 2301, 2302, 2303, 2304 and 2345) use punched paper tape, edge-punched cards or tabulating cards. IBM manufacture machines that use magnetic tape (the Magnetic Tape Selectric Typewriter) or magnetic cards (the Magnetic Card Selectric Typewriter and the Magnetic Card Executive Typewriter).

Most automatic typewriters have a number of features in common.

1. The copies, which are of a very high quality, give the appearance of being typed originals.

2. The master must be typed on the typewriter in the usual way, being recorded on punched paper tape, punched cards, magnetic tape, or magnetic cards.

3. The machine then prints out the typed matter which must be carefully checked for accuracy, corrected, and amended as necessary.

4. As many copies as are required can then be automatically produced from the master—typed at speeds ranging from 145 to 180 words a minute. Each copy will be identical to the master so that no checking is necessary. Various details, such as the name and address of the addressee, can be typed in manually on the copies.

5. If the master is required for future use, it should be numbered and indexed before being stored.

6. Automatic typewriters have a standard keyboard and various function keys such as START READ, STOP READ, EDIT, PARA-GRAPH, TAPE FEED, STOP CODE, NON PRINT, SKIP. Most manufacturers provide a variety of carriage lengths and both fabric and carbon ribbons can be used.

Word processing. Some automatic typewriters are capable of what is known as word processing. Since much routine correspondence consists of sentences and paragraphs that are similar in meaning, a firm owning a word processing typewriter can prepare masters for a series of frequently used standard paragraphs. These are prepared, checked and stored and a handbook compiled which contains all the standard paragraphs. They are numbered and indexed and divided into subject sections. In this way, instead of each letter having to be separately dictated, the dictator need merely give the typist details of the required paragraphs from the handbook and just dictate any additional matter he wishes to insert—which must, of course, be typed in manually in the appropriate places.

Dual pitch typewriter. The IBM Selectric 82 is available in two versions, one with single pitch, the other with dual pitch. The dual-pitch typewriter enables the typist to change from pica pitch (ten characters to the inch) to elite pitch (twelve characters to the inch) merely by flicking a switch. Thus the typist can select either pica or elite, which-ever she thinks the more appropriate for the work, or she can change the type size within a single piece of work, a feature which can give more impact to certain portions that need highlighting.

Dual unit typewriter. This consists of two keyboard units built side by side with a carriage that can be easily moved from one keyboard to the other. The dual unit typewriter is designed for typewritten work which consists of a mixture of prose and mathematical or other scientific symbols. One keyboard comprises letters and the other keyboard provides the required specialized symbols.

Office composing machines. The phrase 'cold type composing' was originally used by the manufacturers of the VariTyper, to distinguish this machine from other typewriters. The expression is now widely used to describe all systems which are not 'hot metal' ones, i.e., the standard method of composition used in printing.

The main function of office composing machines is to produce displayed matter (often using a variety of typefaces, proportional spacing, and a justified right-hand margin) for use with plate making in inplant printing departments.

The IBM Magnetic Tape Selectric Composer incorporates proportional spacing (each letter and character comprising 3–9 units) and the interchangeable golf ball type fonts (available in a variety of type styles) each carry eighty-eight characters. The copy is produced visually and on to magnetic tape simultaneously, corrections being made (as with all magnetic media) simply by backspacing and retyping over the incorrect matter. The copy is then carefully checked, and if extensive corrections or amendments are required, these can be made simply by producing them on a second tape which is merged with the original one during the process of composing. Print out can be on to paper or translucent masters or negatives, from which plates are made. The IBM Magnetic Tape Selectric Composer produces justified copy automatically from the master tape. With the VariTyper the copy must be typed twice. When first typed, each line must finish with a justfication space, as shown on a dial on the machine. This space is adjusted before the second typing by a special device which automatically and evenly distributes the justification space so that line ends are equal.

The VariTyper has no typebars. Instead, the letters and characters are moulded on curved metal segments which swing to the printing point when a character is struck. Two segments can be fitted on to the machine at the same time, so that matching bold face type or italics can be incorporated into the typewritten matter. The segments can also be changed at any time during typing so that several different type

VariTyper 1010

styles and sizes can be used in a single piece of work. Special segments are obtainable for typing in foreign languages, and for mathematical or scientific typing. The VariTyper will produce very high quality masters for *any method of reproduction,* including spirit or stencil masters.

Phototypesetting. Phototypesetting machines consist of a standard typewriter keyboard typesetter and a computer. On the Photon Compositor, a number of function keys are positioned above the keyboard for instructions concerning display (e.g., type style, type size, line length) and for the making of corrections. Phototypesetters differ from other cold type composing machines in that they produce automatic justified copy in a range of typestyles and sizes on photosensitive paper or film (up to ten inches wide), which is then processed to make a printing plate. The Photon Compositor typefaces are drawn on to glass matrix discs, each of which can take eight typefaces (896 characters).

Before the copy is typed it should be marked up for styling. During typing, the matter (32 characters at a time) appears in red against a black background in an illuminated visual display panel situated above the keyboard on the left-hand side. This facility enables the typist to carefully check her work as she types. Faulty matter can be corrected by pressing the KILL CHARACTER, KILL WORD or KILL LINE key—which causes the machine to backspace the appropriate distance, the character(s) at the same time disappearing from the display panel. The correction is then typed.

As each line is completed, it is stored in the adjacent computer. When the typing is finished, the photosensitive paper or film is removed from the machine in a cassette and processed.

Keyboard phototypesetters are used to print books and periodicals, and because of their comparative simplicity and cheapness they will probably take over most of the work produced by hot type printing methods.

Specifications (See also **Bills of quantities** and **Tender**). A specification is a document which details the work to be carried out by a contractor on any particular job. The description of the work to be done and the materials to be used are divided into trades, which follow the order in which the work would normally be carried out. For instance, on a large building project, the specification would begin (after any preliminary paragraphs) with excavation work, proceed to concrete work, and so on, following the order of all the different construction stages.

Specifications are usually typed on A4 paper, using a black record ribbon. If only a few copies are required, carbon copies are usually made. However, if many copies are needed—or in firms where this method of copying is preferred for all copies—they are photocopied from a single typed copy. Line spacing for the paragraphs varies according to preference and the length of the specification. Double or one-and-a-half spacing is obviously more legible, but if the specification is very long, single spacing is often used. The pages (after the first) are numbered at the bottom of each sheet in the centre. In addition, if the specification is long, sub-headings are also numbered (in the left-hand margin) for quick reference.

If a specification is short, when completed it is folded into two lengthwise (folded from right to left): however, if it is long, it is bound in book form and the pages kept flat.

A specification consists of three basic parts:
1. The main heading
2. Trade and sub-headings
3. The body or paragraphs

The main heading consists of a brief explanatory paragraph describing the nature of the work: it always begins with the word 'Specification' (often typed in spaced capitals). This paragraph is always typed in double spacing, regardless of the spacing of the paragraphs in the body of the document. A line of space is then left and the name and address of the architect or builders (if a builders' specification) or engineers (if an engineers' specification) typed in single spacing. Then, following a line of space, the date is typed.

After this heading, the main part of the specification begins. Sometimes there are 'preliminaries': if so, the heading 'Preliminaries' is typed in spaced capitals and underscored. If the preliminaries contain sub-headings, these are typed in closed capitals (in single spacing if running to more than one line) in one of the ways shown in the following diagrams. The preliminaries will be followed by the name of the trade first involved in the work: this and the following trade names should be typed in spaced capitals and underlined, with their sub-headings in closed capitals. If the specification is a long one, each trade begins on a new sheet; but if the document is short, the typing is continuous. Where the paragraphs are typed in single spacing, a line of space should, of course, be left between each paragraph within a single sub-heading and a line of space left between the last line of the last paragraph and the following sub-heading. If the typing of the specification is continuous, an additional line of space should be left before and after each trade heading.

Engineers' specifications are similar in layout to the following diagrams —which illustrate some of the main layout styles for specifications—but it should be noted that the main heading of an engineers' specification is usually centred and displayed, with the traditional method of layout.

The following diagrams illustrate some of the most widely used methods of layout but, as in the typing of nearly all kinds of document, some variations in layout will be found from firm to firm. The typist should always follow the particular style and preferences of her employers. She will be shown typed examples of the documents she is asked to type, and will be able to use these as a guide until she is perfectly familiar with the particular conventions of her employers.

```
              X X X X X X X X   xxxxxxxxxxxxxxxxxxxxxxxxxxxxxxxxxxxxx
              xxxxxxxxxxxxxxxxxxxxxxxxxxxxxxxxxxxxxxxxxxxxxxxxxxxxxxx
              xxxxxxxxxxxxxxxxxxxxxxxxxxxxxxxxxxxxxxxxxxxxxxxxxxxxxxx
              xxxxxxxxxxxxxxxxxxxxxxxxxxxxxxxxxxxxxxxxx

                            xxxxxxxxxxxxxxxxxxxxxxxxxxx) (name
                            xxxxxxxxxxxxxxxxxxxxx       )   and
                            xxxxxxxxxxxxxxxxxxxxxxxx     )   address)

  (date)

  X X X X X X X X X X X X   (Preliminaries or first trade heading)

  xxxxxxxxxxxxxxxxxxxxxxxxxxxxxxxxxxxxxxxxxxxxxxxxxxxxxxxxxxxxxxxxxxxxxxxxxx
  xxxxxxxxxxxxxxxxxxxxxxxxxxxxxxxxxxxxxxxxxxxxxxxxxxxxxxxxxxxxxxxxxxxxxxxxxx
  xxxxxxxxxxxxxxxxxxxxxxxxxxxxxxxxxxxxxxxxxxxxxxxxxxxxxxxxxxxxxxxxxxxxxxxxxx
  xxxxxxxxxxxxxxxxxxxxxxxxxxx

  X X X X X X X X X X X X X X X   (Trade heading)

  XXXXXXXXXXXXXXXXXXXX (Sub-heading)

  xxxxxxxxxxxxxxxxxxxxxxxxxxxxxxxxxxxxxxxxxxxxxxxxxxxxxxxxxxxxxxxxxxxxxxxxxx
  xxxxxxxxxxxxxxxxxxxxxxxxxxxxxxxxxxxxxxxxxxxxxxxxxxxxxxxxxxxxxxxxxxxxxxxxxx
  xxxxxxxxxxxxxxxxxxxxxxxxxxxxxxx

  xxxxxxxxxxxxxxxxxxxxxxxxxxxxxxxxxxxxxxxxxxxxxxxxxxxxxxxxxxxxxxxxxxxxxxxxxx
  xxxxxxxxxxxxxxxxxxxxxxxxxxxxxxxxxxxxxxxxxxxxxxxxxxxxxxxxxxxxxxx
  XXXXXXXXXXXXXXX (Sub-heading)

  xxxxxxxxxxxxxxxxxxxxxxxxxxxxxxxxxxxxxxxxxxxxxxxxxxxxxxxxxxxxxxxxxxxxxxxxxx
  xxxxxxxxxxxxxxxxxxxxxxxxxxxxxxxxxxxxxxxxxxxxxxxxxxxxxxxxxxxxxxxxxxxxxxxxxx
  xxxxxxxxxxxxxxxxxxxxxxxxxxxxxxxxxxxxxxxxxxxxxxxxxxxxxxxxxxxxxxxxxxxxxxxxxx
  xxxxxxxxxxxxxxxxxxxxxxxxxxxxxxxxxxxxxxxxxxxxxxx

  xxxxxxxxxxxxxxxxxxxxxxxxxxxxxxxxxxxxxxxxxxxxxxxxxxxxxxxxxxxxxxxxxxxxxxxxxxx
  xxxxxxxxxxxxxxxxxxxxxxxxxxxxxxxxxxxxxxxxxxxxxxxxxxxxxxxxxxxxxxx
  XXXXXXXXXXXXXXXXXXXXX (Sub-heading)

  xxxxxxxxxxxxxxxxxxxxxxxxxxxxxxxxxxxxxxxxxxxxxxxxxxxxxxxxxxxxxxxxxxxxxxxxxxx
  xxxxxxxxxxxxxxxxxxxxxxxxxxxxxxxxxxxxxxxxxxxxxxxxxxxx
  .
  xxxxxxxxxxxxxxxxxxxxxxxxxxxxxxxxxxxxxxxxxxxxxxxxxxxxxxxxxxxxxxxxxxxxxxxxxxx
  xxxxxxxxxxxxxxxxxxxxxxxxxxxxxxxxxxxxxxxxxxxxxxxxxxxxxxxxxxxxxxxxxxxxxxxxxxx
  xxxxxxxxxxxxxxxxxxxxxxxxxxxxxxxxxxxxxxxxxxxxxxxxxxxxxxxxxxxxxxxxxxxxxxxxxxx

  X X X X X X X X X X X X X   (Trade heading)

  XXXXXXXXXXXXXXXXXXXXXXXX

  xxxxxxxxxxxxxxxxxxxxxxxxxxxxxxxxxxxxxxxxxxxxxxxxxxxxxxxxxxxxxxxxxxxxxxxxxxx
  xxxxxxxxxxxxxxxxxxxxxxxxxxxxxxxxxxxxxxxxxxxxxxxxxxxxxxxxxxxxxxxxxxxxxxxxxxx
  xxxxxxxxxxxxxxxxxxxxxxxxxxxxxxxxxxxxxxxxxxxxxxxxxxxxxxxxxxxxxx
  XXXXXXXXXXXXXXXXXX (Sub-heading)

  xxxxxxxxxxxxxxxxxxxxxxxxxxxxxxxxxxxxxxxxxxxxxxxxxxxxxxxxxxxxxxxxxxxxxxxxxx
  xxxxxxxxxxxxxxxxxxxxxxxxxxxxxxxxxxxxxxxxxxxxxxxxxxxxxxxxxxxxxxxxxxxxxxxxxx
```

Fully-blocked method of layout

```
X X X X X X X X X  xxxxxxxxxxxxxxxxx
xxxxxxxxxxxxxxxxxxxxxxxxxxxxxxxxxxxx
xxxxxxxxxxxxxxxxxxxxxxxxxxxxxxxxx

xxxxxxxxxxxxxxxxxxxxxxxxxx)
xxxxxxxxxxxxxxxxxxx        )     (name and address)
xxxxxxxxxxxxxxxxxxxxxxxx   )

(date)
```

<table>
<tr><td>X X X X X
(Prelims.)</td><td>xxxxxxxxxxxxxxxxxxxxxxxxxxxxxxxxxxxxxxxxxxxxxxxxxxxxxxxxxxxxxxxxxxxx
xxxxxxxxxxxxxxxxxxxxxxxxxxxxxxxxxxxxxxxxxxxxxxxxxxxxxxxxxxxxxxxxxxxx
xxxxxxxxxxxxxxxxxxxxxxxxxxxxxxxxxxxxxxxxxxxxxxxxxxxxxxxxxxxxxxxxxxxx
xxxxxxxxxxxxxxxxxxxxxxxxxxxxxxxxxxxxxxxxxxxxxxxxxxxxxxxxxxxxxxx</td></tr>
<tr><td>XXXXXXXXXXX
(Sub-heading)</td><td>xxxxxxxxxxxxxxxxxxxxxxxxxxxxxxxxxxxxxxxxxxxxxxxxxxxxxxxxxxxxxxxxxxxx
xxxxxxxxxxxxxxxxxxxxxxxxxxxxxxxxxxxxxxxxxxxxxxxxxxxxxxxxxxxxxxxxxxxxx
xxxxxxxxxxxxxxxxxxxxxxxxxxxxxxxxxxxxxxxxxxxxxxxxxxxxxxxxxxxxxxxxxxxxx

xxxxxxxxxxxxxxxxxxxxxxxxxxxxxxxxxxxxxxxxxxxxxxxxxxxxxxxxxxxxxxxxxxxx
xxxxxxxxxxxxxxxxxxxxxxxxxxxxxxxxxxxxxxxxxxxxxxxxxxxxxxxxxxx</td></tr>
<tr><td>XXXXXXXXXXX
XXXXXXXXX
(Sub-head.)</td><td>xxxxxxxxxxxxxxxxxxxxxxxxxxxxxxxxxxxxxxxxxxxxxxxxxxxxxxxxxxxxxxxxxxxx
xxxxxxxxxxxxxxxxxxxxxxxxxxxxxxxxxxxxxxxxxxxxxxxxxxxxxxxxxxxxxxxxxxxx
xxxxxxxxxxxxxxxxxxxxxxxxxxxxxxxxxxxxxxxxxxxx</td></tr>
<tr><td>X X X X X X
</td><td>(Trade heading)</td></tr>
<tr><td>XXXXXXXXXXX
(Sub-head.)</td><td>xxxxxxxxxxxxxxxxxxxxxxxxxxxxxxxxxxxxxxxxxxxxxxxxxxxxxxxxxxxxxxxxxxxx
xxxxxxxxxxxxxxxxxxxxxxxxxxxxxxxxxxxxxxxxxxxxx

xxxxxxxxxxxxxxxxxxxxxxxxxxxxxxxxxxxxxxxxxxxxxxxxxxxxxxxxxxxxxxxxxxxx
xxxxxxxxxxxxxxxxxxxxxxxxxxxxxxxxxxxxxxxxxxxxxxxxxxxxxxxxxxxxxxxxxxxx
xxxxxxxxxxxxxxxxxxxxxxxxxx</td></tr>
<tr><td>XXXXXXXXXXX
(Sub-head.)</td><td>xxxxxxxxxxxxxxxxxxxxxxxxxxxxxxxxxxxxxxxxxxxxxxxxxxxxxxxxxxxxxxxxxxxx
xxxxxxxxxxxxxxxxxxxxxxxxxxxxxxxxxxxxxxxxxxxxxxxxxxxxxxxxxxxxxxxxxxxx
xxxxxxxxxxxxxxxxxxxxxxxxxxxxxxxxxxxxxxxxxxxxxxxxxxxxxxxxxxxxxxxxxxxx
xxxxxxxxxxxxxxx</td></tr>
<tr><td>X X X X X X
</td><td>(Trade heading)</td></tr>
<tr><td>XXXXXXXXXXX
XXXXXXXXXXX
XXXXXXX
(Sub-head.)</td><td>xxxxxxxxxxxxxxxxxxxxxxxxxxxxxxxxxxxxxxxxxxxxxxxxxxxxxxxxxxxxxxxxxxxx
xxxxxxxxxxxxxxxxxxxxxxxxxxxxxxxxxxxxxxxxxxxxxxxxxxxxxxxxxxxxxxxxxxxx
xxxxxxxxxxxxxxxxxxxxxxxxxxxxxxxxxxxxxxxxxxxxxxxxxxxxxxxxxxxxxxxxxxxx
xxxxxxxxxxxxxxxxxxxxxxxxxxxxxxxxxxxxxxxxx</td></tr>
<tr><td>XXXXXXXXX
(Sub-head.)</td><td>xxxxxxxxxxxxxxxxxxxxxxxxxxxxxxxxxxxxxxxxxxxxxxxxxxxxxxxxxxxxxxxxxxxx
xxxxxxxxxxxxxxxxxxxxxxxxxxxxxxxxxxxxxxxxxxxxxxxxxxxxxxxxxxxxxxxxxxxx
xxxxxxxxxxxxxxxxxxxxxxxxxxxxxxxxxxxxxxxxxxxxxxxxxxxxx</td></tr>
<tr><td>XXXXXXXXXXX
XXXXXXXXX
XXXXXXXXXX
(Sub-head.)</td><td>xxxxxxxxxxxxxxxxxxxxxxxxxxxxxxxxxxxxxxxxxxxxxxxxxxxxxxxxxxxxxxxxxxxx
xxxxxxxxxxxxxxxxxxxxxxxxxxxxxxxxxxxxxxxxxxxxxxxxxxxxxxxxxxxxxxxxxxxx
xxxxxxxxxxxxxxxxxxxxxxxxxxxxxxxxxxxxxxxxxxxxxxxxxxxxxxxxxxxxxxxxxxxxx
xxxxxxxxxxxxxxxxxxxxxxxxxxxxx</td></tr>
</table>

Semi-blocked method of layout

Nevertheless, it will be of assistance to the typist if she has practice in typing the different styles of layout during her training, so that her ideas do not become too fixed when she starts work.

If the traditional or semi-blocked style is being used, the left-hand

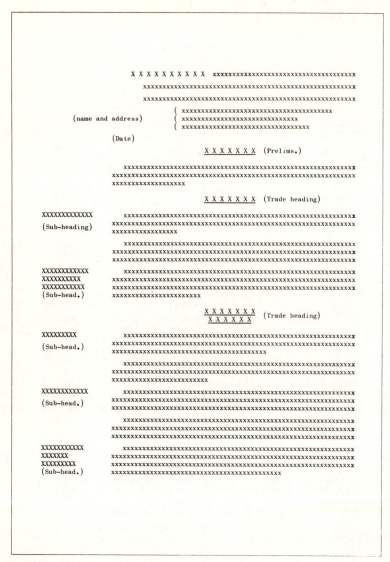

Traditional method of layout

margin stop should be set at the point which will be most frequently used (for the paragraphs) and tab stops should be set where the sub-headings, paragraph indentations (if traditional style) and trade headings will begin: the margin release key and carriage release lever will need to be used to take the printing point to the extreme left of the paper, before pressing the tab bar to obtain the point for the sub-headings.

The endorsement. When a specification is short, the A4 sheets should be folded (and creased) in two from left to right and the endorsement typed in the centre of the surface then uppermost. As with the similar legal endorsement, the folds will all appear on the left-hand edge of the endorsement.

Since long specifications are bound in some way, the endorsement is typed on the front cover.

An example of a specification endorsement follows:

```
            August 19—


        SPECIFICATION OF WORK

          to be carried out

                 at

        29-34 Church Street

            BARNSTAPLE

                for

           Mr William James


                ----


          J Johnson & Co Ltd

        Architects & Surveyors

          60 High Street

            BARNSTAPLE
```

Speed/accuracy tests. Many teachers use speed/accuracy timings as a teaching method throughout the typewriting course. Such timings can begin from about the fourth lesson, i.e., once students have covered enough key reaches to be able to type short sentences (even though the meaning of some of them may be somewhat dubious).

Most typewriting courses begin by introducing the home key row so that the central position of the hands is first established. Other keys are gradually introduced to enable words and meaningful matter to be typed as quickly as possible. The typing of rows of meaningless letter combinations should be kept to a minimum since students find them boring—and such an attitude retards rather than assists progress.

Thus a student often begins her speed/accuracy training by typing short sentences. It is important that speed and accuracy are developed hand in hand and good teachers bear this in mind: one without the other is of no value. The class may first be required to type a given sentence as many times as possible in one minute, the aim being *complete control and accuracy*. Then the same sentence may be repeated once or twice (again for one minute each time) with the main aim of *increasing speed* and making the fingers work as fast as possible. The speed/accuracy drill period then concludes by typing the same sentence again for one minute with the original aim of *complete control and accuracy*. If the operation has been successful—as it frequently is—the student will find that her final typing of the sentence will be both more accurate and faster than the first attempt.

Students enjoy this class activity and it is a strong motivating force. They should be given a specially designed form to keep in their folders to record the date, the number of errors made in the first timing (with speed in brackets), the highest speed attained in the speed timings, and the results of the final accuracy timing—which should be recorded in the same way as the first one. In this way, healthy competition is introduced and fostered and the students compete not only against each other but also strive to improve their own performance.

Timings of the kind just described normally begin with one minute of typing, proceeding to two minutes and then to three minutes. The repeated matter should first be sentences of increasing length, then paragraphs of increasing length and difficulty. It is obviously not realistic to continue with the pattern of accuracy timing/speed timings/accuracy timing beyond a timed period of three minutes. Thereafter the speed/accuracy drill part of the lesson should aim at controlled copy with a maximum error tolerance of two errors for each one hundred words typed (or one error per fifty words and part of fifty words).

Some teachers successfully use 'speed paragraphs' which have to be typed within a prescribed accuracy level in one minute. The class begins with paragraphs of fifteen words, proceeds to twenty words, then twenty-five, thirty, thirty-five, and so on until the highest speed possible is reached by accurate typing. It is sound practice to require each student to 'pass' two paragraphs at one speed before being allowed to attempt the next highest speed.

Often these speed paragraphs are duplicated by the teacher—she providing, say, four paragraphs at each speed. She initials in the right-hand margin when a paragraph has been satisfactorily completed in the one minute, and in this way can keep a check on the progress of each student. The students should always correct their own work, neatly encircling each error: the teacher should check herself before initialling to indicate satisfactory completion of the work.

In speed/accuracy work one counts 'standard words' rather than the actual words typed. A standard word consists of five strokes. Each letter, character, and space counts as a stroke; also each machine manipulation, such as use of the tabulator key/bar for paragraph indentation, and return of the carriage at the end of the line. Some systems count an upper case letter or character as two strokes.

The cumulative stroke count for a passage is given at the end of each line, in the right-hand margin so that the number of standard words typed in a given timing can be easily calculated. If a student ends in the middle of a line she should take the cumulative stroke count given at the end of the last complete line she typed and add on the strokes for the part line. A ruler can be a useful aid here—using the part marked with inches in tenths for pica pitch and twelfths for elite pitch. When the total stroke count has been determined, it should be divided by five to find the number of standard words typed. The number of standard words typed should be divided by the minutes of typing to find the speed in words a minute. For example, 1500 strokes typed equals 300 standard words. If this was completed in 10 minutes, the speed is 30 words a minute. A maximum of one error per fifty words or part of fifty words typed should be allowed for a 'pass'.

Another recognized method of marking speed/accuracy tests is to *deduct ten words from the total typed for each error*. For example, a student who typed 500 words in 10 minutes with 7 errors would be credited with a speed of 43 words a minute.

For speed/accuracy tests the copy should, in general, be of average difficulty; not confined to easy matter—or the students will get a false impression of their ability.

Spirit duplicating (see also **Reprography processes**). With this method of reproduction a spirit duplicating machine is necessary. The master is prepared on special one-sided chromo paper and can be written, drawn or typed—or a combination of all three can be used. The master sheet should be placed with the chromo (shiny) side downwards on top of a special hectograph carbon, with the carbon coating face upwards. Unlike ordinary carbon paper, hectograph carbons can be used only once. Using a spirit backing sheet, the two papers should then be inserted into the typewriter and the master typed through the ribbon in the usual way on to the dull side of the chromo paper. Under the pressure of the typewriter keys, an image in reverse is transferred from the carbon paper to the shiny side of the master.

Special spirit duplicating copy paper is loaded on to the paper tray of the machine. The machine is fitted with a felt pad which is moistened with a colourless spirit by the operator (either automatically or by hand). It is advisable to test the amount of moisture transferring from the pad to the copy paper by passing several sheets through the machine. This 'testing' avoids wasting paper as the test sheets soon dry off, when they can be used again in the ordinary duplicating process. The master is then fitted round the cylinder of the duplicator, the image side uppermost. As each sheet of copy paper enters the machine it is lightly moistened with spirit: it is then pressed against the reverse image of the master and a positive (readable) image thus transferred to the copy paper. Each time a copy is made, a minute amount of the special carbon from the master is transferred to the copy paper. Therefore if only a small number of copies is required, the pressure control should be set at high to obtain the maximum possible density of ink on the copies. If the run is to be a medium or long one, it should begin with the pressure control at 1 and increase one point at a time, the number of copies taken at each position being dependent upon the number required. In this way maximum use will be made of the master. It should be remembered, however, that it is possible to use a master, run off some copies, and retain it for future use, should this be necessary.

The number of good copies obtainable by this method of reproduction is obviously limited—200 being the maximum number generally found obtainable. If more than 200 copies are required, it is necessary to use either a stencil and ink duplicator or an offset duplicator.

One advantage of the spirit method of duplicating—apart from its ease and cheapness—is that the hectograph carbons are available in seven colours. Violet carbons are recommended if only one colour is needed and the maximum number of copies possible is required. As many colours as are required can be used on a single master simply by changing the colour of the carbon at the required position. All the colours can be simultaneously reproduced from the master in a single run (compare **Ink duplicating** on this point). This facility is a great advantage and for this reason the method is frequently used in the preparation of diagrams (for Biology, for instance) or maps.

Points to observe when typing spirit masters
1. The type faces should be clean and in good condition for the production of clear, incisive masters. The number of copies obtainable is, to some extent, dependent on the quality of the master.
2. The platen should be in good condition and free from 'pitting'. Use

of a backing sheet is advisable when typing a master to cushion the effect of any roughness of the platen.

3. With a manual typewriter, the typist should use a sharp, even touch. Any unevenness in striking the keys will show up clearly on the master and the copies taken from it.

4. Lines are best produced on spirit masters by a 4/6H sharp pencil and a ruler.

5. The master should be carefully checked before copies are run off.

Correcting errors on a spirit master. Raise the paper bail and take the following steps.

1. Turn the paper up an inch or so and pull the master gently forward so that the reverse image is visible and accessible.

2. Rest the portion to be corrected on to a spirit master plate and gently remove the error by means of a spirit eraser or a sharp metal blade.

3. Place a strip of unused hectograph carbon of the required colour at the point where the correction is to be made.

4. Replace the paper bail and turn the platen back to the correct position for typing the correction.

5. When the correction has been made, remove the inserted strip of hectograph carbon.

Spirit duplicating masters can also be prepared from a typed or printed original by means of a copying machine.

Square brackets. See **Combination characters and special signs.**

Standard fingering method. See **Fingering methods.**

Statements of account. At regular intervals (usually monthly but sometimes quarterly), every firm sends to each of its customers a 'statement of account'. These are usually typed on specially printed forms—the layout and ruling of which varies considerably.

The *printed* information on statements of account includes:

(a) Name, address, etc., of seller
(b) Ruled columns (there are usually separate columns for Debit and Credit items) and boxes
(c) Terms of payment

As with invoices, the letters E. & O.E. (errors and omissions excepted) are usually printed on statements so that the seller reserves the right to correct any errors that later come to light.

Particulars that are *typewritten* include some or all of the following:

(a) Name and address of customer
(b) Customer's folio number in Sales Ledger
(c) Date of despatch of statement
(d) Balance owing or in credit from previous accounts
(e) Details of goods supplied or returned during the period in question
(f) Date of despatch or return of goods
(g) Invoice or reference numbers
(h) Sub-totals, totals, and final total
(i) Discount

Most statements of account contain a ruled box, etc., for insertion of the customer's name and address so that a window envelope can be used (see **Envelopes**).

Statements of account not only remind the customer that payment is due but also enable a comparison to be made of the buyer's and seller's books so that any discrepancies can be cleared up.

Typing statements of account. The basic rules given for the typing of invoices (see **Invoices**) apply to the typing of statements.

Stencils. See **Ink duplicating.**

Stenotyping. Stenotyping is based on phonetics and words are recorded in a contracted but intelligible form according to the way they are spoken. A stenotyping machine can be used for recording any language with which the operator is familiar.

Stenotyping machines are portable and almost silent in use: they are particularly useful for recording the business at meetings and conferences. The contracted language is recorded on a paper roll and later transcribed on to an ordinary typewriter just as shorthand notes are.

Stenotypists are taught to operate the machines by 'touch' and, unlike typewriters, the keys of a stenotyping machine can be struck with both hands simultaneously. The vowels are positioned in the centre of the keyboard and are struck with the thumbs.

The bands produced from the paper rolls are easy to read and a non-operator can be trained to read and transcribe the recorded material. This feature is a valuable asset if matter must be transcribed quickly—perhaps while a meeting is still in progress. A band can be delivered to a transcriber who can work on it while the stenotyper continues to record the business of the meeting. Often a change of ribbon colour is used to indicate a change of speaker.

Stitching margin. See **Literary work** (*Margins*).

Straight fingering method. See **Fingering methods.**

Striking of typewriter keys. Key striking on both manual and electric typewriters is a ballistic motion, the vital difference being that electric machines require considerably less force than manual ones. Because the keys of an electric typwriter need only a slight 'dab' for an impression to be made, precision of movement of the fingers is very important.

With manual typewriters, a much stronger striking of the keys is necessary, but each strike should be a rapid one with a sharp staccato touch. On no account should the learners 'press' the keys down since another character cannot be made until the previous typebar has been released. Pressing the keys rather than sharply striking them will merely slow down speed of operation and often lead to clashing of the typebars at the printing point (see **Clashing of typebars**).

In the early learning stages of Typewriting, students should be instructed to poise their fingers slightly above the home keys (**asdf**— left hand and **;lkj**—right hand). Before electric typewriters were so widely used, learners were often taught to *rest* their fingers on the home keys—but with electric machines this would obviously produce disastrous results. However, for many experienced typists this habit of resting the fingers on the home keys has become so ingrained that it is often an impediment to their changing from manual to electric machines. Once high typewriting speeds are reached the positioning of all the fingers over the home keys becomes intermittent, although the central position of the hands over the keyboard is largely maintained, and whenever there is a pause in typing, the skilled operator will automatically find her fingers hovering over the home keys.

This central position of the hands is important in touch typewriting because, from it, the individual fingers acquire the skill to move in the right direction in mastering all the key reaches.

When striking the keys there should be as little movement as possible in the wrists and hands. Movement should be restricted, as far as possible, to the fingers only, but mastery of independent finger action takes a considerable amount of practice, particularly with people who have not been used to moving their fingers separately for any length of time. It is for this reason that young people who can play the piano often master independent finger action comparatively quickly.

When using manual typewriters, many learners experience difficulty in securing uniformly dense impression of the characters. Until they have had a great deal of practice, letters struck with the weaker fingers— particularly the little finger of each hand—appear fainter than letters struck with the stronger fingers, with which independent finger action is easier to master.

Suffix drills. See **Drills**.

Superior (raised) characters. (See also **Inferior (lowered) characters.**) Superior characters are raised half a space above the normal typing line. The half-space mechanism, interliner or variable line spacer are used for this purpose. Superior characters are used for algebraic formulae, footnote signs, etc. Examples follows.

$$x^2 + y^3 = z^4$$

```
In his latest book* Mr Turner describes . . .
```

Tabular work. See **Display** and **Column work without column headings** and **Column work with column headings.**

Tabulator. See **Parts of a typewriter.**

Tabulator drills. See **Drills.**

Tailpieces. These are decorative endings to articles, programmes, book chapters, sections, etc. They vary in decorative content and some examples follow:

```
                    o

                  o:o

                o:o:o

              o:o:o:o

            o:o:o:o:o



              :-:-:-:-:

              --ooOoo--


          *************
```

Teaching yourself to type. See **Learning to type.**

Technique drills. See **Drills.**

Technique errors. See **Errors, their cause and remedy.**

Telegrams. A telegram may be sent either by telephone (consult Dialling Instruction booklet for appropriate dialling code) or by handing a completed telegram form in at a post office.

In the business situation it is advisable to use a telegram form since, by taking a carbon copy (either on plain paper or on another telegram form) an exact copy of the message can be filed. Telegrams may be handwritten in ink, in block letters, or typed—the latter method usually being adopted in an office, where a supply of telegram forms should always be kept.

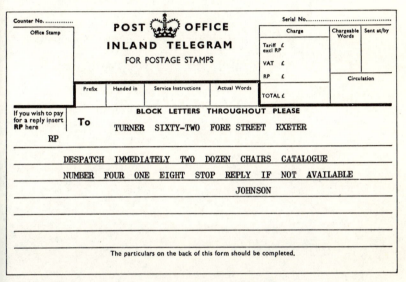

Inland Telegram form, with message clearly typed

The telegram message and particulars should be typed all in capital letters (with two or three spaces between words, for clarity). The message should be as concise as possible since the charge is dependent on length, but the meaning must be *clear*. Only essential punctuation marks should be inserted and these must be typed in word form. Numbers should be given as words and there should be no salutation or complimentary close. If a telegraphic address is used on the telegram, the typist should type the full name and address of the addressee on the carbon copy, for filing. A telegram should normally be confirmed by letter, posted on the same day that the telegram is sent. Often a second carbon copy is taken for this purpose and enclosed with the covering letter.

Television scripts. TV scripts, like radio scripts, are a specialized form of typing and comparatively few typists will ever be required to type them. As with many typewritten documents, there are some variations in styling and layout.

An excerpt from a typical television script follows, together with a list of points to note.

```
                              -4-
        31.          INT.          OLD PEOPLE'S CLUB          DAY

                    (THIS IS A LARGE ROOM WITH SEVERAL TABLES PILED HIGH
                    WITH ARTICLES. CARDBOARD BOXES, PAINTINGS, ETC.,
                    WITH OLD AGE PENSIONERS WORKING AT THEM.

                    THE PRINCIPAL, MRS. WEATHERBY, A HANDSOME WOMAN OF
                    FORTY-FIVE, IS CONDUCTING THE NEWCOMERS ROUND. SHE
                    PUSHES MRS. HALLIDAY BESIDE A SHARP-FEATURED SMALL
                    WOMAN.)

        MRS. WEATHERBY: This lady is making cardboard boxes. Mrs.
        Williamson, show Mrs. Halliday how you do them.

        MRS. HALLIDAY: We've met.

                    (PAN WITH MRS. WEATHERBY AS SHE GOES OVER TO GRAN AND
                    TAKES HER ARM, LOOKING FOR A SUITABLE INTRODUCTION.

                    SHE REACHES A ROBUST LATE-SIXTIES HANDSOME MAN NAMED
                    MARSHALL, SMARTLY DRESSED, SMOKING A CIGAR, ENGAGED IN
                    A LOVE/HATE RELATIONSHIP WITH A BASKET OF RAFIA WORK.)

        GRAN: Please! Do carry on. (POINTS TO BASKET)

        MARSHALL: I was afraid you'd say that.

        GRAN: Of course, if you have a car, and plenty of spare time,
        you could be doing more important things.
```

MIX TELECINE
L.S. of an open old Rolls
speeding through the
countryside, with four
people in it: MARSHALL,
GRAN, MRS. HALLIDAY and
O'MALLEY.

END TELECINE

```
        32.          INT.          DAY          B.P.

                    (MARSHALL IS ON HIS FAVOURITE THEME, BUT NO-ONE IS
                    LISTENING. THEY ARE ALL ENJOYING THE COUNTRYSIDE.)

        MARSHALL: We're cluttering up the earth. Ought to be done
        away with, everybody over sixty.

                    (Sound dubbed: Car skidding)

                    (MARSHALL'S EYES NEARLY POP OUT OF HIS HEAD AS HE
                    SWERVES LEFT AND RIGHT.)

        The idiot! He nearly killed me!
```

Points to Note

1. The script is divided into 'frames' and each one is numbered and underscored.

2. Each number is followed by information which 'sets the scene'.

3. The typing, which should be on one side only of A4 paper, allows a wide left-hand margin. Dialogue, general instructions, and sound effects are typed on the right-hand side of the paper: *visual* information is placed on the left-hand side—and it is here that the producer adds his camera directions.

4. The names of the characters are typed in closed capitals, underscored and followed by a colon. In this example, their dialogue begins

on the same line as their name: alternatively, the dialogue begins on the following line, starting at the same point as the name.

5. Dialogue is typed in single spacing with a line of space between each speech and effect.

6. General directions are typed in capital letters and enclosed in brackets: they begin an inch to the right of the dialogue margin.

7. Special sound effects are typed in lower case and enclosed in brackets: they begin at the same point as the general instructions.

8. Each page should be numbered both at the top and bottom, in the centre of the sheet.

9. Abbreviations are used. In this excerpt the following occur:

INT. Interior

L.S. Long Shot

B.P. Back Projection

Telex. Modern business and industry must have quick and reliable communications. The postal, telephone, and telegraph services all play a vital part in meeting this requirement.

The postal service provides the main means of written communication—and for many business matters the written word is essential. However, the post is relatively slow. The telephone gives immediate service, provided the called party is available, but lacks the often necessary authority of the written word. The telegraph service provides written communication but cannot compare in speed with the telephone. The problem of providing *immediate* printed or typed communication has been overcome by the telex (short for telegraph exchange) service. It was developed particularly for business purposes, is expanding rapidly, and connection can be made with other telex users in nearly every country in the world.

A teleprinter looks something like a large electric typewriter. As can be seen from the illustration of the Teleprinter No. 15, its keyboard is basically the same as a typewriter's and anyone who can type can also operate a teleprinter with very little additional training.

Many trained typists may become telex operators through expediency or choice, but since the work is repetitive, success in it requires a particular kind of temperament. The telex system and technique will be briefly described for the benefit of typists interested in this kind of work.

The operating procedure of a teleprinter is very simple. You first press the 'dial' button on the dialling unit (see illustration), when the green bulb will light up to show that the circuit is ready for use. You dial the wanted number and are connected almost immediately. On connection, the distant teleprinter automatically sends its 'answer-back' code, so you can check that you are through to the right number. You send you own 'answer-back' to let them know who you are, and then

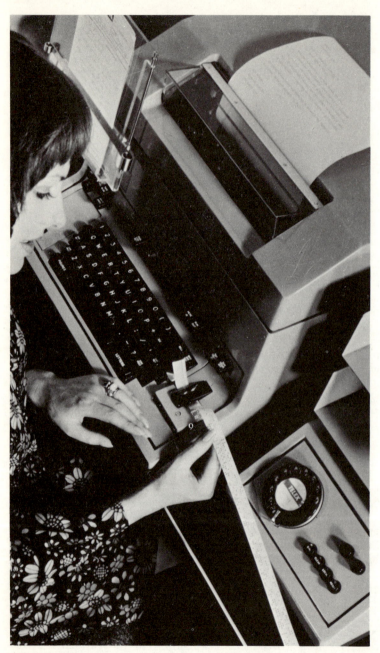

Teleprinter No. 15

type your message, which appears simultaneously (all in capitals) on the machine you are calling. When you have finished, to confirm that you are still connected and that the whole of your message has been received at the distant end, you send your 'answer-back' code and obtain the code of the distant machine. Pressing the button marked 'clear' on the dialling

Keyboard layout of the Teleprinter No. 15

unit disconnects the apparatus from the exchange. Incoming and outgoing messages can be identified by using a bichrome ribbon.

A telex machine does not have to be attended all the time by an operator. It receives messages automatically—even outside office hours—provided that it is connected to the power supply. This is an obvious advantage to firms that deal with overseas countries where, because of time differences, the working day may coincide for only a short time.

The language used on teleprinters is usually condensed, as on telegrams, conveying only essential information. Call charges, like STD telephone rates, are based on the distance of the transmission and the time used. Increased efficiency and saving of costs are obtained by automatic transmission—now an integral part of the Teleprinter No. 15 (although the model is available without this facility).

Automatic transmission enables users to send messages by means of punched paper tape at a constant speed of about 70 words a minute. The tapes are prepared while the machine is 'off-line' (not actually transmitting) and no call charges are being incurred. By this means it is possible to prepare and check messages before starting to pay for line time, thereby keeping the call time and consequent charges to a minimum. When you transmit the prepared message you simply insert the tape, flick a switch and the machine automatically sends the message. The tapes can be used over and over again if necessary—which is useful if the same message has to be sent to several destinations.

Telex messages should be prepared on the standard message forms available from the Post Office. To assist the telex operator, difficult or unusual words should be printed in capital letters.

Paper is fitted to the teleprinter in rolls. 'Multi-ply' paper can be used to obtain up to six copies. It is essential that the machine is regularly checked to ensure that it has an adequate supply of paper—particularly at the end of the working day when incoming messages may be received out of office hours.

The Post Office produces a directory of all subscribers in the United Kingdom and it is also possible to obtain international telex directories—vital for firms needing to contact overseas organizations.

Tender (see also **Bills of quantities** and **Specifications**). A tender is a quotation for a particular job of work and a formal indication of the willingness to accept the terms of the Contract if and when the tender is accepted.

A form of tender is usually sent out to an interested contractor, together with the bill of quantities and any other relevant documents. Tenders vary in wording and layout but a typical example follows.

```
THE   PROPOSED   ERECTION   OF
        AN OFFICE BLOCK
             at

   . . . . . . . . . . . . . . . . . . . . . . .

   . . . . . . . . . . . . . . . . . . . . . . .

   . . . . . . . . . . . . . . . . . . . . . . .

             for

   . . . . . . . . . . . . . . . . . . . . . . .


   F O R M   O F   T E N D E R
```

```
The Borough Architect
County Hall
LIVERPOOL

Dear Sir

I/We, the undersigned, do hereby tender to
construct, complete and maintain for a period of
six months, the whole of the works comprised in
the above Contract and to supply all materials,
plant and labour according to the true intent
and meaning of the Conditions of Contract,
Drawings and Bill of Quantities which I/we have
carefully inspected and to the entire satisfac-
tion of the Architects in the said Conditions of
Contract mentioned for the sum of...............
. . . . . . . . . . . . . . . . . . . . . . . . . . . . . (£_____).
```

I/We undertake and agree within fourteen days after acceptance by the Employer of this Tender, to execute a Contract prepared by the Architects of the form mentioned in the Conditions of Contract for the due and satisfactory performance of the Contract.

And I/we further undertake to complete and deliver up the whole of the works within .... weeks of the date of signing the Contract

AS WITNESS my/our hand(s) this ....

day of ....

Signature ....

Address   ....

           ....

           ....

Signature of Witness

           ....

Address   ....

           ....

           ....

The Employer does not bind himself to accept the lowest or any tender.

LABOUR RATES

Schedule of Labour Rates for which the Contractor requires Adjustment of Cost as Clause 24/B (1), and for Daywork Prices as Clause 8 (b) (ii) of the Form of Contract.

      Tradesman .... p per hour

      Labourer .... p per hour

Declaration   The Tender is based on the preceding rates which are current at the date of tender.

Date of Tender ....

Signature of Contractor ....

              ....

Time. Increasing use is being made of the international 24-hour clock to state the time. In these days of frequent international travel the method is clearer for all concerned. It is used for all air, rail, and other traffic timetables, in many offices and walks of life, and is, of course, the normal way of telling the time on the Continent and elsewhere.

The 24-hour clock. This spans the twenty-four hours from midnight to midnight. It always includes four figures, the first two representing the hour and the second two indicating any following minutes. It is followed by 'hours' or the abbreviation 'hrs' (with or without a following stop, depending on the method used of typing abbreviations). For instance, one minute after midnight would be typed as 0001 hrs and one minute before midnight would appear as 2359 hrs. Midnight itself, however, must always be represented by the word. Mid-day is typed as 1200 hrs and it follows that any hour before ten would begin with a nought and any hour between mid-day and midnight would carry on from the twelve for the first two figures which indicate the hour. For example:

    0540 hrs (5.40 am)
    0900 hrs (9.00 am)
    1330 hrs (1.30 pm)
    2115 hrs (9.15 pm)

The four figures always included in the 24-hour clock are usually not punctuated in any way. Sometimes, however, a stop is used to divide the hours from the minutes as in 14.20 hrs (2.20 pm).

The preceding examples are spoken as follows.

    0540 hrs (oh five forty hours)
    0900 hrs (oh nine hundred hours)
    1330 hrs (thirteen thirty hours)
    2115 hrs (twenty-one fifteen hours)
    1420 hrs (fourteen twenty hours)

The traditional method of telling the time. We often say 'eight o'clock in the morning' or 'eight o'clock this evening', although when typing letters or other formal documents, these times would be represented as:

    8.00 am (or 0800 hrs)
    8.00 pm (or 2000 hrs)

When using 'am' or 'pm', the preceding number is always typed as a figure, as in the above examples. However, if one is typing the time using the words 'o'clock', figures are usually given as words. Increasingly, nevertheless, figures are used before 'o'clock', as in the following example.

```
There were 24 men and they all set out at
8 o'clock in the morning.
```

Timed typewriting. There is a tendency to think of timed typing mainly in relation to working from straightforward printed or typed copy. This aspect is dealt with under the separate entry **Speed/ accuracy tests.**

Many teachers find that their students tackle speed/accuracy tests with alertness and speed. They are all keyed up and ready to begin typing the moment the teacher says 'start now'. However, once production typing is resumed they lapse into a comparatively desultory attitude to work and speed is not considered important. In the office situation, however, *production speed is of prime importance.* Also, students will find it difficult to pass their typewriting examinations unless they can produce speedy and accurate work.

Therefore, in the typewriting learning situation it is very important that students are made aware of the constant need to produce each typewriting task as speedily as possible and to a mailable standard.

To a large extent the speed at which we do things is habit. For instance, we dress in the mornings or walk along the street at a pace which has become habitual. Unless a conscious mental effort is made to do things at a faster rate, we tend to plod along with things at the same pace. The same is true of production typewriting. We have to train the mind to tackle each new task at a rate that represents a genuine endeavour to make use of all the speed at our command.

Some suggestions follow to help train students to tackle production tasks as quickly and accurately as possible.

1. At regular intervals, time the class *for one or two minutes on production work.* Get them to see how much they can type of, say, a letter, or a report from manuscript in this time.

2. Train them (by timing) to type an envelope in ten seconds or less.

3. When typewriter ribbons need changing, see how many of the class can do this in one minute. Before beginning the timing, ensure that the worn ribbon has been completely wound on to one spool.

4. Give regular, general tests consisting of more than one task. The length of the tests should be geared to the lesson time available, and the material given should be based on previous instruction. This is a useful lead-up to 'mock' examinations.

To achieve the best results, the teacher should do her part by carefully marking the work and keeping a systematic record of performance. The results should be interpreted in terms of student needs and necessary help given on an individual, group or class basis.

Title page. See **Literary work.**

Titles, decorations, qualifications, forms of address, etc.
An employer often leaves his typist/secretary to check on titles, decorations, qualifications, and forms of address. If in doubt, she should always refer to a reference book or telephone an appropriate person who would possess the correct information about a person's qualifications, etc.

Some of the more common titles and forms of address are given on page 257–8, set out in the open punctuated style. A more comprehensive list will be found in *Titles and Forms of Address* published by A. & C. Black. A typist should possess a copy of this book if her employer corresponds with many titled people. The list is for use in formal correspondence: if the relationship were informal, the wording would be correspondingly less formal, particularly for the salutation and complimentary close. Increasingly, titled people do not object to, and often prefer, less formal wording. The typist should consult her employer's wishes, however, before deviating from traditional practice.

The correct order of precedence for notable persons in Great Britain is given in *Whitaker's Almanack*.

The typist should ensure that she types decorations, honours, and qualifications in their correct order after titles (if any). As a general rule they are listed in order of importance, which is as follows.

1. *Decorations and honours*, e.g., (Military and Civil)	VC (Victoria Cross), MC (Military Cross), DSO (Distinguished Service Order), CBE (Commander of the Most Excellent Order of the British Empire)
2. *Educational qualifications*, e.g.,	PhD (Doctor of Philosophy), MA (Master of Arts), BA (Bachelor of Arts), BSc (Bachelor of Science)
3. *Professional Titles*, e.g.,	FRCS (Fellow of the Royal College of Surgeons), FRSA (Fellow of the Royal Society of Arts), ACA (Associate Member of the Institute of Chartered Accountants)
4. *Member of Parliament*	MP (last because it's not permanent!)

An example including one each of the above is: Mr J Matthews, VC, MA, FRSA, MP.

Educational and professional qualifications are usually omitted except in formal correspondence.

Title	Form of Address	Salutation	Usual Complimentary Close
Archbishop	His Grace The Lord Archbishop of—	My Lord Archbishop	I have the honour to be, my Lord Archbishop Your Lordship's obedient servant
Baron	The Right Hon Lord—	My Lord	I have the honour to be, my Lord Your Lordship's obedient servant
Baroness	The Right Hon Lady—	Madam	I have the honour to be, Madam Your Ladyship's obedient servant
Baronet	Sir Malcolm—, Bt.	Sir	I have the honour to be, Sir Your obedient servant
Baronet's Wife	Lady—	Madam	I have the honour to be, Madam Your obedient servant
Bishop (with seat in Lords)	The Right Rev The Lord Bishop of—	My Lord Bishop	I have the honour to be, my Lord Bishop Your Lordship's obedient servant
Countess	The Right Hon The Countess of—	Madam	I have the honour to be, Madam Your Ladyship's obedient servant
Duchess	Her Grace The Duchess of—	Madam	I am, Madam Your Grace's most obedient servant
Duke	His Grace The Duke of—	My Lord Duke	I am, my Lord Duke Your Grace's most obedient servant
Earl	The Right Hon The Earl of—	My Lord	I have the honour to be, my Lord Your Lordship's obedient servant
Judge	The Hon Mr Justice—	Sir	I am, Sir Your obedient servant
Knight	Sir James—	Sir	I am, Sir Your obedient servant
Knight's Wife	Lady—	Madam	I am, Madam Your obedient servant
Lord Mayor	The Right Worshipful The Lord Mayor of—	My Lord Mayor	I am, My Lord Mayor Your obedient servant
Lord Provost	The Lord Provost of—	My Lord Provost	I am, my Lord Provost Your obedient servant
Marchioness	The Most Hon The Marchioness of—	Madam	I have the honour to be, Madam Your Ladyship's obedient servant

Titles, etc.

Title	Form of Address	Salutation	Usual Complimentary Close
Marquess	The Most Hon The Marquess of—	My Lord Marquess	I have the honour to be, my Lord Your Lordship's obedient servant
Mayor (Mayoress)	The Right Worshipful The Mayor (Mayoress) of—	Sir (Madam)	I am, Sir (Madam) Your obedient servant
Minister of Church	The Rev J—	Reverend Sir	I am, Reverend Sir Your obedient servant
Viscount	The Right Hon The Viscount—	My Lord	I have the honour to be, my Lord Your Lordship's obedient servant
Viscountess	The Right Hon The Viscountess—	Madam	I have the honour to be, Madam Your Ladyship's obedient servant

Messrs Used when addressing a partnership (e.g., Messrs Watson & James), although it is often omitted if there are three or more names (e.g., Stimpson, Lock & Brown). A limited company is an impersonal legal entity so the name of such a firm should not be preceded by Messrs. However, if personal names are included, Messrs is sometimes used in practice, e.g., Messrs Lamb & Martin Ltd. Messrs should not be used if the name of a firm begins with The (e.g., The Fenton Electrical Co.) or a title (e.g., Sir James Browning & Co.). The typist should follow the practice of her employers in the use of Messrs, since some firms deviate from what is generally considered good usage.

Mr and Esq One or the other should be used when addressing a man: it is incorrect to use both. Esq is considered formal and meaningless by many people (it once denoted an owner of property) and Mr is now in more general use.

Ms A form of address suitable for both married and single women.

Sen and Jun (or Snr and Jnr) Used to distinguish between a father and son with the same first name. It is typed before Esq (e.g., John Mason, Jun, Esq) when this method of address is preferred to Mr (Mr John Mason, Jun).

Unmarried Sisters Unmarried sisters should be addressed as in the following example—The Misses C & J Simpson.

Young boy	A young boy is addressed by his first name and surname (e.g., Henry Hull) or his name is preceded by Master—e.g., Master Henry Hull: the latter form is dying out.

Touch control adjuster. See **Parts of a typewriter.**

Touch typewriting (development of, and meaning). As you sit at your typewriter and 'touch' type with speed and skill, have you ever stopped to question the basis of that skill ? You probably remember the insistence of your teacher that, among other things, you sat correctly, positioned your fingers over the home keys, and typed without looking at the keys or typescript, keeping your eyes on the copy. Possibly it has never occurred to you that mastering typewriting ever involved anything different: but the development of 'touch' typing makes an interesting study.

The first practical typewriter was manufactured by Remington in 1873 (see **History of the typewriter**). At first little interest was shown in it and early sales were slow. However, an astute minority saw the potential of the new 'writing machine' and by the 1880s young ladies were being shown how to type.

The earliest typewriting instruction consisted of sitting the 'students' at the machines, showing them how to manipulate the then clumsy apparatus—and letting them get on with it by the best means they could devise for themselves. Speed and accuracy were the sole objectives and it mattered not one bit whether the students used two, four, or all their fingers and whether or not they looked at the keys or typescript. The 'sight' method in general use required neither textbook nor teacher because the typist's speed and accuracy, like Topsy, just 'growed'! In fact, the 'teacher's' main function was to check papers for accuracy.

One of the early sight operators of great speed was an American called Frank McGurrin. It is said that he was told in the later 1870s that a young lady could type rapidly, using all her fingers, *without* looking at the keys. McGurrin decided that if a girl could do such a thing, he could too. Within a year of hearing the story, Frank McGurrin could type at upwards of ninety words a minute without looking at the keys and using all his fingers. Having accomplished this feat, McGurrin learned that the story that inspired it was not true. However, he made history by becoming the first skilled practical exponent of 'touch' typewriting.

Speed championships were held each year in America and these brought about many and rapid improvements in typewriter construction and led to a questioning of the best techniques for operation. The typewriting championship of 1888 was a significant one. Basically it was between Frank McGurrin and another man called Louis Traub. In fact it was a contest between the two methods of typewriting—'touch' (McGurrin) and 'sight' (Traub): and between the two kinds of typewriter—the single keyboard (McGurrin) and the double keyboard (Traub). Before the shift key was introduced in 1887, some typewriters had two sets of keys, one for lower- and the other for upper-case letters. Traub used the Caligraph—the leading double keyboard typewriter of the time and he typed with only two fingers of each hand. McGurrin used a shift-key typewriter and, of course, by this time was a first-class 'touch' typist, using all his fingers and seldom looking at the keys. McGurrin was the decisive winner of this championship and proved conclusively the superiority of the single keyboard typewriter and the 'touch' method of operation.

The following year (1889) Bates Torrey of America published *A Manual of Practical Typewriting*, and described the method advocated in it as a 'touch' system. Obviously the lesson learned from McGurrin's defeat of Traub in the previous year was a powerful one for, since the publication of this manual in 1889, the teaching of 'touch' typewriting has never looked back. Many of the early teachers of typewriting, however, were largely ignorant of educational and skill psychology and although insisting that their students did not look at the keys when typing, instead made them learn by rote and recite the order of keys on each bank of the typewriter! Presumably it was assumed that with this knowledge, students would be able to find their way around the keyboard without the aid of sight! Memory of this kind, of course, plays little part in the learning of typewriting. So important was it considered that the students did not look at the keys, that they had to grope around underneath a cumbersome metal shield which stood over the keyboard. It is now generally recognized that such 'aids' retard rather than assist mastery of typewriting skill.

Gradually, after publication of *A Manual of Practical Typewriting*, there emerged a systematic approach to the teaching and learning of typewriting: teachers became aware of the different methods of mastering the keyboard and the importance of correct habit formation from the start. By about 1910 the guide key positions of the two little fingers on **a** and **;** had become established and this was accompanied by the almost permanent positioning (until high speeds are reached) of the fingers over the 'home keys', as the middle bank of letters is known. By about 1920 keyboard fingering had become standardized, with a few minor exceptions (see **Fingering methods**). Each finger was assigned a certain group of keys and the right-hand thumb used for operating the space bar.

Although there are still differences in the method and order of teaching the typewriter keyboard, the basic concepts are the same—all fingers of both hands are used and the students are instructed either not to look at the keys at all, or only in the *initial* learning stage. Most skilled typists would probably say that they are 'touch typists' and that they always type without looking at the keyboard. But this notion, which is fondly cherished by skilful typists about their own performance, is not as true as they think.

The sense of touch is one of the five commonly accepted senses—hearing, taste, sight, touch, and smell. Our sense of touch can tell us that something is rough rather than smooth, made of cloth rather than metal, but it has practically nothing at all to do with typewriting. It can only tell us that we are touching typewriter keys—not *which* keys we are touching. Therefore, the term 'touch typewriting' is, in fact, a complete misnomer. Typewriter keys are objects in space and the two senses that are best fitted for the perception of such objects in space are *touch* and *vision* combined.

However, it is kinesthesis (muscular sensations) on which virtually all acts of skill are based (*kinesthesis* from the Greek *kinetikos* (to move) and *aisthesis* (sensation). W. L. Jenkins in *Handbook of Experimental Psychology* (1951) states:

'Kinesthesis—the sense of position and movement—is probably the most important sensitivity man possesses. Without kinesthesis a person could not maintain erect posture, let alone walk, talk or engage in other skilled activities. Yet the existence of kinesthesis is not popularly appreciated and the word has no counterpart in common language.'

Visual control is, in fact, important while a person is learning a new perceptual motor skill. As his performance becomes automatic as a result of numerous repetitions, 'feel' (kinesthesis) becomes the more important factor. However, vision remains important, certainly in the perceptual motor skill of typewriting, and even very highly-skilled typists glance at the keys and what they are doing more often than they probably think.

Various experiments have been carried out in America to ascertain the part vision plays in the mastery of motor skills. All the experiments showed that vision is desirable in the early learning of motor skills and that the beginner should not attempt to rely solely on his muscular sensations, as this leads to increased errors. Thus the teacher of typewriting who strictly insists on 'touch' typing from the start is retarding rather than accelerating acquisition of the skill. Typewriting appears to be the only skill in this world that sighted persons are asked to learn as if they were blind. All beginners at typewriting—no matter how insistent the teacher may be about typing without looking—occasionally look at the keys or the typescript. This is not wilful misbehaviour: there is a definite need of vision for guidance and confirmation in the early stages of learning.

Fast, highly-skilled typists are perhaps not aware of the frequency with which they fleetingly glance at the keyboard or typescript without any interference to speed. They depend on vision far more than they think. Again, experiments carried out in America showed that there was no significant effect on speed when typists were deprived of the assistance of vision—but the effect on errors was enormous. Beginners more than doubled their errors whereas those with speeds of 85+ showed a 35 per cent increase in errors.

A good 'touch' typist who has been well trained will, of course, only seldom glance at the keys and typescript. It is important that the teacher explains to her class of beginners what they are doing and why—and what the ultimate aim is. Constant looking at the keys or typescript is impermissible for copy typing and transcription. However, it should be explained to the class that 'peeping' in the early learning stages is natural and desirable and that as the stimulus-response bonds build up the need for this will become less and less. The frequent 'peeping' that keen learners do after even several weeks of instruction attests to the slowness with which dependable kinesthetic sensations develop and the very real need for the support of vision. As with so many things in life and in learning, the transition process is a gradual one.

Transparent paper holders. See **Parts of a typewriter.**

Transposition. See **Errors, their cause and remedy.**

Twenty-four hour clock. See **Time.**

Type basket. See **Parts of a typewriter.**

Type-face styles. Typewriter manufacturers have their own special 'founts' or styles of type-faces and thus there are numerous kinds available.

When purchasing a typewriter fitted with standard typebars, one must select the type-face required. However, with some sophisticated typewriters it is possible to use a variety of type-faces on the one machine. For instance, on the Varityper the different type-faces can be easily and quickly changed. This machine has a keyboard but no typebars, the impression on the paper being produced by characters on strips of metal which are fitted to a central pillar and can be changed at will. Most IBM 'golf ball' typewriters are fitted with a detachable typing head which looks like a golf ball (hence the name). By changing the

ELITE is the other more usual business type style.
Clear and neat for good appearance.

A B C D E F G H I   1 2 3 4 5 6 7 8 9

SMALL MICRO is even more condensed, with three
additional characters, making seventeen in all.

A B C D E F G H I   1 2 3 4 5 6 7 8 9

COPY ELITE is sharp, crisp and eventoned. It is
suitable for correspondence and reproduction.

A B C D E F G H I   1 2 3 4 5 6 7 8 9

CONGRESS PICA is the largest of the shaded types.
Gives a clean, impressive printed appearance.

A B C D E F G H I   1 2 3 4 5 6 7 8 9

COPY PICA is sharp and crisp but the slightly
wider spacing makes for easier reading.

A B C D E F G H I   1 2 3 4 5 6 7 8 9

DOUBLE GOTHIC PICA. IS MAINLY USED FOR BILLING AND
ADDRESSING, BECAUSE OF ITS CLEAR CARBON COPIES.

A B C D E F G H I   1 2 3 4 5 6 7 8 9

*ITALIC ELITE BOLD is similar and smaller – quite
distinctive and clean in appearance.*

A B C D E F G H I   *1 2 3 4 5 6 7 8 9*

*Script is the perfect personal type style, for
it resembles beautiful handwriting.*

A B C D E F G H I   *1 2 3 4 5 6 7 8 9*

Examples of the different type-faces offered by one manufacturer alone

typing head to suit the particular purpose, a variety of type-faces can be easily used within a single piece of work.

Typewriter and manuscript correction signs. A typist will often be called upon to type a fair copy from a corrected typewritten draft. She therefore needs to be familiar with the commonly used signs employed, which are set out below. The marginal sign should be written on the same line as the correction, in the margin nearest the correction: if more than one correction appears in a single line, the marginal signs should be written in the same order as the corrections, reading from right to left (on both sides of the paper).

Sign in Margin	Sign in Text	Meaning
⊙/	⋀	Insert colon
⁏/	⋀	Insert semi-colon
⸴/	⋀	Insert comma
⸴/	⋀	Insert apostrophe (or superior figure or letter as shown)
2/	⋀	Insert inferior figure or letter as shown
⸴/ ⸴/	⋀	Insert single quotation marks
⸴⸴/ ⸴⸴/	⋀	Insert double quotation marks
/-/	⋀	Insert hyphen
/—/	⋀	Insert dash
caps/	Three lines under word(s)	Use spaced capitals
caps/	Two lines under word(s)	Use closed (unspaced) capitals
uc/	Underline or strike through letter(s) to be altered	Change from lower to upper case, i.e., use shift key
lc/	Underline or strike through letter(s) to be altered	Change to lower case
NP/	⌈	Begin new paragraph immediately after bracket sign
run on/	⌐	Do not begin a new paragraph, i.e. just 'run on' and start a new sentence

264

Sign in Margin	Sign in Text	Meaning
stet/	_ _ _ _	Let it stand. Type word(s) with broken line underneath them although crossed through or altered
	Cross through letter, word or words	Omit
	Cross through letter, word or words	Omit and close up the space
trs/		Transpose. If necessary, number the words 1, 2, 3, etc, to make order clear
		Close up space
eq #/		Equalize the spacing
raise/		Raise as indicated
lower/		Lower as indicated
	at right of words to be moved	Move to the left
	at left of words to be moved	Move to the right
		Straighten margin
		Move matter as indicated to position shown in text
(words required)/		Insert words given in margin at point indicated
		Insert full stop

Typewriter maintenance. See **Care of the typewriter.**

Umlaut. See **Combination characters and special signs** (*Diaeresis*).

Underscore fractions. See **Fractions** and **Mathematical typing.**

Underscoring. The underscore key is an upper-case one, normally situated on the top bank of keys, in conjunction with the lower-case figure 6. Each time it is struck, it produces (below the typing line) a line the full width of a character space. The successive use of this key produces a continuous line and thus underscores the required word or words.

The following points should be observed when using the underscore key.

1. The word or words to be underscored should first be typed. Then the carriage should be returned (by means of the carriage release lever) until the first letter of the word or words to be underscored is above the printing point. The shift key (or shift lock if more than two or three characters are to be underscored) should then be depressed and the underscore key struck as many times as required. If continuous matter is being underscored, the underscore should not be omitted between words. Initial and final punctuation marks may or may not be underscored.

2. The hyphen key should never be used for underscoring.

3. Underscoring is used in typewriting to emphasize particular words just as in printing this effect is achieved by the use of italics. If matter is being typed for the printer, underscoring indicates that italics should be used (see **Emphasizing words**).

4. Foreign words or phrases that have not been anglicized are sometimes underscored.

5. The name of the author or authority at the end of a quotation, or the name of the poet at the end of a poem is often underscored.

6. Subject headings are frequently underscored. Note that in manuscript or typescript draft copy, double underlining indicates that the heading should be typed in closed capitals (with one or two spaces between words). Treble underlining requires spaced capitals (with three spaces between words). A typed subject heading should never be underscored more than once.

7. The underscore key is used for ruling figure or money totals in column work. When the total is preceded by the £ sign, the underscoring should not extend above or below it in the ruling. Final totals are usually double underscored, using the interliner or variable line spacer (see **Money**).

8. The underscore can be used effectively to produce ornamental borders for programmes, etc. (see **Ornamental typing**).

9. Column headings in boxed tabulations should not be underscored.

Universal keyboard. See **Arrangement of the keyboard.**

Variable line spacer. See **Parts of a typewriter.**

Vertical centring. See **Centring—horizontal and vertical.**

Vertical column headings. See **Column work with column headings,** (f).

Window envelopes. See **Envelopes.**

Word frequency: its significance in typewriting. The frequency with which words are used is an important factor to take into account in the learning and teaching of any repetitive skill (such as Shorthand and Typewriting) based on the English language.

English is a very rich language containing something like half a million words. The working language of most people, however, is only a small fraction of this total. A fact which few people realize is that a mere *ten* words make up *25 per cent* of normal English connected prose: these words, in alphabetical order, are:

a, and, I, in, is, it, of, that, the, to

Another important fact is that *sixty-nine* words comprise *50 per cent* of ordinary English connected matter. These, again in alphabetical order, are:

a	but	her	me	or	there	what
all	by	him	more	our	they	when
an	can	his	my	out	this	which
and	do	I	no	she	time	who
any	for	if	not	so	to	will
are	from	in	now	that	up	with
as	had	is	of	the	us	would
at	has	it	on	their	was	you
be	have	its	one	them	we	your
been	he	made	only	then	were	

There have been several investigations into the frequency with which English words occur. Perhaps the best known are by Dewey, Horn and Thorndike. The shorthand textbook, *The New Course* (Pitman), for instance, uses almost exclusively the two thousand most common words in the Horn list.

Dewey analysed 100,000 words of everyday connected English, the passages for consideration being taken from a variety of sources. His findings are to be found in the book *Relative Frequency of English Speech Sounds* where he lists 1,027 words—all of which occurred at least 11 times in the 100,000 words studied. Dewey recorded the number of times each of these words occurred: they range from the most common word in the English language, 'the', which occurred 7,310 times, to the word 'worse' which occurred the minimum 11 times.

There were considerable differences in the findings of Dewey, Horn, and Thorndike. For instance, the word 'loan' is included in the first 400 words of the Dewey list, but only in the first 2,500 most common words of the Horn list, and the first 7,000 words of the Thorndike list. Similar variations were found with other words.

All Pitman Shorthand writers will be familiar with the 700 Common

Word list (and derivatives) and the passages composed solely by use of them. In deciding upon the first 500 most common words, only words common to all three lists were selected. The additional 200 words were all high-frequency words chosen for two main reasons: their demonstration of shorthand principles, and their *meaning*—so that interesting matter could be composed using only this very restricted vocabulary.

In analysing the Dewey, Horn, and Thorndike lists, the factor of frequency was found to be significant for only the first 500 words. The most common 69 words (which, as already stated, comprise approximately 50 per cent of ordinary connected prose) were not in dispute and recurred with such high frequency because of the pattern of the English language. Beyond the 500 mark, however, considerable variations were found which resulted largely from the subject matter under scrutiny and the particular writers concerned.

It has been estimated that the basic 700 Common Words of the Pitman list make up approximately 68 per cent of normal connected English—and if one takes these words together with their derivatives, the figure rises to 80 per cent. When one considers that the vocabulary of the 'average' person contains approximately 15,000 words, these percentages are enormous, taking into account the small number of words involved.

Word frequency should always be seriously taken into consideration in teaching and learning Shorthand and Typewriting. Pitman Shorthand places considerable emphasis on the 700 Common Words. Their importance is reflected in the fact that Shorthand teachers are frequently instructed to dictate and drill these words to the point of 'overlearning'. By this it is meant that the stimulus-response bonds of the learners should be developed to such a high degree for these words that the response (i.e., writing of the Shorthand outline) becomes an automatic one to the stimulus (hearing the word dictated). In the early learning stages, the processes of thought and reasoning come between the stimulus and the response—but with frequent repetitions, the length of the 'thought' stage is gradually cut down until it can be finally omitted. Since the 700 Common Words and their derivatives comprise approximately 80 per cent of normal connected English, such treatment is laudable.

In Typewriting, however, the 700 Common Words do not generally obtain the same intensive attention. Nevertheless it is just as important in Typewriting as in Shorthand to build up an 'automatic vocabulary' at as early a stage as possible. When the learner is first introduced to the different keys, she types each one individually as a single-letter response. In time, when she types words and sentences, she will gradually be able to type the more common words each as a *single* response. For instance, the word 'the' will first of all be typed as three separate responses on a stroke-by-stroke basis. After typing this word on numerous occasions, however, the typist will type it as a *single* response (it will become part of her 'automatic' vocabulary) and she will be scarcely aware of the fact that she is typing three separate letters.

There are a number of ways in which the 700 Common Words list can be used to speed up the process whereby these important words become part of the typist's automatic vocabulary. The following are some suggestions.

1. They can be divided into groups to correspond to the various reaches to be taught in each lesson covering the introduction of the keyboard—so that from as early a stage as possible they are given special attention.

2. A duplicated list of the 700 Common Words and their derivatives could be prepared, dividing the words into groups of twenty or thirty. Typewriting classes could be given regular five-minute drills on each list. In addition, such a list could be used for carriage-return drills and practice in typing columns of words. Alternatively, the class could sometimes take one of the groups of words and use it as a 'warming-up drill' at the beginning of a typing session.

3. The typewriting teacher could duplicate passages composed solely of this restricted vocabulary—which could then be used as straight-forward copying exercises or speed/accuracy tests.

All the above uses will help ensure that the 700 Common Words become part of the students' automatic vocabulary at as early a stage as possible. This, in turn, will help improve the speed, accuracy and general efficiency of the typist.

Word processing. See **Special-purpose typewriters.**

Words commonly mis-spelt. See **Drills.**